I0024562

Keep the Bones Alive

Photo courtesy of Aline Abdala.

Keep the Bones Alive

MISSING PEOPLE AND THE SEARCH
FOR LIFE IN BRAZIL

Graham Denyer Willis

UNIVERSITY OF CALIFORNIA PRESS

University of California Press
Oakland, California

© 2022 by Graham Denyer Willis

Library of Congress Cataloging-in-Publication Data

Names: Denyer Willis, Graham, 1979– author.
Title: Keep the bones alive : missing people and the search for life in
    Brazil / Graham Denyer Willis.
Description: Oakland, California : University of California Press, [2021] |
    Includes bibliographical references and index.
Identifiers: LCCN 2022002100 (print) | LCCN 2022002101 (ebook) |
    ISBN 9780520388512 (cloth) | ISBN 9780520388529 (paperback) |
    ISBN 9780520388536 (epub)
Subjects: LCSH: Disappeared persons—Brazil. | BISAC: SOCIAL
    SCIENCE / Anthropology / Cultural & Social | SOCIAL SCIENCE /
    Sociology / Urban
Classification: LCC HV6322.3.B6 D36 2021 (print) | LCC HV6322.3.B6 (ebook)
    | DDC 362.870981—dc23/eng/20220224
LC record available at https://lccn.loc.gov/2022002100
LC ebook record available at https://lccn.loc.gov/2022002101

30 29 28 27 26 25 24 23 22
10 9 8 7 6 5 4 3 2 1

For the missing

All author's proceeds from this book are donated to Mães da Sé

Contents

Illustrations

Acknowledgments

I wish this book were the result of careful deliberation, quiet thought, and an "Aha!" moment or something like that. Instead, it pains me to say that ills and violence made this book necessary. In January 2016, the Egyptian state disappeared Giulio Regeni, torturing and killing him before leaving him on the street. Egypt has denied it ever since, in one of the most absurd political foils imaginable. Giulio was a doctoral student the year I arrived at Cambridge, a brilliant student and one of the first PhD students I would engage with as a full-fledged academic. He was of the kind that unnerves you with their gregariousness and smarts, but with a sincere humility and concern for others. I hope this book is a finger in the eye to all governments and leaders—Egyptian, Italian, British, American, and Canadian, especially—who in full knowledge of what happened to Giulio, and what continues to happen to others, enable this and other disappearances with arms transfers and a manifest preference for capital over human life.

I would also like to acknowledge murderous policing in Brazil, and elsewhere. Over the last decade, Brazilian police—like many others—have become more deadly, and more disastrous, overcoming virtually any objection that their work is *not* of the genocidal proportions so deftly described by Abdias Nascimento. While I've been more sensitive to the class conditions of Brazilian police in the past, the rise of Bolsonaro has revealed the clear tensions between liberalism's patience with policing and a lucid recognition that police institutions cannot be placed apart from structural inequality, the governance of its basic assumptions, and the ongoing making of race, death, suffering, and disappearance in prisons and more. That Bolsonaro presides over another kind of mass killing through inequality now, via COVID-19, is yet more convincing proof that the world really does need to exhaust its fetish for militarism, police, and everyday hierarchy.

Against countervailing forces, good and not so good, others have enabled me to write this book. I am deeply indebted to everyone who gave this monograph the varied kinds of space and support for the elaboration that it has needed, whether collegial, financial, with reading, invitations to speak, or by thinking with me about Latin America, ethnography, and politics. To those, too, who allow me to think with them as they've undertaken study alongside me, pushing me to question my assumptions and to think and do better every day. In particular, to:

Maha Abdelrahman, Jaime Alves, Jude Browne, Samira Bueno, Katerina Chatzikidi, Max Curtis, Diane Davis, David Doyle, Kristen Drybread, Alex Fattal, Gabriel Feltran, Anthony Fontes, John French, Jeff Garmany, Thomas Blom Hansen, Marcia Hattori, Max Horder, Iza Hussin, Amy Jaffa, Gareth Jones, Ieva Jusionyte, Shamus Khan, Gray Kidd, Sian Lazar, Charlotte Lemanski, Ben Lessing, Renato Sérgio de Lima, Beatriz Magaloni, Kate Marshall, William Mazzarella, Flávia Medeiros, Karen Morton, Chloe Nahum-Claudel, Cleia Noia, Yael Navaro, Kevin Lewis O'Neill, Enrique Ochoa-Kaup, Leigh Payne, Anthony Pickles, Sarah Radcliffe, Robert Samet, Jason Sharman, Finn Stepputat, Jonny Steinberg, Madiha Tahir, Rebecca Tapscott, Winifred Tate, Sharika Thiranagama, Anna Villareal, Sarah Wagner, Queens' College, the Centres for Latin American Studies and Development Studies, and the Department of Politics and International Studies at Cambridge. With primacy, Laurie Denyer Willis.

Parts of this manuscript have been adapted with permission from work published in *Economy and Society* (50:2, "Mundane Disappearance," in the introduction), *Public Culture* (31:3, "The Exceptional Prison"), and *Comparative Studies in Society and History* (60:3, "The Potter's Field"). Special appreciation to Samira Bueno for permission to use our work "The

Exceptional Prison." I thank these journals, their editors, reviewers, and unsung managing editors for being so thoroughly generous with their time.

I save all of my thanks and admiration for Debora, Neide, Mariana, Matias, Otávio, Sandro, and Viviane, as well as others who are not explicitly named but who agreed to be a part of this work, who I hope feel that their words and continued time spent with me give life to a more ample struggle for recognition of their children and loved ones, Kaio, Felipe, Madalena, and Samuel. And to never forget. Seguimos na luta e na busca.

Introduction

GONE

Neide fixes her deep brown eyes on mine; linear, and piercing. I'm suddenly unnerved. "You're here now, but if you were to disappear here, now, *ah meu filho* [my child] . . ." she laughs, ill at ease, but full of assertion. Her gaze shifts, the focus dissipates. One day, in 2008, Neide's son Felipe walked out the door of their home. He said he was going to return a motorcycle with a friend of his. He was never heard from again.

Between twenty thousand and twenty-five thousand people go missing in São Paulo every year, or so a prosecutor and the newspapers tell me. Many of them are found, one way or another. Thousands of others are not.

I sit with Neide in the living room of the house she built from scratch with her husband on the south side of São Paulo. Neide's house—put in place brick by brick, mortar on mortar, a new room one year, another one years later by her husband's hands—is around the corner from one of the fluid urban capillaries that connect the informally urbanized periphery with the downtown of this global city of around twenty-four million people. She told me to tell the minibus driver to drop me by the big Y intersection, after taking the metro, a bus, and a short walk. In the other direction the capillary courses down to the Billings Reservoir, a dammed body of heavily contaminated urban water that feeds into the Pinheiros

1

River, a thread of brown liquid that moves back through the city, past the crystalline towers along United Nations Avenue—the height and light of so-called global harmony.

For Neide, everything changed when night fell and Felipe didn't come through the door. Soon, there was trauma. She speaks of depression and dejection mixed into every stride of the searching. Reiterated trauma. When he didn't come home, Felipe was still vividly present. His absence was generative, affective, brimming in what, to others, might seem like silent emptiness. Where he might have spoken or laughed in a family conversation, nothing was audible. Instead, there was melancholy, an individualizing but nonetheless collective reminder of the unfulfilled expectation of his presence, borne in excess by Neide. Such silences were not of solace or of coming to peace. What Neide describes is a smile that should be there, the warmth of eye contact, of someone's distinctive smell, of knowing how they sit and hold a fork or spoon between their fingers at the lunch table.

Soon emptiness started soiling everything surrounding it—any conversation, the euphoria of a song, a birthday party. Shreds of happiness and contentment always caving into guilt. Materials and moments are the crux of his memory (figure 1). Other things are also gone. The emptiness Neide describes is not just of Felipe's presence in his absence, but also of the way that a sensation of emptiness carried her own life away with it. Neide had worked for a law firm doing minor paralegal tasks. After Felipe vanished she tried to muddle through, but in the end she lost her job. Eventually, her husband did as well. Soon after, then, Felipe's disappearance was also an absence of money. His material emptiness, which had become her emotional emptiness, now became emptiness in the family purse. Soon, there was an emptiness in their stomachs.

But, as it turned out, even more emptiness was possible. A kind of political emptiness, as though the state that would help to find Felipe had itself gone away. Felipe had been a high school student. And, as with every student in the municipal public school system, when he was absent from school, parents would hear about it. Sometimes the *assistente social* (school extension worker) would call to ask where he was, why he wasn't in the classroom. "They would harass us," Neide said. The first thing these municipal employees would always ask was, "Is there a problem at home?"

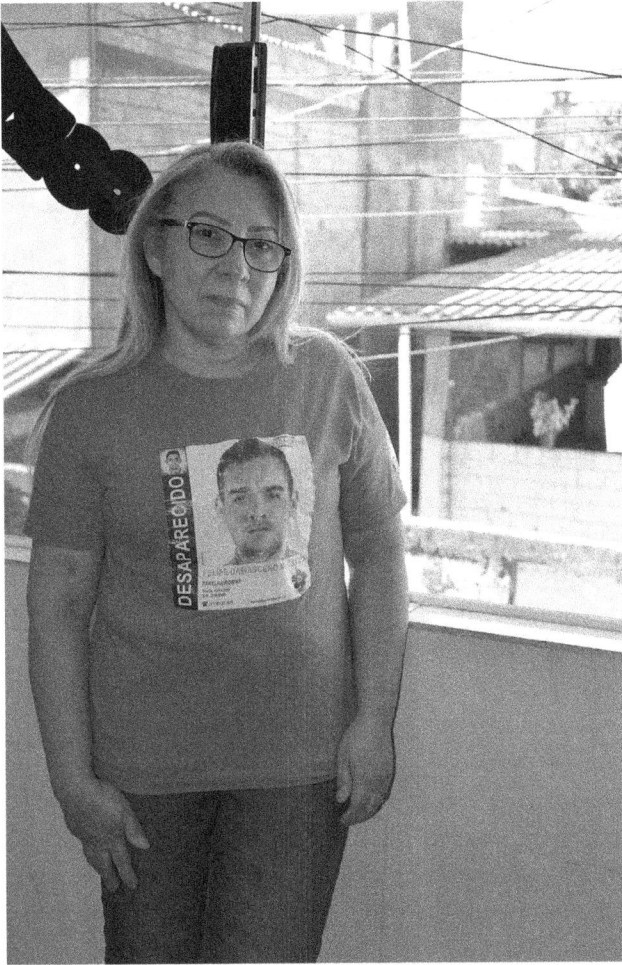

Figure 1. Neide (photo courtesy of Aline Abdala).

And then, five or six months after he disappeared, Felipe's school principal called. The extension workers had escalated the issue. Neide told him that Felipe was gone, he'd disappeared. The principal was shocked. He'd heard nothing of the matter. In a nanosecond his inquisitiveness about Felipe turned to awkwardness and withdrawal. "After he hung up," said Neide, "I never heard from him again." It was like the principal, too, had disappeared.

This shift of the principal and the school system from inquisitive to abrogated resonates in Neide's words, even years later. As she puts it, "But where is the extension worker now to help me? Where is that group of people, from the Concelho Tutelar, that is supposed to be so concerned about child welfare? They do nothing, but say that they do. But if I was ever to spank a child, the police would be there the next day."

They cared when he was occasionally absent from school. But they don't care when he is completely absent. Neide traces the sensation with her words, speaking around the way that their "care" was, really, an effort to control. That care is now gone, and not just from the school. State agencies that are supposed to care instead show indifference, resignation beneath the filed paperwork. With some important exceptions, she's found very few who will join her in the search, outside of other mothers and a handful of fathers she has come to know because their sons and daughters have disappeared, too.

The widespread indifference to searching for Felipe is shrouded in other kinds of doubt about what might have happened. When Felipe disappeared he was with a friend, a young man that Neide didn't know. Both he and Felipe vanished. So, for Neide, this wasn't just a problem of finding Felipe. It was about finding both of them. One would likely hold the key to knowing what happened to the other. But Neide was surprised to not find a willing partner in the other man's family, who reacted very differently. They didn't do much searching, and she could never really account for why. Sometimes they would say that they didn't have enough money to do it. That seemed the justification; they would do it when there was enough money. But they certainly weren't without the acute trauma of loss. As Neide put it, the mother seemed like she would only shout, "I want my son! I want my son!" She was groundless, untethered, but apparently totally disinterested in finding him.

"You know those kinds of people that never really open their mouth?" says Neide. "That don't really want to share anything with you? And so, she just never wanted to say anything. She would just keep shouting, 'I want my son! I want my son!'" They often wouldn't pick up the phone, and they wouldn't open the door when Neide came by. People spoke of her as being depressed. One time, to Neide, her husband wrote off her inconsolability as "a problem of depression." Neide had a hard time not reaching out, not trying to share in the effort and not uniting forces to find the two young men. It seemed so obvious to her, so important. She still can't get her head around why they "weren't interested." Where had their desire to search gone?

At some point, Neide was contacted by the Public Prosecutor's Office and told to leave the mother alone. Neide doesn't know how the prosecutor came to know, or why *this* was important enough for an institution that usually doesn't work at street level to intervene. This intervention from on high, concerned with someone *searching* and not with the disappearance itself, was striking to Neide. Rather than assembling a search party to find Felipe, she was threatened for asking questions—or maybe the right questions of the wrong people. The Prosecutor's Office, it seemed to her, was asking her to stop the search.

Neide has been everywhere else that could possibly help her. An NGO— Mães da Praça da Sé (Mothers of the Central Square)—for parents of missing children, gives out a prepared and photocopied list of places to look. She's been to each of their suggestions what feels like hundreds of times in these last ten years. To places like her neighborhood police station, where they record it but dismiss his disappearance as "not a crime," noting under their breath and in pseudonyms and posture, that he was a young man who wasn't always at school who was driving a motorcycle in a poor neighborhood. "Maybe he wasn't an angel," they imply. To the missing persons unit, which exudes disinterest and an affective film of bureaucratic violence. They drawl, "Did you find anything?" when she returns each time, hoping that their job has been done for them. To the morgue, which smells of a heaviness of decomposition that sticks to the fibers of her clothes. To public cemeteries—especially those for the indigent—with their routine processes of interment, disinterment, and disposal. She follows any hint of what I call "mundane mass graves," tracking any community whispers about a new one being found. She's been beneath every urban underpass, where struggling people congregate for shelter, that she's seen and could think of. She talks of São Paulo's infamous psychiatric *manicômio* and of the newer, partially private, and mysterious rehabilitation centers—home to the homeless, mentally ill, and dying persons left there by police, by hospitals, by families and by neighbors.

She has found nothing. She pins her hopes on Felipe maybe walking right back in through the front door—one day.

"Eight people are registered as disappeared per hour in Brazil in the last ten years," shouts a 2017 newspaper headline. One person every seven and a half minutes. The International Committee of the Red Cross (ICRC), which has worked on efforts to trace missing people around the world since the Franco Prussian War in 1870, says eighty-two thousand people are reported missing every year in Brazil. Numbers are approximate, and there is a battle over them.[1] Many people reappear, having been tracked down and returned or their body found—an argument often used to minimize urgency around the thousands that never do. Unlike "political disappearances" in historical moments, occurring amid crisis, war, and outright contestation for political power, which have been well studied, counted, and disinterred, this kind of mundane disappearance is made apolitical and treated as banal.[2] The numbers, which collapse the missing dead, the missing alive, and the missing in search of life, elsewhere, just don't seem to count. Mundane disappearance, existing outside of systemic crisis, is yet to be marked as a political problem, even as its condition as mundane is necessarily a question of power. Why?

For the ICRC, as for others, the project is to make this kind of disappearance political, through enumeration and population delineation. But numeration can feel like a project of containing a cloud in a football net, or using a pitchfork to move a pile of rice. The affects of disappearance, its varied violences, and systemic productions are not captured in the numbers. For those who search and hope, those who have disappeared are not easily assigned to death, to life, to violence, or even to politics.

In this city and state—which would be the fourth-largest country in Latin America if measured by population—other numbers describe what surrounds disappearance. Over 4.2 million chattel slaves were trafficked into Brazil in the transatlantic slave trade, the largest amount of any nation in the Americas. Still today, according to the Brazilian government, there remain at least 3,524 *quilombos* (Maroon communities) created by slaves who disappeared from plantations, fleeing to build new societies. Urbanists describe how greater than 60 percent of the city of São Paulo urbanized informally, in spite of the state rather than through regulation, redistribution, and an attention to life. Police statistics show that every year, police kill between seven hundred and eight hundred people in the city, 75 percent of whom are typically young Black men. São Paulo's prison population has grown by 2,144 percent since 1983—from 9,972 to 233,755. An organized crime group now controls all but seven of the state's 178 prisons, 28 of which have been built since I wrote the first sentence for this book in 2016. That organized crime group is now present in each of Brazil's twenty-six states, plus Bolivia and Paraguay. The rise of this organization from the historically violent and informally urbanized parts of the city and through the prison system coincides with a homicide decline in the city of around 80 percent, which, in real terms, means at least six thousand fewer intentional deaths per year. Journalists have written about thirty-five mass graves discovered around the city since 2007. The Immigration and Customs Enforcement Agency (ICE) of the United States detained seventeen thousand Brazilians at one land-border station alone, El Paso, Texas in 2019.

Alongside all of this, how might one make sense of the equivalent of a small city disappearing every year—if indeed it actually is? What does such mundane disappearance—the nebulousness of no body, no life, and no death—tell us about a contemporary political condition that holds some life as so devoid of value that it can disappear and not be pursued? While apparently passive, disappearance is an acute condition, speaking to the blurring of political nonexistence and material disappearance, with the former a necessary condition for the banality of the latter. Some people will be pursued by the state when they disappear. Most others, like Felipe, are not. It seems that politics—the state, popular urgency, an affective desire to collectively pursue the absent, protest in the streets—has itself gone missing. And yet there is a search.

Over the course of this book, I will describe three claims. First, disappearance is a generalized assumption tied to capitalism as a system that inscribes inequality on human life, as though an ethical or universal truth. In this sense, disappearance cannot be disentangled from a condition that sees human value relative to what it can(not) produce, make, or do—a constant comparative gesture embedded with value-laden difference. This differs from an understanding of disappearance as political only when someone is yanked off the street, rendered away by cloaked figures because they were members of a political organization, or were actively contesting a political regime. Always political, disappearance—today—works through indifference and forgettability for some, but a spectacular outcry for others,

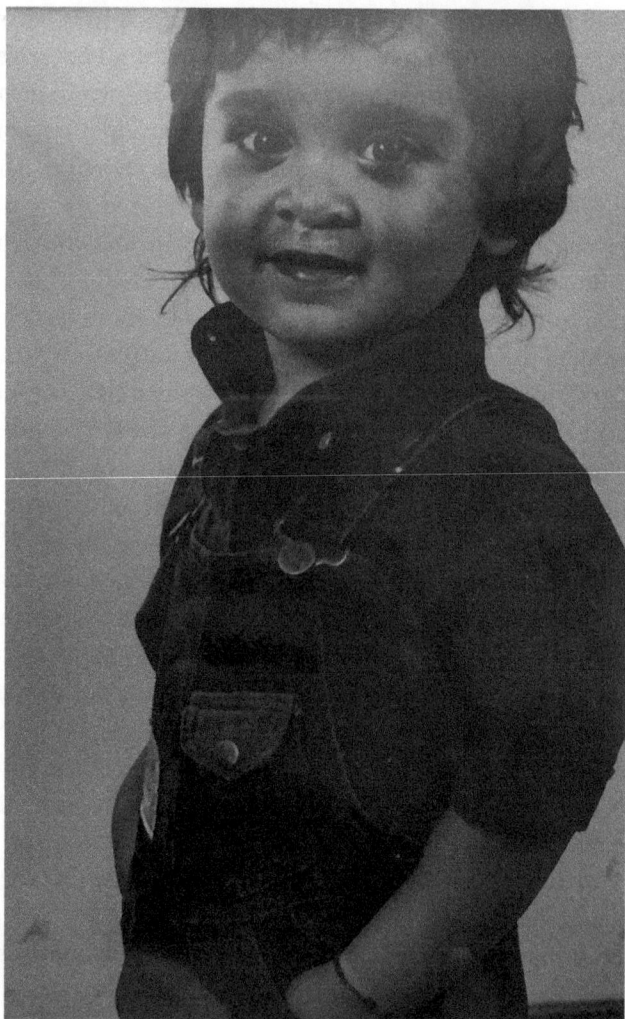

Figure 2. Felipe at age five (photo courtesy of Neide).

each of whom are understood, relative to the other, to be worthy of either pursuit or nonexistence. Here, then, "the disappeared" are not a discrete population, solely to be counted or numbered, one category of wrong among many. Rather, disappearance is itself *the* political reason, defining a prison system where people get lost and can't be found, and working as a defining characteristic of life and social death. In other words, disappearance is more than being denied humanity, it is a way of everyday knowing, succumbing, and surviving, in a global condition where there are too many bodies for capital's use, a need for some life to be maintained, and where bodies must be understood as useful in the service of accumulation. To mark mundane disappearance as a political problem is to implicate the kind of politics that presides over inequality as assumed and unquestioned. Mundane disappearance is central to capitalism's order and forms.

Second, this does not mean that someone vanishing doesn't matter. It has preconditions. The aftermath of Felipe's disappearance reasserts social and political order, affirming the inequity of life; an act of non-pursuit written on the face of a resigned police detective or through a spectacular public hunt for an innocent White child. An absent search, a mother or father left to search alone, performs inequality, where saving those who must not disappear also shapes the person who *can* disappear: the disappearable subject. In this way social and political order should be understood as being reasserted not only at the time of death, as Bloch and Parry (1982) once argued, but also even where the relationship between time and death is unknown, and unknowable. In doing so, material disappearance works as a discursive social category—"he disappeared," "they vanished," "he's gone"—dependent already on whether someone could be understood as disappearable, and independent of what might actually have "caused" their disappearance. *Who* makes people disappear, why people disappear—or flee—works at a second order of importance, behind an understanding of their already absent value, or of their supposed position as threatening to the status quo. Supposition about who the disappeared are, what they may have done, and why they do not deserve to be pursued, conditions the scope of a search—or lack thereof.

Third, an ethnographic focus on disappearance of both kinds reveals a *search for life*: a world of weeping tied up in the political economy of mass incarceration and dehumanizing racism. Within the assumptions and uneventfulness of disappearance there is an unmistakable search for life; mothers and fathers fighting to prevent bones being incinerated, collectivity at muted gravesides where commemoration of life is a criminal act, in the toil of everyday disinterment with care, and via distinctive organizations that take an opposition to mundane disappearance and sub-humanity as their starting point for a different assertion of lives that matter. Mothers unite, struggling to mobilize against all odds. Other people, who are contained in the prisons that are a materialization of the mundane ethics of disappearance, are emboldened to monopolize conditions of life and death on different terms. Such searches for life are tenuous and tricky, walking a knife's edge between reasserting the importance of some lives, and denying such recognition to others—including in the making of mundane mass graves.

Disappearance is not, then, a condition of absolute foreclosure. This banal paradigm is revelatory of a tenacious resistance to letting people be disregarded; to contesting the very idea that some people matter less than others. Though disappearance may imply absence and nothingness, it speaks immutably of a fight for a better politics; an ethos of determination to not let disappearance define the status quo. Against efforts to forget, to let the absence of people become the absence of memory, there is astonishing movement. As I will show, this takes everyday shape in flight, in collective organization, in violence, in a dogged devotion to recast disappearable subjects as worthy of being human, and in a call to never let people be forgotten. To keep the bones alive. Looking closely at who disappears reveals the indomitable efforts to radically reassert the importance of life in the bleakest conditions, however unnerving, illiberal, or counter-ethical. *The search*, then, is a means to appreciate what disappearance creates in subjectivity, will, and possibility.

In narrative form, this book is organized around two intertwined themes: disappearance as a political assumption, and, people searching. The narrative follows both, with empirical struggles, constraints, successes, and violence tracing the assumptions and practices of how disappearance functions as banal in the political status quo. Along the way, the reader will encounter the historical arc, spaces, people, institutions, trajectories, and inhumanity that shape contemporary disappearance, and how conventional but not inevitable political solutions like prisons and police produce this accelerating regime of disappearance. The chapters follow this pattern, leading from the moment of someone vanishing, to speculative answers about where the search ends.

The narrative unfolds as follows: "Disappearance and the Search" places the contemporary resurgence of missing people in context, describing how *vital* the two ideas and practices have been in the making of Brazilian political order, attending to what has changed and what has not. "Keep the Bones Alive" follows the efforts of mothers and fathers, individually and collectively, to search for their disappeared, placing the dehumanized ethics of disappearance alongside the lives of a son and mother, Kaio and Débora. "Unearthing Life" takes the reader to the cemetery for the urban poor where the unknown and unclaimed are buried, introducing the work and toil of Otávio, a gravedigger. "Disappearance and the Cemetery" points to the centrality and use of the cemetery of the urban poor in the making of political order, *especially* via disappearance, across historical moments and material forms. "The Usefulness of Capricious Knowledge" shows that the cemetery is only one instance of passive governance and selective rationalization of bodies within the state, inquiring into the medical examiner and into the uses of bodies in the production of knowledge and science. "The Disappearable Subject" trains a lens on prisons, and especially one just for police, to show the ways that direct and exterminatory violence works alongside the politics of disappearance. "From Disappearance, Presence" places a collective search for life within this exterminatory violence, showing how violence and mass incarceration generate new sociality.

"Muted Martyrdom" looks more closely at this rationale, and the way the Primeiro Comando da Capital (PCC) continues to function as a collective search for life, by focusing on the work of death and commemoration at the graveside. In "Make Live, Make Disappear," I reveal that this form of belonging has its own regime of disappearance and searching. The organization answers some questions about the missing, but it poses new ones by causing others to flee and search for a new life elsewhere. "'I Just Want to Live'" invites answers to the enduring question, *but where did they go?* I introduce Matias, an asylum seeker in an ICE detention center run by a private detention company named CoreCivic. The search leads people like Matias in many directions, cloudy and crisscrossed as they are, away from mundane mass graves, from being buried in a pit by police, to the anonymized streets of the city, into Microsoft's facial recognition database for the United States' ICE, and, ultimately, into a patterning of global political order that also takes disappearance as its starting point.

1 Disappearance and the Search

In Brazilian law, disappearance is just a *fato atípico*; an "atypical occurrence." It carries no notion of atrocity.[1] The "atypical" sits alongside the positivist "typical" in Brazilian jurisprudence, where the latter works through four enmeshed normative premises: *conduct, result, relationship of causality*, and *legal typology*. These four principles, forged in a global colonial legal pact premised on bodies as the pith of knowing, require a linearity between intent, outcome, effect of action, and the ability to categorize according to codified doctrine. The "atypical," by contrast, is the absence of these complementary and necessary conditions.

Another way of locating the absence of legal reason amid everyday rationality is through a foundational writ: habeus corpus. Bring the body. Brazilian legal theory—derived from hegemonic Western legal theory— holds that if a body has been deprived of liberty, and for such a condition to be contested as unjust, the body must be brought to court for *it* to attest to its own condition of deprivation. Such a logic of deprivation of liberty vests its premises in the materiality, voice, or representation of the body to the state. The absence of a body untethers the ability, and any substantive demand, to claim "deprivation of liberty." Without a body there can be no deprivation of liberty, by fact of law. Thus, "atypical."

How does one come to know who someone is, even when a body *is* found? One way to end the search is forensic analysis and DNA testing, which are available. Private tests are the quickest, but they're inaccessible on a moment's notice for anyone scraping by. The medical examiner can do it too, but there always seems to be a queue, murky knowledge, and arbitrary answers. Even where this supposed silver bullet might matter most, it gets tripped up by a bevy of banality: the body as a site of evidence now can't be found; a body was misnamed; the body was already buried, nameless, under a numbered wooden stake; there are bones found among many other bones, commingled. Some bones and remains are alive with political agency and the capacity to govern or disrupt governance.[2] Many others, however, are ungrievable.[3] They lack the ability to haunt, to politicize.

And yet, the "adverse non-event" of disappearance moves quietly through the most political of spaces and logics. A given case, or body, can trace pathways to mundane mass graves, to the indigent cemetery or "potter's field," through the medical examiner's room (Instituto Médico Legal [IML]), and through the affective existence of loved ones left behind. Or it may not. And it may, or may not, also move through the "alternative tribunals" of the PCC, an organized crime group, in and out of para-police death squads and murderous policing, or in the gossip and normative silences that surround all of these. Crucial, too, is the weight of the supposition that it *may have* been any one of these things, and it almost doesn't matter. Talk of disappearance assumes a life of its own. Silence and unwillingness to join the search speaks.

Disappearance seems a perfect post-truth category, a political shrug at something that shouldn't have happened, might not have anyway, and that can't really specify anything if it did in any case. So well subsumed within capitalism's enactment of life as inequitable, to have disappeared is to be politically evident of nothing much in particular, and to fit within a banal category of human (non-)existence that is neither life, nor body, nor death. This kind of disappearance, in a state of political banality rather than crisis or atrocity, or historical retrospect, also extracts the body as a site of contestation, evidence, and rationality. Where the body cannot be the basis of evidence, "missing people" allow for the reproduction of distinctive kinds of political indifference or disavowal. This works even as the social experience of coping with those who are no longer there—but could one day return—is wrought with a lucidity of supposition, a clear but often whispered normative rationale, and an abyssal depth of atomized suffering for those left behind. But if disappearance can be both politically disavowed and simultaneously socially avowed and understood, its empirical condition is at least partially materialized in landscape. New but banal terrains of burial outside the cemetery have emerged in São Paulo, and throughout Latin America as a region, mass graves of a mundane kind for their inability to rupture political discussion as other mass graves can.

The way disappearance happens, and why it is important, wasn't always this way. Far from it. A recognition of the basic assumptions of mundane disappearance might be critical in the present, but its shifting characteristics and responses over time—who is pursued when they disappear, why, with what justifications—means tracking it and its ethical assumptions across historical moments. Indeed, disappearance underpins the very development of countries like Brazil, especially in terms of institutional codifications, contested territorial expansion and settlement, violent pursuit and disavowal of populations, and the crystallization of abject and violent relations between the ruler and the ruled. Disappearance is embedded in some of the most basic assumptions of capitalist territorialization and constantly incomplete "state formation" as a mode of power, from past to present.

Attending to disappearance in a historical arc offers a renewed view of political power and the practice of power and order. The fractious relationship between ruler and ruled, in the dualized light of fugitivity and capture amid chattel slavery, is materially inscribed on the landscape and in enduring institutional, social, and political forms. Here, disputed state formation cannot be understood in terms of overcoming or eliminating contesting parties. Rather, it is in the expansion, settlement, and spatiality of power deployed in pursuit of the flight of the disappeared—from the Indigenous settlement, the slave-labor gold mine, the sugar plantation— and their attempted capture. The variegated back-and-forth efforts to disappear from political oppression, slavery and its spaces, and the vigorous and violent efforts to recapture and reassert order, necessarily pushed the spatial, moral, and epistemic boundaries of politics itself, expanding territory in a production of space written through the social relations of disappearance and searching.

Focusing on Brazil in particular reveals a long arc of disappearance and the search as particularly inseparable from lived politics, both in crisis and banality. The history of this territory, to become Brazil, is written through the pursuit of bodies that disappear, and their attempted capture, century after century, region to region. The problem transcends not just space but projects and moments of governance, perhaps especially on the frontier. From the blurry forced labor and indoctrination logics of early Jesuit, Franciscan, and Carmelite missionary outposts, funded through the use of Indigenous "labor" in the search for wild cocoa in the Eastern Amazon basin, to the *mocambo* "safe havens" of runaway slave Maroons, the colonization process worked in dialogical lockstep with containment and a desire by the contained to flee and search for life beyond.[4] "By far," writes Stuart Schwartz (1996: 103), "the most common form of slave resistance was flight." Flight was quite simply the most obvious way of not getting worked to death; it was the way out.

Disappearance worked at different scales—individuals fleeing the plantation or the mine, Maroon communities forming, other communities vanishing, perhaps obliterated, perhaps starved or dead of disease. Each surrounds a desire, materialization, or practice of "getting out" of a violent system to search for a better life, or being eliminated by it, that pushed outward into the hinterlands in a "civilizing" process. As Flávio dos Santos Gomes (2002: 470) alludes: "Fugitives—blacks, Amerindians, and military deserters—played a leading role in the pursuit of freedom. Through their own acts, they reinvented the meanings and constructed views of slavery and liberty. Moreover, they colonised swathes of the Amazon, particularly those on the international colonial borders. Settlers arrived. Ships cast anchor. Economic calculations were made. Forts were built. Boundary markers were put in place. Laws and regulations were sent. Several kinds of adventures were beginning for the men and women in those parts." Such lines of flight and settlement in a search for life led in almost every direction, outward from the plantation, mine, and settlement, and from (and into) the city.

This is not solely a question of space or territorial expansion, either. Even the much nationally celebrated settler colonial "pioneers" worked through a logic of disappearance. *Bandeirantes*, private bands that hunted down Indigenous populations, moved westward through what is today

São Paulo, Minas Gerais, and Paraná states (and then northward). They did so to steal Indigenous lives to enslave—while in the process expanding the "frontier" in a search for mineral deposits that germinated settlement. The effect was alternately to disappear whole populations, "depopulating areas" by stealing lives while causing others to flee. Those who fled sometimes "took shelter" in Jesuit missions that "besides actually 'rounding up' willing indigenous groups, welcomed other indigenous groups who fled *bandeirante* fury."[5]

Moreover, the "sheltering" of Indigenous populations in missions made them, in particular, an appetizing target for hunting parties. "One cannot imagine a more tempting prey for slave traders," wrote Abreu (1998) of the missions. Why steal populations with unintelligible language, incomprehensible mores who attack violently, when ". . . nearby, well sized villages with people schooled in the art of peace, and accepting of authority" (2:111–13) could be invaded? The very idea of human domination over nature, which assumes the conquest of "civil" populations over the Indigenous, cannot be understood without disappearance, flight, and capture—all entwined in forms of searching.

Analytically, following where someone who disappeared, fleeing, may have gone, trails both why they fled and what they may have fled to, and why. Analytically thickening such efforts to "get out," disappear, and search for a better life is of vital importance for seeing the vivid ways that disappearance has and has not transformed across historical moments. Yuko Miki (2012: 495) writes of Benedito, "a slave who disappeared from prison in a flamboyant escape," in late nineteenth-century Brazil. After Benedito freed himself from handcuffs by smearing them with sheep fat, he vanished in the night—and likely to (and with the help of) the nearby fugitive slave community, a *quilombo*. The police officer investigating the incident "grimly acknowledged that arrest would be difficult. . . . He was certain that Benedito would be impossible to capture because he was likely protected by a local *quilombo* in the city district—and possibly many others" (496).

Histories like these reveal a vital relationship of complementarity between disappearance and searching for life, both empirical and conceptual. In a single case, disappearance and a search exist, and with contrasting meanings. The search was both an effort to obtain life, for slaves, and a means of domination, for masters and their hunters wanting to reobtain their property. The difference between the two rests in one's position and perspective of political and social order. For the slave, like Benedito, to abscond from the plantation and its prison logic was to flee a system, a life of violent domination, a bleak and foreclosed world where slaves were cheaper to replace from the slave ship than to invest in for more than a handful of years. This was a system where their life was not recognized as human.

For the slave owner, someone disappearing was both a crisis, and much foreseen. It required a search; in this case a violent pursuit to reclaim lost labor and to patch the cracks in their political order. These "man-hunts" weren't single-issue problems of individuals, or an offhand concern (Chamayou 2012). The disappearance of someone who had fled was made to redefine the rule by making the fleeing party reappear after a grand and raucous search, for all to see—and to be punished publicly and spectacularly at its conclusion.

And yet, it wasn't even the case that slave owners worked to eliminate, to obliterate, the very possibility of disappearance. Rather, some masters let slaves try, as part of a technique of domination. "Owners usually treated the first flight less severely than subsequent attempts," Mary Karasch (1987: 303) describes, "because they regarded it as part of the seasoning in process, and the new slave earned a valuable lesson: running away was grounds for punishment." Disappearance from the plantation, or from urban chattel, was both a threat, and useful to demonstrate the power of the search.

Having hope for a better life, and a history of attempts to flee in search of it, also made slaves cheaper. For the Jesuits, who saw humanity and the possibility of salvation in the Indigenous population but denied such recognition to African slaves, failed "seasoning in" was attractive. As one seventeenth-century friar in a remote northern state put it while writing to a slave seller, "Admitting that the [Black slaves] here have nowhere to escape to, it would be convenient if there were a few who could be [sold] more cheaply because of this wrongdoing."[6]

Disappearance and the search were far from peripheral to political life. The logics of constant disappearance and searching shaped social relations and space in systemic ways, recasting the very meaning of the plantation, the city, and political orderliness itself. In nineteenth-century Rio de Janeiro, "the city and nearby hills were overrun with runaway slaves"

(Karasch, 1987: 304), patterning how space and security were enacted. Not just spatial, though, Amy Chazkel (2020) has written of how the constant inability to control runaways shaped the very temporality of society, where nightly curfews kept fugitives and the enslaved from blending in the sensory disorder of the night, to overrun the daylight. On the fringes of the plantation, the mine, and the city, police and bush-hunting *capitães do mato* scoured the landscape, returning to punish the disappeared with monstrous spectacle. That someone like Benedito would disappear under cover of night was both a critical logic for his disappearance and well subsumed into the curfew response that sought to rationalize the terms of the search for the disappeared.

All of this meant that disappearance and the search were countered by a barrage of intersecting and contesting interests. Disappearance was so common that it gave way to distinctive institutions of capture, some of a "third-party" or twilight variety, like the *capitães do mato*. These groups, made up of quasi-free former slave and Indigenous militias, were put to work—per head captured—in the scrubland and forests for those in flight.[7] Amid police who might deny their ability to do anything, or on the resignation of slave owners to try to get the police to help, hunting parties could be easily deployed. Slave owners, their patrols, one slave owner upon another, groups of Maroons, and *capitães* were part of a complex and often disassociated tapestry of theft, violence, and capture—from each other.

The contested relationship around disappearance and the search was further complicated by blurred relationships between some slave owners and fugitive slaves. Amid such a terrain of political disorder, pragmatism was important. Miki (2012) shows that slave owners would protect their interests, both from incursions by fugitive slave communities and from other owners, by other surprising means: allowing some Maroons to settle on their land to avoid being found. By doing so, these land owners could accrue free labor, in return for shelter, food and munitions—and a cut of their "criminal" proceeds. From this protected position, the disappeared like Benedito could then steal livestock, staples, and other property from neighboring areas, leveraging a safe haven overseen, at least informally, by a patron.[8] To disappear was to elide within a different sphere of governance, becoming a shadow in plain sight, protected from the search.

Brazilian politics was, and remains, alive with disappearance and searching. Seeing politics in these terms allows for a consideration of all these crossed lines, the varied violence implied, and the internally contradictory nature of everyday politics made through human inequality. Crucial things have changed over time and with at least two key distinctions for how disappearance and the search must be understood. First, both have been subsumed into a dominant logic of passive ordering, from actively hunting for missing slave labor to letting labor disappear. A manhunt to recapture labor is no longer necessary, nor does it allow for a punitive public spectacle and social pedagogy that absent Black lives and labor will be tracked down. Labor is now compelled in other ways. Subjects are now, already, "disappearable"; their condition of being policed in life but unpursuable in disappearance is evident in non-provision of biopolitical care and ill attention to particular bodies as not worth saving. Disappearance is a systemic assumption that is written through absent policy and inconsistent provision of life-giving infrastructures. The poor are left to disappear, unless one builds a house out of scraps, toils in the informal economy at all hours, or overcomes the disease and diarrhea that happen in the absence of biopolitical techniques of making live. Here, the favela itself is built on the uncertain and shaky landscapes of disappearance as the political condition. Such places that are built, communally, exist against this political assumption *as a materialization* of an enduring search for life.

Unlike in the past, an active manhunt is reserved for other populations, the pursuit of whom is cast as necessary to right wrongs, to maintain innocence, or to bring justice to bear. The spectacularity of these kinds of pursuits, the force of which comes in part from a public reimagining of the horror of the event, leaves audiences verklempt but demanding. This search is necessarily to demonstrate the worth of some lives, discursively constructed, and backed up by helicopters, ground-penetrating radar, "search parties," and a kind of volition that opens the floodgates of funding.

Second, the logics of disappearance have urbanized in dominant form and space. Today disappearance exists in dense human conditions, where spaces of disappearance and of populations who can disappear, or who might want to disappear, are contiguous with the city. Such spaces, like the favela, are alternately unattended to, with people allowed to disappear,

and policed with murderous violence under the guise of a search for criminals. And yet, then, as now, rural and chattel, versus urban and incar-
cerated, disappearance derives from an ethical condition and patterns of
economic subsistence at the margins. Spaces and populations, subsisting
from the outside, are required to be "parasitic, based on highway theft,
cattle rustling, raiding, and extortion" (Schwartz, 1996: 109).

In the city, where class, race, and inequality are entangled in everyday
and proximate relations of use and accumulation, the spectacularity of
the search for the wrongfully disappeared functions as a performative and
affective device. The search disentangles lives whose absence reasserts the
imperative of their presence for lives that matter. While nonetheless a bru-
tal simplification, the search for the absent worthy—including their discrete selection from a world of disappearances—becomes an acute means
for navigating and reproducing inequality in the city, further justifying
the differentiation between who can be held as property and who should
hold property.

Under these ethical conditions, most of those who disappear are situated as omnipresent threats, socio-spatial types of ill will, with populations guilty by association with criminalized urban spaces. This notion
of criminalization circumscribes the will not to search for a person who
has vanished, serving to further invalidate them by virtue of their own
material disappearance. The absent need to search for those who disappear mundanely, like Felipe, flows from this assumption, derived from and
reproducing a systemic logic. The search for life out of a systemic assumption of disappearance is not just a search for *a* life, but for an appreciation
of all such lives, contesting the precondition. It is a search for a politics
of life that would overturn their disappearance—the disappearance of
others—as the ethical starting point.

Reframed relative to understandings of power, Foucauldian scholarship has called for an appreciation of population and sovereignty as the
power to make live and let die—to attend to some lives and refrain from
attending to others. Weberians till the conceptual soil of monopolized territories of violence in an active and state-centric understanding vested
in institutions, bureaucratic regimentation, and territory. Others, like
Achille Mbembe, have asked for an analytical return to the politics of
death as the enactment of power, and to what the conditions of death and

suffering make evident about politics. While advancing aspects of these interpretations, here I attend to what might be missing, conceptually and materially from too much emphasis on death, the state, or "letting die." My concern with what is "gone," what is no longer there or disappeared, and who can disappear, is a threefold concern about (a) the limited conceptual engagement with how "missing people" matter in the ways that states, sovereignty, violence, and political order are reproduced; (b) a way to think about what is now materially somewhere, though elsewhere, and how power manifests when they can't be found—and apparently don't need to be found—and, last, (c) that mundane disappearance might reveal distinctive and under-recognized patterns of organization, power, and space.

On the one hand, to not control bodies—to let them disappear—implies a weakness of political authority, an absence of power. The conventional "monopoly on violence" frame, which associates political order with the power to use violence and death to make or preserve a status quo, implies that politics works through death, punishment, and their specters, and that it does so mundanely. All deaths are political; politics, governance, works through death in mundane ways, but on different terms. For some, there is an active assertion of death-worthiness for some populations. Daina Berry (2017: xiii) calls this current moment of videos of police killings of Black populations "the historic spectacle of black death," where the death of Black men and women is a public and political rehearsal of ritualized lynching that reiterates a historic political regime of violence against Black bodies. In this vein, Mbembe (2003: 12) writes of "necropolitics," the power of de jure states to decide who may live and who must die. Or, as he questions, "Imagining politics as a form of war, we must ask: What place is given to life, death, and the human body (in particular the wounded or slain body)? How are they inscribed in the order of power?"

On the other, inaction *is* political power: it is the power of the political to differentiate between populations in a comparative exercise replete with violence and lifesaving. Here power is understood as operating in a way that both absolves itself and maintains order, in an ongoing and sharpening paradox of freedom and containment, active killing and passive engagement. Here, to be sovereign is to decide these terms of violence and death, including and especially through the evocation, omission, and ambiguity of law—of "letting things happen." Daniel Goldstein (2016: 6) writes of absent-presence, a mode of sovereign rule that "imposes certain kinds of legal and social regulation but neglects others, making the state into a phantom, at once there and not there, a ghostly presence." All of this happens under a global cloak of deregulation, where political paring back works upon particular populations and spaces, depressing labor conditions and labor value through non-provision. While there is not much new about positive attention to labor and workers since the end of the Cold War, these questions are especially aggravated in the current historical moment and the "outright win" of liberal capitalism. Or, as Werner Bonefeld (2010: 19) puts it, "The free market is thus endorsed as a stateless sphere under state protection."

Like Ruth Wilson Gilmore (2007) understood of the United States' "prison fix" in the early 2000s—where prisons became a solution to excess labor, land, and un/employment in American deindustrialization—disappearance should be seen as a kind of fix to a series of contemporary crises of global capitalism. Alongside increasing reliance on prisons as a local fix, and a means of disappearing, in São Paulo and Latin America mundane disappearance is surrounded by acute crises of excess labor, concentrated land ownership, export-oriented economies increasingly dependent on services for employment, and a constant ambiguity about state capacity to govern populations and market. Allowing people to disappear decreases labor value, redresses surplus labor, reduces pressure on unequal land ownership, leaves global capital unperturbed while advancing lower costs, and allows the state to eschew its involvement in ordering society. Like a prison fix, a "disappearance fix" disorganizes communities, disrupts households, and allays collective mobilization across space and time. It describes a regime of global spatiality underwritten by a specific kind of securitization: keeping depressed labor in place, outside of countries and zones of concentrated wealth, while enabling capital to get to it—when it so desires.

Disappearance and the search. These two conceptual concerns about political order must be brought together under these conditions. Political order requires both pursuit and resignation, an active and a passive. To be disappeared is to be both materially, socially absent *and* politically present. Countless people are never registered at birth. Here people can be both left to disappear *and* the subject of direct forms of violence that would obliterate any potential political contention. This means existing in both an easily predated *and* a politically expendable condition, where disappearing is always logical, possible, unexceptional. Sometimes, though, disappearance becomes spectacular as "political disappearance." In the micro-historical terms of the late twentieth century, and the active pursuit for real or imagined insurgents, Brazil and Latin America saw mundane disappearance elided by the "political disappearance" associated largely with an undisappearable middle class. People seen to have been *actively* disappeared by state, paramilitary, or akin actors *became* the paradigm of disappearance, obscuring all other forms, populations, and modes of power that have made disappearance mundane for some, before, during, and after Cold War violence.

Such a condition of constant disappearability is articulated through a discourse of freedom alongside practices of unfreedom, or containment.[9] "Capitalism appears to be about the 'freeing of labor,'" write Peter Geschiere and Francis Nyamnjoh (2000: 426), "as a necessary condition for creating a mobile mass of wage-laborers; yet in many instances it has also brought with it determined efforts to compartmentalize labor, imposing classifications—ever changing, but all the more powerful—in order to facilitate control over the labor market." Freedom is not for those who, as Jaime Alves (2019) has written, contain the "specter of Haiti." These are the "new wretched of the earth," Mbembe (2017: 177) writes, those "to whom the right to have rights is refused, those who are told not to move, those who are condemned to live within structures of confinement—camps, transit centers, the thousands of sites of detention that dot our spaces of law and policing. They are those who are turned away, deported, expelled; the clandestine, the 'undocumented'—the intruders, castoffs from humanity that we want to get rid of because we think that, between them and us, there is nothing worth saving."

And yet, they must not only be not worth saving; they must also not be a danger to the status quo. These people are "already missing 'persons' in a bio-political system that appropriates migrants from the south as exploitable bodies for labor," wrote Robin Reineke from the United States–Mexico borderlands in 2016. Or, expanding further in a global and historical arc, "Colonialism needed to move large populations of people—slaves and indentured labor—to work in mines and on plantations," writes Arundhati Roy. "Now the new dispensation needs to keep people in place and move the money—so the new formula is free capital, caged labor. How else are you going to drive down wages and increase profit margins?"[10] Disappearable subjects are told not to move, to stay in place, and, simultaneously, to disappear from the political map. "This ambivalence of freedom," writes Immanuel Wallerstein (2010: 172), "pervades [capitalism's] politics, its culture, its social relations." With freedom for some must come containment for others. The everyday practice of containment is written through mundane social exchanges, spoken tropes of deservedness, affective refusals to intervene and to help with a search.

This is not a question that should be limited to Brazil. It is a global condition. Under settler colonialism Indigenous populations in Canada, Australia, and Brazil, among others, are enabled to disappear through a confluence of veiled assimilation policies, suicide, the absence of basic infrastructures, and material disappearance after engaging in "dangerous professions" such as urban sex work on the streets of idyllic global cities like Vancouver. These slow violences of settler colonialism, what Elizabeth Povinelli (2008: 521) calls the forms of dying that are "cruddy, cumulative and chronic," can't be so easily accounted for in outright state-centric political terms. As Lisa Stevenson (2012: 592) evokes by drawing on bureaucratic documents on the Canadian North, this kind of cruddy violence speaks of the ongoing colonial project's preference for a "disturbed Inuit population over a dead one." Better still for the colonial project is the analogous category, the indigenous who disappear.

After all, disappearance offers the project the ability to absolve itself from, on the one hand, having to account for illiberal lethal violence and, on the other, from the minimalist but costly techniques of maintaining the condition of "being disturbed" and institutionalizing. Such a logic is about both political indifference and the bottom line. You don't have to kill and create political upheaval, or bear the price tag of cumulative hospital stays or an "Indian residential school"—including the burden of making mass graves within—if a person ceases to be present in material form. After all, without a means of knowing, of bureaucratic rationality and record, there is no evidence of wrong. Or, to paraphrase Melissa Wright, without someone's proof of existence, and without a crime, there is no injustice. Why not just let them cease to exist, to disappear into a space of what she calls "epistemological ignorance"?[11]

There is a vital distinction between the way that disappearance works internal to settler colonial states and, external to them, at the seams of global inequality. In the border spaces between wealthy regions and populations that seek to escape conditions of mundane and material disappearance, a different iteration of disappearance as bordering is made to work through forms of non-human "environmental deterrence" (De León, 2015). It is here that people searching for a better life confront the violence of states that otherwise passively deny their humanity. On the margins of especially privileged settler colonial regions—Europe, the United States and Canada, Australia—landscapes and seascapes are employed as violent terrains where bodies will never be found. And if they are, the bodies will bear the vestiges of what biologically killed them—often water, or the absence of it. Here, the politics of death deploys H_2O as a weapon that both kills and assumes the role of antagonist—dehydration did it—on a case file. So while Losif Kovras and Simon Robins (2016: 9) argue that "death is the border," disappearance is a governance sleight of hand, and ethically a washing of hands, to deny people success in their search for a better life.

And yet, writ large, disappearance is unavoidably a resurgent problem because it leaves material and spatial traces. The practice of bordering around places like "Fortress Europe," the "American Homeland," or "No-boats Australia" works through efforts to dislocate both the enumeration of bodies and the structural conditions that compel people to flee from elsewhere. This is true whether in the ways that environmental deterrence turns the desert of the United States–Mexico borderlands into an open grave (De León, 2015), the southern shores of the Mediterranean into mass graves (Zagaria, 2019) or, in Brazil, allows armed groups to govern space and produce and reuse their own burial plots. What these spaces have in common is a ubiquitous rationality of missing people as politics, where the missing are not known and don't need to be known, yet their condition seems known by all.

The "mundane mass grave," whether in São Paulo or a few miles from San Diego, and the logics that make it happen imply a further change in the marginalization of premature death from political life, such that these spaces can exist and be "discovered" by the state, used once more, then discovered yet again, to be then used again, ad nauseam. In São Paulo at least thirty-four such mundane mass graves have been discovered since 2007, containing people that have *by definition* disappeared, whether or not they were ever reported to the state as such. Similar to how it happens in other places like Mexico, these burial spaces are not the subject of routine and rigorous investigation by the state. It costs too much for the kinds of bodies found—and what is implied about their deservedness *just because* of their presence within—to be identified, rationalized, categorized, and recognized as human. Such a process of knowledge pursuit reveals a paradox for any state agency—to investigate the existence of a mass grave is to concurrently unearth layers of state apathy, a generalized politics of disappearance, and the use of this condition by other, violent, groups to *actively* disappear people.

The burden of searching, of finding—and sometimes even of the process of unearthing—falls on the shoulders of those tirelessly in pursuit of loved ones. In Mexico, where mothers and family members search with "suspended grief" (Schwartz-Marin and Cruz-Santiago, 2016: 485), and in São Paulo, most mundane mass graves have been found by citizens searching for the disappeared, from anonymous tips, word of mouth, or some form of happenstance. Only exceptionally are they found by the state in a process of investigation for these spaces themselves. These spaces are only thinly the subject of investigation by state agencies. Their existence is alternatively denied or shrugged off as exceptional, as "not mass graves," or as isolated incidents. Little will exists to recognize such spaces as a category of their own, of knowledge or of counting—with some revealing exceptions, as I hope to show.

In this shroud of state indifference to the contemporary disappeared and to the burial sites where some are found, a technique of power operates. Disappearance is nonetheless transparently a method of ordering. Whether carried out historically by the state, or ending in a mundane mass grave dug by members of an organized crime group, the power of disappearance rests in how it is read and understood in social relations. "When you disappear," Paulo Malhães, a former colonel, testified to Brazil's Truth Commission in 2014, "you cause an impact much more violent [than death] in the group. Where is he? I don't know, no one saw, no one knows? How? How did he disappear?" In the 1970s Malhães ran a torture and disappearance house in Petrópolis, a city in the hills outside of Rio de Janeiro.

He confessed to both torture and disappearance, speaking increasingly openly about it—including to the Rio de Janeiro State Truth Commission. Less than a month later, at the height of the commission's activities, he was dead in a "home invasion" in his gated community, the details of which were posted on a prominent military chat website before it even hit the news.

Disappearance is a social phenomenon par excellence, whether amid war, Cold War, or everyday life. Where did she go? Are they in a mass grave? Even where there is no "rational" way to know if "punishment" or violence actually "caused" the disappearance, supposition and innuendo do the work. Was Felipe taken by the police? By a death squad? By organized crime? Hunch works to affirm the outcome, not to contest its most insidious but under-spoken assumptions. "He must have done something wrong," they say. "He had been missing school." Perhaps you, reader, are already caught thinking that Felipe was probably involved in bad things. He was driving a motorcycle underage, after all. Or maybe that he was a member of the PCC, the organized crime group so prominent in particular spaces in São Paulo and beyond. Or that it was police that took him—after all, Neide describes being followed and watched for months after by men. Once, they made a gun, aimed at her, with their thumb and forefinger. "Pow," their lips said as she passed by on the bus.

Under these conditions, who or what *made* someone disappear, "forced them to disappear," or made them flee, becomes a second-order concern. That it may be organized crime beneath significant parts of the story of disappearance is a seductive answer, a simplistic easy-out. The "bloodthirsty criminal," or organized crime as a whole, is a compelling but fallacious figure playing out an intoxicating storyline that holds the criminal responsible for his own demise, being ethically irretrievable. It also makes the problem of disappearance a problem of "criminals," further centering the state as a superior solution. But the first-order concern remains: a need to focus on the generalized condition of disappearance that allows someone to be cast as a criminal *after* they disappear. Disappearance is simultaneously capitalist, political, spatial, and racial before anyone ever vanishes. It is this larger foundation—that some people can disappear without political rupture—that strengthens organized crime, giving it legitimacy.[12] If we are, for a moment, compelled to believe that Felipe "was involved," or that he might have "done something," his disappearance is both enabled and shut to scrutiny. This starting point already inters him, making him the subject of mundane mass graves and forgettability, disallowing Neide's search as anything worth accompanying.

Instead, pointing to the preconditions of disappearance that surround Felipe's absence enables something much different—a search for individuals *and* for a politics of equitable life. Felipe's disappearance is a fix for capital and the status quo insofar as it is the conclusion. And yet, it isn't. It reveals a new crisis and worry for defenders of global inequality: he and the tens of thousands of others who have gone missing may not be dead, buried, or fading away. Instead, they may have set out on a different path, to cross the spatial threshold of global inequality or to join new forms of counter-ethical collective life, both new kinds of crises that must be fixed.

2   Keep the Bones Alive

It is a weekday afternoon when I meet a group of mothers and fathers outside a courthouse in São Paulo. They are gathering with white T-shirts, this time, to protest a new initiative from the mayor's office—an effort to privatize the city's cemeteries. To do so, the municipality had sought permission to clean them up, bringing them into respectable order before publishing a formal solicitation of interest for private corporations to purchase the city's twenty-two public cemeteries. As part of this process, the municipality sought permission to clean out a number of *ossuários* (bone houses) containing the "unidentified and unclaimed" remains of sixteen hundred people. The capacity of this bone house is "totally spent," they wrote, and these bones, whose "identification was lost because of changing environmental conditions" within the bone house, should be taken to another cemetery and incinerated. These mothers and fathers protest the potential transformation of the cemetery, the expulsion of bones from it, knowing that such a possibility might further disappear their sons and daughters. They fight to keep these bones alive.

The new businessman mayor, later to be governor, had realized, it seemed, that death is big business. The ability to be buried in one of the city's ornate central cemeteries, ringed with razor wire and adorned with statue-like mausoleums and remembrance tombs, is a commodity par excellence. In the long arc of privatization of public goods and services, even the most basic material conditions of life and death—burial—would not be spared. They are another crucial and ongoing iteration of what Francisco Ferrándiz (2019) calls "funerary apartheid," the condition of spatial segregation continued in death, accelerating and widening just as it is in life.

It is not typical for this group of mothers and fathers to protest here, so directly in front of a courthouse, or to push back against public policy with a collective voice. There are countervailing pressures, and a less obvious target for their claims. Instead, they are usually elsewhere, searching the city, the morgues, the cemeteries, and *abrigos*. Sometimes they spend their Sundays at the central church square. It is because of this gathering at the Praça da Sé that they have become known, echoing the Argentine Madres de la Plaza de Mayo, as the Mães da Praça da Sé (Mothers of the Central Square). But unlike the Argentine Madres, these Brazilian mothers cannot frame their loss in the past tense, politically or otherwise. The mundane political conditions that surround their disappearance are ongoing, the protagonists far less clear. For all of the violence of the state and its indifference, it may have been, but probably was not, the state that "caused" their sons and daughters to vanish. Like the Argentine Madres, though, they've found a shared experience, searching in the spaces of disappearance around the city.

On this occasion, though, their interests and concerns can converge, both in place and in political objective. The reason that they've come to the courthouse, with austere pictures of their sons and daughters on their shirts, is because among those sixteen hundred bodies could be their missing son or daughter—to be tossed, nameless, into the city's single public crematorium and incinerated. They know these cemeteries well, having spent hours, days, moving through them, questioning the unnamed bodies within, fretting about the temporality of an everyday policy of disinterment and disposal from public cemeteries—after three years, if someone doesn't pay—which is far too soon for their search.

Neide is there, as is a mother named Mariana and a father named Sandro, as well as a woman named Débora. Débora is a tall Black woman with a glowing smile, whose dark curly hair drapes over her shoulders.

She wears a white T-shirt over a sweater, with a full chest-sized picture of her son, Kaio (see frontispiece). On this day she had taken some time to prepare herself before taking a bus, train, and subway ride into the center of the city. People seem to congregate around her. She's there to convey his image, one that might inspire others to help the search. She hopes that she might be on television or in a newspaper photo. Someone seeing that might recognize Kaio and call in.

Kaio has been missing for around six years, since 2013. Later I visit her at her house in a municipality on the outskirts of the city proper, somewhere far past the Dr. Oetker factory and the outer highway rings. Having moved away from the community where Kaio disappeared, Débora now lives in a public housing block at the end of a street. In front of her house the road continues onto a dirt path, with houses made of scraps of wood on the other side. Her housing block is old, but it follows the conventional style. There are two blocks adjacent to each other connected by walk-up stairways. A gate and wall surround its perimeter.

Kaio is gone. He wasn't murdered; or, maybe he was. He wasn't taken by police, though it's possible that he could have been. He went out with a friend that Débora didn't know, a guy nicknamed Magro ("Skinny"). He never came back. The last time she heard from him was the next morning when she called him. "I'm in the middle of something," he said. "I can't talk now."

Débora has so many questions. What was he in the middle of? Who is Skinny, and what did he do? Or what does he know? Where is he now? What did they do to Kaio? Or is he out there, walking somewhere, in search of something?

When I see Débora at her house, she's shrunken back a little. Her hair is pulled back and up. She is in a well-worn sweater. She seems exhausted. Her smile is ephemeral. Débora has searched everywhere. She went to the police station to file a report. She's been to morgues, to cemeteries, to institutions for the socially abandoned. She's walked, and walked, and walked.

Débora's suffering is individual but systemic. She is alone, but the condition of being alone is produced. It fits within a long, aching, and deeply political history of violence. Some mothers in these conditions become radical, conjuring the force, against the odds, to contest the conditions of violence that seek, incessantly, to bury them. Fábio Araújo (2012) tells the story of a mother in the Brazilian city of Vitoria whose son disappears from a police station after being arrested. Days later, a burned body appears at the morgue. After cobbling together resources, the poor family manages to have a DNA exam carried out on the body. Months later, it comes back positive. In rage, this mother takes the burned and decomposing pieces of her son from the morgue. She takes them on a tour of all of the relevant state institutions—police, public prosecutors, the public security secretary—stopping at each to expose the rotting pieces of the body of her son. She publicly exposes it, in all its visceral, affective, and sensorial violence. The charred pieces of body stink, the sight of burned flesh jars the eyes, the sound of wailing shoots like pins through the ear. The violence is out of place in the city. This mother is furious. She places all of the blame for this violence on the state.

This could have been Débora, or Neide. But it isn't. At least not in such defined ways. Instead, they are of a different category. This is similar to how Dána-Ain Davis describes mothers of young men killed by police. These mothers "breathe between tears and work; awaiting relief from the flooding memories of their children and how a child's cheek felt against their lips. These women settle uncomfortably into boxes of suspended reality—needing reminders that they are still alive. Being the mother of a slain child animates nothing but unbearable weight" (Davis, 2016: 10).

Débora is also different because Kaio is gone, not dead. She doesn't know if it was the state; if it was, as she puts it, "that silver car that was driving around slowly," or if it was the PCC, a criminal organization that controls the region surrounding her former home. What she carries is a particular kind of sequela—"a subsequent infection." Christen Smith (2016b) writes about the sequelae—multiple continuous violences that follow from the first—for Black women like Débora they are the reverberating, gendered, and affective infections that appear and nag to the point of exhaustion.

Smith's interlocutors are, like Araújo's, mothers of sons murdered by the state. These sons have been found, giving only the most mitigated amount of finality. For Débora, and the thousands of mothers like her, the sequelae accompany her like a gnawing parasite on her search for a body and justice. This is a process of slow violence that continues to push Débora and others like her to the end of their rope.

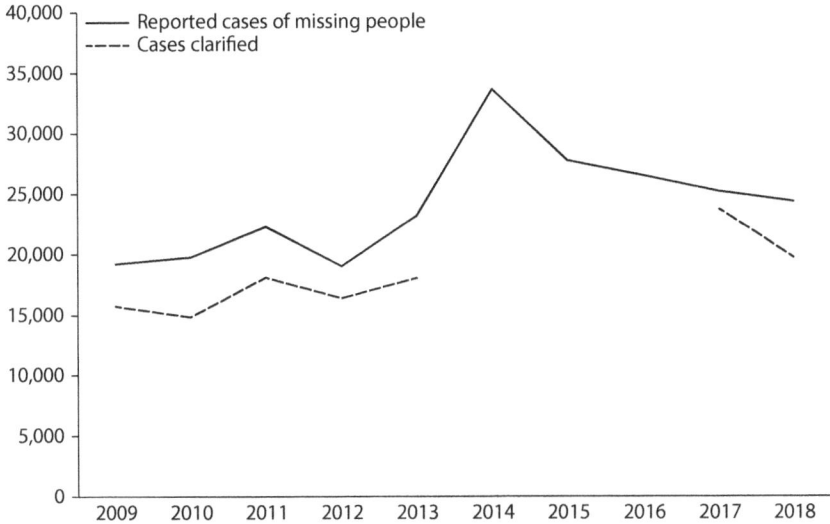

Figure 3. Reported cases of missing people in São Paulo State (graph by author with data from the Public Prosecutor's Office of São Paulo).

"They say 'you are so strong,' but we aren't strong," Débora breathes. "Not strong. We just learn to deal with this kind of situation. It isn't easy, easy to have to deal with this. And we have to find . . . I don't know from where . . . the strength to deal with it."

Some commit suicide. Others "can't talk now" because it is a bad day, week, or month. Many are slowly consumed by ache, by those conniving illnesses that prey on faltering and depressed bodies. They don't show in public. It takes far too much energy—which is misdirected anyway. Their energy, when they have it, gets plowed into their search. They look through hundreds of images of the most mutilated bodies, to inspect the disfigurations carefully, in case misshapen parts of a body might actually be hiding their child beneath. They rush to the morgue when a rumor spreads on Facebook, WhatsApp, or elsewhere that a body or bones have been found. They both want and don't want to know.

One of the bodies that Débora once saw pictures of still speaks to her. It could have been him. The police found the body of a young man in the forest, covered in dirt, surrounded by weeds. There are a handful of photos—only three or four. Débora mulls over one photo in particular. She keeps it on her phone, and she shows me. The body is completely swollen, its features smoothed out from the swelling. Almost totally unrecognizable.

"They found this body," she says, "and all they do is take pictures. They don't even clean it up. It is all covered in dirt." She describes the political materiality: "It was there in the middle of the scrubland, beaten up, murdered. And they make their judgment . . . é um lixo [it's just a piece of garbage]." Four or five photos exist to document the body. That's it. The body is nameless, by definition disappeared from somewhere.

But there was hair. Hair like Kaio's. This was years ago now. "If I could have paid for a DNA test, I would have," she says. She couldn't afford the few hundred dollars at the time. It annoys her endlessly still, this picture of a supposedly nameless *indigente* and how it was treated. "It doesn't matter if it was a *mendigo* or a thief; . . . there has to be dignity. They need to do their work properly."

In a way, all of her experience with an untrustworthy state goes way back. When Kaio was born at a hospital in São Paulo in 1996, nearly adjacent to the international airport, he was almost switched at birth. As she put it when we were speaking about Kaio's early childhood:

DÉBORA: He was a chubby little baby, strong, very beautiful. There was even a funny incident when I was leaving the hospital. They almost mixed up two babies. And I almost took the wrong baby home. . . . It was lucky that I noticed. . . . He was always healthy, happy, with a huge heart. He loved little children, loved them.

GDW: Wait, so the nurses dressed the wrong baby and gave it to you to take home?

DÉBORA: Yes, yes, that's right they dressed the baby and delivered it right to me. He was really chubby when he was born, and this other baby was really skinny. 'Oh my,' I thought, 'the baby is really different now.' So I had a good look and realized this wasn't actually my baby. I took its little foot out of the sleeper and looked at the little bracelet on the leg. And it was the wrong baby. So I took it back and the nurses lost their minds, begged a thousand apologies. I went right into the nursery myself, found him and got him dressed, then took him home.

Outside the hospital, Kaio was surrounded by a nurturing extended family. His grandfather was a boilermaker, employed for most of his life by

Figure 4. Kaio (photo by Débora).

a businessman with a small private company that made fire extinguishers. Though he had little formal education, he functionally ran the company. He knew all of the ins and outs of how it ran—and especially how to work the boiler. Though never unionized, Débora's father was well enough off and had consistent enough pay that he could buy land and build homes for the family and to rent out. Beneath the flight path, he bought a patch of land on a street corner. It was plenty ample, and on weekends he slowly built five homes on it—each fairly small and with only a couple of rooms— one above the other. He would come and go from work on a bicycle, always leaving at 4 a.m. They also built a curbside shop that would later become a corner bar that Débora's mom would manage.

When Débora and her husband married they went to live with her parents, and the extended family lived all together in this series of little homes. Birthdays for them and others were always together, very festive; Grandma always made a cake, and everyone would crowd around to sing "Happy Birthday" to whoever was celebrating. For years and years, things continued this way, with everyone happy and managing well—largely subsisting on the one regular pay check of Débora's father, the low-margin shop that it made possible, and the bits of rent coming from the growing extensions on the house.

That all changed when Débora's husband tried to kill her. In a fit of jealousy, he stabbed Débora seven times. She barely survived, passing through multiple reparative surgeries on her intestine, which had been severed, and to drain her lungs, which had filled with fluid. In recovery, after nine days in the ward, she left the hospital and chose to search for safety elsewhere. She took the children to find a safe place to get by, far from him. They landed in a city several hundred kilometers distant, where Débora did her best to lie low while trying to making ends meet.

It was around this time, following the move, that Kaio sought solace in drugs. With Débora struggling to manage in a different set of conditions, and now with multiple things to fear, she had few immediate solutions. A year on, she moved with the boys again—this time to live with her mother-in-law in a home near the coast. By this time, her ex-husband had pledged to help her get Kaio back on the straight and narrow. His violence against her became a second-order problem, and as he swore that it would never happen again, it seemed the best solution possible for her. With all of the difficulty the move had presented, and with Kaio and his brother now advocating for her to take their father back—but threatening to hurt him if he was ever violent again—it was perhaps her only real solution.

However, it was from this town on the coast that Kaio would eventually disappear.

Kaio's "is a difficult case," a public prosecutor named Viviane tells me. Viviane is White, and her persona and background stand in stark contrast to most of the people who come to her for help finding those who have gone missing. Her hair is golden, with dark layers, and the sharp edges of her black pantsuits and jackets lend an air of authority and formality. On first meeting, most would not dare call her by her first name. Prosecutors are some of the highest-paid public servants in Brazil, with salaries that easily afford a life behind private security gates and walls. But Viviane has chosen to take on the work of investigating disappearance as a professional and ethical mission, to allow her life to be pervaded by the uncertainty of disappearance, its subterranean politics, and all that this entails.

Being a prosecutor typically means two things as a starting point—passing an extremely challenging and competitive public exam after having completed a law degree, and being willing to do a particular kind of political arithmetic. Prosecutorial work in Brazil is heavily influenced by political interests that shape the contours of what each prosecutor may or may not pursue in terms of proactive work, especially if it has the potential to tip the apple cart. Politically sensitive topics that might cast high-profile figures in harsh light often meet quiet ends, sometimes—perhaps especially—after much effort has already been invested in unearthing key findings. Viviane, as with every other prosecutor I've met, has been told to take a case she has become personally invested in for years and bury it.

For the most part, Viviane has been able to work on questions of disappearance freely, however, because few expect her to find anything especially disruptive. Most understand this as a question of the poor, people whose personal problems, backgrounds in shady activities, or work as criminals have something to do with their unknown whereabouts. The answers are already axiomatic. And so, lacking any political worry, Viviane has had a green light to keep working on the issue.

Kaio's case, Viviane says, is one where the body could be in a clandestine grave somewhere. *Cemitérios clandestinos* (clandestine cemeteries) have proliferated in Brazilian cities, and indeed across Latin America more generally. But these spaces are really neither "clandestine" nor "cemeteries," being widely recognized as both commonly utilized for the disappeared and not places of commemoration. Instead I call these spaces "mundane mass graves," since their banality denies the idea that they are secret or that knowledge of their existences motivates a deliberate search or investigation by police.

Moreover, these burial spaces are specifically antithetical to commemoration. Rather than being spaces of memory, they are spaces designed to make people forgettable. Being buried here, outside of a state cemetery, is both an act of spatial governance—occurring in areas where the state rarely goes and rarely chooses to go—and a specific way to sever the living from the dead. Those who are buried in these spaces are put here so they shouldn't be found, removing the means for others to make life out of their death or their remains. Mothers, however, are undeterred.

In Mexico, mothers organize bake sales and raffles to fund their search for mass burials in the landscape, and on the outskirts of cities like Vera Cruz. Sometimes mundane mass graves become particularly apparent in public discussion, owing to a systemic kind of rupture. Starting in 2009, almost immediately after being awarded the 2016 Olympics, police in Rio de Janeiro embarked on a new public security policy that sought to remove "drug gangs" from informally urbanized but strategically located hillside favelas proximate to event venues. Called "pacification," this policy slowly, iteratively, and contentiously sought to retake control of spaces governed by these highly racialized and prison-rooted "gangs." This highly exceptional effort driven by the hosting of the Olympic games revealed something all too unexceptional. The "discovery" of burial fields in these recently "pacified" spaces. Police came across such spaces atop hillsides in at least seven different favelas during the early years of the policy. Many surely never made the news. In these fields, residents speak widely of such spaces as known but off limits, places used to kill and bury those believed to have transgressed rules about crime in the community, those accused of sexual violence and "snitching," among other deemed wrongs.

São Paulo has never seen an "exogenous" rupture like this that so dramatically (but very temporarily) remade the state's association with spaces that it had long absolved itself from, and what this might reveal about the scope or scale of mundane mass graves that dot the city. Here they exist nonetheless, well subsumed in everyday politics, created and used routinely, though usually containing smaller numbers of people, commonly two to four, rather than tens or hundreds as elsewhere. The internet and news websites are flooded with videos of police discovering, unearthing, and haphazardly examining their contents. And so, too, is YouTube, which has cellphone videos, even, of multiple people being made to dig their own graves before being shot, killed, burned, and buried. These spaces are said to be the product of the PCC, a group emergent from the prison system and now widely associated with a major decline in violence.

But not all mundane mass graves are the product of organized crime. Rather, they seem to exist as part and parcel of a systemic deregulation of life and death that has allowed people, bodies, and body parts to be used for science and accumulation. Mundane mass graves have been found on the grounds of hospitals and universities. These kinds of spaces aren't just the product of those operating in a sphere of state deregulation and inattention to bodies and life, but also of para-state entities themselves, that, in varying ways, have a long history of asserting political order.

Para-state death work functions sometimes in quite public and spectacular ways, and other times in the terrifying uncertainty and hollowness
of the lack of outcome. A lurid recent case, made public, followed how
an off-duty *guarda municipal* (low-level city bylaw officer) created fake
social media profiles of young women to lure five young Black men. He
then coaxed them to a location where he killed each of them, buried them
together in a pit and covered them with lime to accelerate decomposition.

Viviane has this kind of material space top of mind when she thinks of
Kaio's case, but she is very cautious about expressing it as a finality. No one
really knows. She has been working with Débora since he disappeared,
helping to connect dots within the bureaucracy, providing information
when it becomes available, and keeping herself accessible on WhatsApp.
Viviane knows, though, that there is plenty of reason to believe that Kaio,
who had recently come through a substance-abuse program, had fallen
afoul of people close to the PCC. There is no denying the PCC and its work,
which operates around what it calls a *paz entre ladroes* (peace among
thieves) of "good criminals" working through a particular "ethic of crime."
This work is both about asserting life that matters amid the country's
dehumanizing inequality and dramatic turn to mass incarceration, and
redefining lives that do not matter. It is around an assertion of the latter
that the organization asserts and codifies an identity, finding and punishing those whom it asserts are unethical criminals, persistent rule breakers,
or sexual miscreants. With one hand for care and the other for punishment, scholars such as Dias and Darke (2016) liken the organization to
the techniques of statecraft. Not all agree. Karina Biondi (2017) speaks of
it as a rhizome, evoking the way the organization eschews hierarchy and
has a multiplicity of connections in its enforcement of prison and urban
periphery order. Gabriel Feltran (2018), by contrast, sees the PCC as a
kind of highly masculine "brotherhood," like the Masons.

Whichever way, the PCC governs through a series of internal checks and
balances, punishing those who break its rules while, at the same time, "taking care" of those killed by police or while doing its "business." As I describe
elsewhere (Lessing and Denyer Willis 2019), it keeps highly organized
internal records of whom it punishes and why, and tracks its membership by bureaucratizing rule-breakers with "criminal criminal records," in
which every case file has at least twelve identifying fields used in order

to keep track of who is associated, who is not, and whether someone is a trustworthy fee-paying member, a kicked-out and delinquent former member, or someone that did something so severe as to constitute murder. Viviane knows, too, though, that this kind of supposition is a problem. It feeds the cycle of assumption and provides powerful fodder for people to deny the missing as worthy of a moment's notice.

Viviane fears that when Kaio told Débora he "was busy" when on the phone, he was with Skinny at a PCC tribunal, where members and a "judge" (senior PCC members on the phone in prison) and "jury" (made up of those involved in one way or another in a particular case) discuss whether someone has broken rules—and, if so, how they should be punished. But this process is absolute. Once a resolution is found, there is no turning back—for anyone involved. If Kaio had been on the wrong side of that judgment, he could very well be in a mass grave somewhere. At the same time, Kaio might have recognized this possibility, seeing its equivocated justice and totality coming toward him, and fled—like many others before him—with great haste.

The conditions surrounding this whole case are far from clear, and much of what Débora has encountered in her search muddies the water further. For example, when searching for Kaio, Débora struck up against a local drug boss. Débora thought that he knew something about Kaio. He was exceptionally arrogant and bothersome about it all. Fearless, Débora would openly call him out in front of others. And whenever in his presence, for he was often at the bar of a friend of hers that she would help clean, she would glare at him, staring him down and disagreeing with him on everything he would say. All of this scared her local friends, who were afraid that her fearlessness toward this man would lead to bad things.

And yet Débora got to know a different local drug boss—not a rival of the former—who showed concern for Kaio's disappearance, and who said he would see if he could find out more. As she describes it, they even developed a kind of friendship, with no hostility. But before he had time to tell Débora what he had found out about what happened to Kaio, he was arrested. He vanished into the prison system.

But it wasn't just Kaio and the local guy that disappeared in all of this. Skinny has since vanished, too. Viviane and Débora now know that he was in prison for a brief time but was untraceable even for people with access to the state's criminal justice databases. They later discovered that he'd been released almost right around the time that Viviane had filed an order to bring him in for questioning -which is still outstanding. It is possible, say both Viviane and Débora, that Skinny is himself on the run for doing something violent to Kaio that he wasn't authorized by the local crew to do. If he had broken these rules, his own life might be on the line. He could also still be in prison, or now back in prison, hidden within a labyrinth of unknowns inside the state itself.

Even Skinny's connections to the community seem to have evaporated to some degree. Skinny had lived with his mother, a person of very modest means, in the same neighborhood. Débora had come across her a couple of times. She, too, left the community soon after and Débora wagers that "her son's life made her life complicated, too." There are few answers as to where she went, or why.

Even if Kaio is in a mundane mass grave somewhere, the generalized anguish Débora gets from the state while searching for such a place stings. "Clandestine cemeteries" do not exist as investigative category that might allow for a dedicated state entity with specific techniques and methods to search and find them. And in case records, they are not written or described in bureaucratic or easily identifiable or consistent terms, making searches for numbers and aggregating data more difficult for those who have access and the desire to try. This equivocation of law, of how it is thinly but selectively deployed, runs like a seam through Kaio's disappearance, the meager investigation by the missing persons unit, and the absence of ethical concern when she speaks to others that should have the power to do something about it.

To make sense of this omission, Débora sometimes casts her search for Kaio alongside other cases of disappearance around the same time and place, especially involving people whose acute absence generated public consternation, and a massive search party. An incident like this happened just prior to Kaio going missing. The missing person happened to be a journalist. He was a White man, recently retired, who had traveled to the region to negotiate the sale of a piece of family property near the ocean. He vanished. His disappearance was out of place, just as Kaio's was to Débora and the rest of her family. And yet this man's family succeeded in elevating his disappearance in public discussion. They mobilized contacts

in the media, whose framing of the event revolved around the distinctive-
ness of this life, and of how important and known he was. The disappearance generated major headlines. Police found the man's body quickly,
within a few days. For Débora this was troubling, too, because all of the
effort expended to find out what happened to this man, showing that it
was indeed possible to pursue and to know, revealed an egregious contrast
with Kaio's disappearance.

They found the man's body in the kind of place that one person searching, or even a small group, would never come across. It took a manhunt
of larger proportions. Débora draws the comparison by referencing the
impossibility of finding people or clues in all of the *valas* ("trenches" or
pits) where the earth has been unsettled around her former neighborhood. The amount of digging required to reveal what the earth could be
hiding seemed boundless. They found the journalist by first finding the
man that he was last seen with. With time, and whatever else the police
did, this man confessed to killing the reporter and burying him. He took
them to the place.

Of course, there is no guarantee that Kaio was killed or buried anywhere near the town where they lived. Others suggest to Débora that it
is just as possible that Kaio's body, unidentified, might have been found
somewhere else, disappearing soon after into the uncertainty of state
bureaucracy and burial in a potter's field for indigents. If the body that
speaks to Débora was actually Kaio, he would now be in such a place. But,
six years on, his bones would have long been taken out of the ground, put
into a numbered plastic bag, and stored in the dark corner of a cistern-
like space—if not already incinerated. There, with limited identification
attached, they might have been slowly washed from memory by "environmental conditions."

It was for all of these reasons that Débora, Neide, and the other
mothers and fathers of the missing came to the steps of the courthouse,
in protest. And while the protest was partly about finding some finality
for their children, it was also transcendental—keeping these bones alive
in a bleak moment for an undefined future moment when the bones, and
their missing, might be recognized as human. The mass cremation and
disposal of those sixteen hundred unknown bones, which sat in bags in
a dank, leaky tomb, evident of nothing in particular, could one day be

identified, reclaimed, and put to work in a different political commitment to life from death.

In the end, with the help of Viviane and others, they succeeded. A higher court granted a stay, admonishing the city for its efforts, while finding that the unidentified remains could not be incinerated. For the moment, at least, the cemeteries would not be privatized and the bones within would not be incinerated, which would have made any future identification impossible. This, it seemed, was victory.

3 Unearthing Life

One afternoon, I stood beside a row of open graves in one of the city cemeteries for the urban poor and indigents, where caskets are allotted fifteen minutes each for burial. In this section of the cemetery where I stood, the caskets aren't for nameless paupers; they come with families, social ties, wailing. The gravediggers carry a table with their names on a piece of paper And yet the treatment of these bodies struck me as being hardly different from those buried nameless on the other side of this cemetery, a quiet corner for indigents without many visitors. Here, where families bury loved ones at an industrial pace, the difference between the *vala* and a grave seems negligible somehow. Disappearance is mixed into the soil, among and of the bones.

In an open grave, next to the one being filled by pallbearers and family, was a bone, as though placed there intentionally; it had been left behind during a routine disinterment that morning. Gravediggers and others walked around the edge of the grave as they placed the new casket beside it in the ground. Some of them looked in, noticed the bone, and moved on. No one mentioned it or pointed it out to anyone, as though it was as normal and unexceptional as other vestiges of disinterment, like the ornamental flowers and broadleaves people left. Some of these—like the leaf of *costela de Adão* ("Adam's Rib," or *Monstera deliciosa*)—lay around as metaphors of bone-like materiality and the biblical violence of the place. But this was not just a bone, some vestige of Adam, it was a worn old femur, the largest bone in the human body. And yet it was there, evidence of nothing, apropos of nothing. Just a remnant of unidentified bones.

Ten minutes later that lingering femur had a new casket placed on top of it. I was left to wonder. What really counts as the beginning and the end of the pauper's grave, the potter's field, or a mass grave, when all bodies of the urban poor are buried in places where bones are jumbled, left behind, treated like soil?

Asking how people disappear means looking to the material places where dead bodies usually go. It means, especially, looking to the burial places where the unknown meet those whom governments decided should not be known, and to the mixing that occurs between the two. The "potter's field"—indigent cemetery, pauper's burial ground, pit grave—is a category and practice that has existed for centuries. The idea is this: it is where the most worthless are buried, usually in "communal" conditions. It is a location where the everyday techniques of governance, and their by-products, are slowed and made material.

Take the case of New York City. Here an entire island—Hart Island—is a potter's field. It is abstracted from public view. Yet the bodies buried here have been actively predated and "cared for" in a range of ways. Insurance firms, old-age homes, hospitals, and the prison system shape the subjects of a condition where the inability to pay to be laid to rest defines the result. At Hart Island, *New York Times* journalist Nina Bernstein (2015) wrote that these bodies are buried in mass graves dug by industrial machinery and filled in by labor—prisoners—paid fifty cents an hour, often after "benefitting science" at elite NYC medical schools. The bodies of the potter's field—as with those who bury them—are deeply marked by race, evidenced as much in their lives as in their ultimate condition of material disposal. Historically, this is especially acute: the potter's field is where victims of lynching, hanging, and racialized violence are put in their place. But not only these; the potter's field is decisively shaped by governing logics as they shift over time.

And yet, in some places, potter's fields are also spaces where disinterment is standard and political massacres of past and present blend together in human fragments. Acute in Latin America, direct and indirect violence leads straight to tirelessly churning urban cemeteries that are sowed, unsowed, and sowed again. São Paulo is a case in point. Little seems sacrosanct or well ordered in the potter's fields here. Dogs traipse by. Bits of coffin are everywhere. Scraps of button-up shirts lie partially buried all around.

In one of these terrains, Otávio digs, day in and day out. Otávio is paid by the city to dig graves. On one of the days that I see him, he is disinterring in the cemetery's section for children, spoken of as *anjos* (angels). Pinched between his thumb and index finger is a tiny rib bone. He turns it over and back again to see both sides. "She was a little Bolivian," he says. To our side, on the edge of the earth he has just removed, are a number of thin straight sticks, turned black after three years beneath. He has pulled these out first. It looks like they were used to wrap the small body for burial. Otherwise, there is no casket to be seen.

Otávio is a slender Black man. Behind him is a row of six or seven open graves carved out of São Paulo's ochre earth. He's disinterred these so far this morning. This is routine, cyclical work. Digging up the bones of *anjos*—dead children. All of the remains in this field, and in the fields for adults that surround it, were put in by him or one of the other *coveiros* (gravediggers) around three years previous. Such is the mundane cycle of interment and disinterment that accompanies a free burial provided by the city, hinging on 1,095 days as roughly enough time for complete decomposition. At the foot and head of these graves is a ridge of loose earth piled, shovelful by shovelful, to the side. This afternoon it will be shoveled back into these graves, on top of another little body. In the meantime, these graves are open and ready.

We chat as he pulls out other tiny bones—parts of a cranium, leg, and arm—putting them in a gray plastic bag. He finds little woven yellow-and-white mitts or booties. Too small to tell which. They must be made of polyester. They didn't degrade. Otávio says he makes sure to put things like this in the bag too. "It helps the family to know that these are the right bones." If they come to collect them.

He digs a little farther with his hand in a blue latex glove. "Sometimes you find snakes," he says. "You know it is a snake because it doesn't come out." He mimics a snake moving with his hand over the dirt in a squiggly motion. "Do they bite?" I ask. "No," he chuckles, "or at least that's what they say! Frogs are different, though. They can fill you with terror. They jump out abruptly when the dirt is unsettled from on top of them. There is one *coveiro* that runs away when this happens," he says, laughing aloud. "It freaks him out. He can't handle the idea of something jumping from the earth. In this job you can't think. You just need to do it," he says. "Just dig. Just pull out the bones. Just put people in. The rest can never stick to you. Otherwise, you're done for. *Senão, você fica louco* [If not, you'll go crazy]."

In my own laughter about the frog—it is kind of horrifyingly funny—I step back into the ridge of soil. When I do, I notice a stark white bone emerging from the loose dirt on one of the berms. It is an adult bone, clearly. I point it out to Otávio. "A back bone?" I ask. It is kind of spiny. He thinks it isn't. "Maybe part of the knee. Like this," he picks it up and mimics where it might fit on his own body. After a moment or two of conjecture, he takes it, picks up a shovel and walks to an adjacent row of graves. He chooses one that is partly open, wedges the shovel in, and places it back underground, still within the terrain of the *anjos*.

The cemetery that Otávio works in once followed a grand plan, a dream-work of modernist government bent on progress through infrastructure, orderliness, and design. This is recognizable in vestiges. At the original entrance there is a boulevard, with two lanes, trees in the island and on either side. They reach high, significant on the landscape. The road was once paved with tarmac up this boulevard, which leads to a tower. One could imagine the original material rendering of this place as a planned space with ideals. High modernist planning made in a historical moment of centralized schemes to improve the human condition, where the creation of space intends to reformat social practice.

Much has changed since. While the external form or material shell slowly withers, its internal and surrounding components have been changing with dynamism. The cemetery grew as the city urbanized, expanding into two parts, each with a separate administration and spatial domain. The original gate, which had a planned car park and a gently sloping road through the walls, has been locked shut. Outside this gate, a man lives under a piece of plastic wrapping, fastened to a wall opposite. The mundane flow of people, and the lack of subsequent political investment, has taken its toll on the original vision. That grand plan remains in appropriated fragments. Today, on city maps, the cemetery is represented by blank space and a series of "+" signs denoting something undefined within. to indicate grave markers. There are no internal details represented, as though it is empty, or its contents are unidentifiable.

But Otávio hints to me that this isn't just an abandoned space. There is important order in the cemetery that comes from these vestiges of planning, which remain useful for making work a little easier. Along the edges of each *quadra*, lines of trees remain, some flourishing and others fading. The trees are important. They serve as orientation markers for how to locate rows and burial locations. When the burial spaces of soil become grassy mounds, and the granite plaques become jumbled, the trees are static: Two trees up, six graves in, one row above. Dig there.

In the somber conditions of São Paulo's cemeteries for the poor, the commemoration of life and death matters a great deal. Most families manage to cobble together enough funds for a basic funeral package. This typically includes a small salt-and-pepper-colored granite plaque engraved with two brief phrases of text, as well as date of birth and date of death. For an additional sum, a small concave button-like oval picture of the person may be fastened on the plaque. Also included is a small prefab candle shelter, typically then placed at the foot of the grave, where families may put votive candles or other long-burning artifacts. The plaques are not usually finished by the time the burial takes place. They are brought by someone a few days later, polished and new, and placed at the head of the grave. In the topography of the place, verdant and bumpy amid the ochre, their dates of death also later become a compass for where someone like Otávio should disinter. When it comes time to disinter, these plaques become waste.

They aren't just waste, however. They become a means for asserting dignity in other ways. The road, once smooth tarmac, is now broken up along most of the boulevard, and in most other thoroughfares. This is especially true of the intersections that lead down the hill, serving to channel torrential rains that make cars skid up the pasty ochre mud. One afternoon, I walk with Otávio toward the administration building for a lunch break. The road at the crest of the hill here is still mostly intact. But as we turn to walk down, it's broken apart. "Erundina paved this," Otávio says, as though he knew I'd noticed the near absence of the road. Little rivulets once formed in the rain have grown into gullies. They eventually funneled water beneath the tarmac, washing out the aggregate beneath. Where there once was asphalt with a proper foundation there are now a series of gulches running down and across the road. Cars must swerve around them, or drivers must find strategic traction on their edge, leading them nearly into the trees and burial plots.

Luiza Erundina is a former city mayor, elected in 1988, just as Brazil was creating a visionary and people-oriented new constitution. She became a national senator five mandates in with the most prominent socialist party (PSOL). Recently but fleetingly, she presided over Congress after corruption charges ousted the sitting member in 2016.[1] While other prominent leftist parties and leaders have moved toward the center, she hasn't. Now called "elderly," she detests the idea that age should hamper her dedication to a socialist world.

"Damn them," she said when asked in 2020 if she should retire, "You know, if you lose your life project, everything loses meaning. And my life project doesn't finish in my lifetime. My project is to dream of another future. I don't want to change São Paulo and Brazil, I want to change the world. My dream, of a socialist society, fraternal and equal, sadly won't happen in my lifetime, I'm conscious of that. But if I don't do my part now, this kind of society won't ever happen." She concluded saying, "The dream that moves me, all of the transformations that society needs, doesn't age."[2]

As a mayor and since, Erundina had an incisive political vision for the urban poor. Humanizing the city's cemeteries became a necessary part of her focus. Herself a migrant from the arid hinterland of a poor northeastern state, a region dominated historically by the slave economy and sugar monoculture, she recognized the life of the poor, earnestly and politically, even in death. This translated to the value given to infrastructure projects that targeted the political conditions and materiality of death for the urban poor. Otávio's cemetery became a reflection of her political urgency. Roads were paved, infrastructure renewed and burial conditions improved. Where once a fetid urban brook flowed in the cemetery, new culverts were put in place and covered with cobblestone. She had the same attention and concern for other cemetery spaces, including one where she revealed a Cold War mass grave.

Otávio must be right, I thought. The gulch-ridden road hasn't seen political attention since. It certainly appears that way. Brazil's most recent iteration of counter-hegemonic politics, evoked in the rise of former president Luis "Lula" da Silva, a man who evolved from a machine worker and labor organizer to be head of state, did many things to mitigate inequality—targeting the poorest, mitigating hunger, enabling pathways into higher education for the Black population. At the same time, many say that though Lula started "red," his political movement shifted decisively to the center, becoming a darling of what became commonly called Latin America's "pink tide."[3] Many have since declared those policies successful, at least in filling bellies, getting many more kids to school, and growing the economy. But just as Lula's larger political agenda placed comparatively more money into the hands of the middle class in the form of things like international scholarships, with less than $30 a month in conditional cash transfers for the poorest, he shied away from any systemic and structural questions about the conditions of life and death for the poor.

Over the course of fifteen years, Lula and his successor, Dilma Rousseff, advanced a number of progressive policies. But they also invested heavily in policing and prisons. Unlike prison construction, which boomed during the years of their government, never did a cemetery appear in the government's two "accelerated growth program" stimulus packages, known as PAC1 and PAC2, with their combined investment of 2.1 trillion Brazilian *reais* (US$1 trillion in 2009). While some gains were made, this "left" politics only marginally attenuated major biopolitical questions such as the provision of adequate health care and life infrastructure, preferring more workable tinkering solutions done through public-private partnerships.

Violence rose to its highest levels in recorded history through Lula's and Dilma's presidencies, new prisons were built, and an ad hoc federal police force was created.[4] Thus more pressure was placed on the cemetery in these years, which was not met by new expenditure or recognition of such material questions of life and death infrastructure.[5]

For nearly thirty years, the streets of this cemetery, its political infrastructure, have been left in a shambles. The roads are now almost useless, especially in the rain. People still die and must be buried when it rains. Though cars can usually pass, anyone who must walk this road when it is muddy ends up with red muck caked on their shoes and fancy dress or trousers. And, of course, many people who come here don't drive. Not by a long shot. It is another order of humiliation to arrive at the graveside, caked in the same terracotta earth used to bury a loved one, with your best clothes totally soiled.

Otávio and the other gravediggers are conscientious. These amorphous but material injustices settle heavily on the shoulders of those who work here. They recognize the humility and humble backgrounds of those that come to their cemetery. Broken infrastructure shouldn't go unaddressed. It should be mended, somehow. Their will to continue, to push on, to try to build something better can be framed in different lights. For some, Otávio digs as Erundina does, toward a horizon with a future but undefined redemptive. In all of his careful digging, collecting, and bagging of booties, he unearths life from death, keeping memories alive against all countervailing force.

In the meantime, he needs to make space for more people in the cemetery. He cares for them, with each bone in a bag, each polyester booty saved, part of a conscientiousness. And yet capitalism condemns him to dig at an ever faster industrial pace, keeping time with ever-accelerating conditions.

This regime of governance by indifference cannot obliterate all kinds of agentic and emergent organization. There is life in the ruins of this mode of capitalism, and in the ruins of political inequality. There is Black life emergent, historic and contemporary. There is life before the future redemptive, in the present, in the incipient political space, another future, among dead bodies.

These questions coalesce, at least partly, into material form. Much is produced in excess in this disassembly-line space; there is an abundance of waste as a result. New dumpsters are filled and taken away every day with the remnants of routine disinterment; things like bits of clothing, old shoes, faded flower arrangements, huge chunks of wood, plastic spinney wheels and laminated medium-density fiberboard coffins that burst apart when wet.

Not everything is waste. Much becomes useful. The granite grave plaques are heavy, hard to dispose of and durable. The same is true of concrete candle shelters. If not broken, they can be reused. These most weather-resistant of materials, and other formidable pieces—old coffin handles, solid chunks of coffin, and sometimes even bones—are excellent pothole filler. Cemetery workers have taken to gathering up these fragments, which tend to lie around anyway, to patch up the gaping washouts in the road. They do it every so often, using the material outcomes of political indifference to make life just a little more bearable for those who need to grieve.

My conversation with Otávio digresses. His wife hasn't been well. He commutes by bus from hundreds of miles away to work in the city cemetery during the week. She remains at home, with regular trips to the public hospital in the city for treatment. Her condition is serious but chronic, having declined of late. And the doctors told her some months ago that they didn't have the supply of blood to keep treating her illness with blood transfusions. Not enough people choose to give blood to the public health system. They are running dry. Blood is a commodity in São Paulo, to be mined or purchased. And though Otávio's wife having to halt transfusions would mean a slow and painful death, the hospital people had one solution: gather your friends, gather your family, gather whoever cares about you, and get them to give blood.

Otávio did. His fellow gravediggers and their families rallied, rolled up their sleeves and gave of themselves for her life. They mined for blood. They gave enough to patch the infrastructural failures of a health system reserved for those who cannot afford an alternative—or who must avoid the cheap and predatory private alternatives. While the gravediggers, and Otávio, could just as easily have ended up burying her, they mobilized, used their tactics to leverage an alternative: more life for Otávio's family. Their agency saved Otávio's wife, for a while at least. And they've once again bent, but not broken, under the weight of shock and pressure.

I walk with Otávio from the Quadra dos Anjos. We are headed toward the administration building, which is across a valley and up the other side. "There isn't even a bathroom here," he says, "which is terrible when you get a pain in your stomach." "So you have to find some place to hide?" I ask. "Except there isn't any," he says. "Anywhere you go, you are visible to someone." I try not to imagine what it would be like to see a gravedigger shitting on the cemetery grounds, in obvious discomfort. What would families think? "Even one of those ones that they have for events," he says, reflecting on what should be possible. "Like a portable toilet?" I say. He nods.

That Otávio and other gravediggers must shit on the very earth where others are buried—and perhaps in sight of others who are burying their loved ones—is a damning empirical truth. Otherwise, the only place even remotely obscured, where one can be discrete but in discomfort, is the eucalyptus grove, near the vulture signpost.

Like elsewhere in Latin America, São Paulo's cemeteries for the urban poor are full of vultures.[6] They are just there always, their interest in scattered trash and meat indistinguishable. In this place where bones are similarly indistinguishable from the semi-submersed sticks fallen from draping tree canopies, a vulture is much more than a material presence. They go unmentioned and seemingly unnoticed by *coveiros* and visitors alike. Not that they would be welcome amid the marble tombs of spectacular and wealthy cemeteries. Even their presence and symbolism seems entirely lost on those bureaucrats or NGOs who would try to remake the cemetery as a more welcoming space under minimal-budget logics.

Rather than exorcise the vultures from the cemetery, managers made an effort some time ago to reclaim them as "natural," mitigating their presence and symbolism in a place of human bones. Down the hill from the most heavily used cemetery fields, managers put up a series of "ecological trail" signs in a reforested grove of eucalyptus trees. Those visiting the cemetery might want to understand the local flora, they must have surmised. Nature is peace. But besides being the best place for a gravedigger to alleviate a terrible bellyache, this grove has since grown to make these signs invisible behind tree trunks. Looking around, I see that the first has fallen down. Only a post remains. The second is a photo of the *urubu*, that nefarious-looking character without a feather on a red-stained head, beak protruding. The sign reads:

Popular Name: Urubu

Scientific Name: *Coragyps atratus*

Characteristics: Feeds from dead animals and other decomposing organic material. Their habitat is throughout Brazil and they live in groups.

Débora and the other mothers speak with an intimate familiarity of Otávio's work, though they have never met each other. They have been here many times before. Débora and Otávio are contiguous, as people witnessing bodies and bones, and working through an everyday effort to unearth life and keep bones alive. Débora's effort to find a way to do a DNA exam on the body of the man who looked like Kaio ran into all sorts of problems—some of which may have run off of Otávio's shovel. With money, doing a DNA test is straightforward, in theory: "Go to the cemetery, get the bones, and do the exam privately, just like that," as she says. But without money, she hasn't been able to do it. That body continues unidentified but alive in Débora's mind, and on her phone. Her attachment to the possibility of that body, those bones, being Kaio, "That doubt stays with you."

Even when Débora was looking at the photo in the station, the body was already in the ground, buried. "They wait fifteen days, but sometimes even fewer, I think," she laments. Then they bury them and there is no way to see them in the flesh. Even as we speak, that photo, that body, are of a kind of history. "If they jumbled it all up when they disinterred, putting the bones in the bag, didn't put it away properly . . . there is no way."

Débora may never find Kaio, but she will keep searching. Her narration of the search for Kaio in the body of the unidentified young man moves through Otávio's world, through a vivid description of the minimal management of bodies on the cheap. "It takes its toll on us," she says, this "solitary search," "You'll go crazy," says Otávio. He may never find people coming to reclaim the bones of their children, but he will keep bones alive for those who search.

4 Disappearance and the Cemetery

"Have you heard of the Vala de Perus?" Débora asks. The *vala* that Débora revisits in her mind's eye is a Cold War–era mass grave within one of the city cemeteries. This cemetery, also known as Dom Bosco, was especially consecrated for the indigent, understood by authorities as those unclaimed by family or with no acquaintances after their death. But this cemetery worked as a kind of shroud for what existed within it. Beneath the rhetoric of the *indigente* was a direct, political kind of intervention. The political void that surrounds the nameless poor, a space that rarely begs larger questions, could be used to obscure things—people, bodies, a violent political project—that *did* beg larger questions. From the early 1970s, in the midst of a US-supported Cold War dictatorship, police and military men like Coronel Malhães tried to make suspected dissidents disappear here, placing them in this and analogous spaces of namelessness, excising their bodies as sites of contestation while instilling fear in their social relations by tossing them amid hundreds of socially dead indigent bodies.

There is a great deal of important scholarly work on the disappeared and on the ways that states have made people disappear. Rightly, much of this literature links disappearance to political crises, massacres, and recent historical events attending to the techniques of Cold War insurgency and counterinsurgency. It documents the continuing search for mass graves of states, para-states, rebel groups, and those working in the interstices. The Madres in Argentina; Indigenous communities throughout Central America; populations in Southeast Asia and in the Balkans; and families of real or perceived "insurgents" in Chile, Brazil, and other places, all give evidence of these conditions.[1]

The missing in Latin America have been a central concern over the past five decades. Much of the focus in Latin America, and beyond, has been on Las Madres de la Plaza de Mayo, a group of mothers and grandmothers of the disappeared in Argentina. This group, which every Thursday occupies a central plaza in Buenos Aires, seeks a resolution for their missing relatives, who were taken, it is widely believed, by the Argentine military government in the 1970s and '80s. In Brazil, similar concerns focus on a comparatively small number of men and women, 243 disappeared, during Brazil's dictatorship from 1964 to the mid-1980s.

The extensive work on disappearance in Cold War Latin America engages very directly with the politics of dead bodies, or, put differently, with the political potentiality of dead bodies. The perpetrators of this violence sought, at least partly, to obscure the finality of the act for fear of people holding them to account. As Ferrándiz and Robben (2015: 1) write, there was a "deliberate commingling of remains in unmarked graves." This effort was not just to make individuals absent from their political fight, but also to remove the political remnants contained in the materiality and symbolism of their bodies. In making them disappear they created symbolically nameless subjects, what I think of as "political indigents," hidden amid a generalized politics of disappearance, which hinders their becoming martyrs for a cause against the seated political project. Disappearance was about stripping away political resistance as an act committed by individuals, and political resistance as a social category.

A focus on reclaiming particular kinds of bodies lost in battles of the past or in the crises of the contemporary is a search, too, for the political consolidation of the liberal democratic present. The proliferation of disappearances and mass graves, and the study of both, give evidence of the ways that a historical exception can come to justify a norm while creating new silences. While this work of finding history is vitally important, it can further bury the quiet and ongoing centrality of mundane disappearances to everyday political order. Here, the cemetery is an infrastructure that reveals the evolving and enduring relationship between disappearance and politics. In what follows, I would like to show that, across historical moments, the cemetery reveals how disappearance works in its different modulations and in striking spatial patterns of terrestrial layering and proximity.

"How is it possible that police were killing and burying people without anyone seeing it?" Débora laments. Her narrative reaches back to history, to what is often framed as a different political moment, passed now, where mass graves were transparently a political question. The mass grave at Dom Bosco cemetery looms over what she is usually concerned with—today's dead and disappeared—and traces a substantive point: the practice of disappearance as a political condition has never actually gone away. For mothers like Débora, the cemetery remains a place for searching, where answers might be found in the foreground of a Cold War mass grave. Here, and especially in terrains where nameless bodies are buried, mothers investigate, gravediggers bury, and history is at work. And so is politics, still, decisively. Centered on the state or not, cemeteries are the infrastructure of political order, and the shifting material terrains of dead bodies are the shifting material terrains of political order—whether inside city cemeteries or not. Cemeteries are, by their very nature, terrains of both political making and political disappearance, of the enactment of commemoration for some and the disposal of others who are not known or should not be known.

In *The Work of the Dead*, Thomas Laqueur (2016) argues for a recognition of the "age of the cemetery," where the ways that cemeteries change and are used is an expressly political question. People respond to the political uses and spatial reformatting of cemeteries and the changing burial conditions they imply, mobilizing, creating new forms of sociality—like burial societies—and remaking the conditions of life in the process. Laqueur's focus is the reorganization of cemeteries in the nineteenth century, where a decline in churchyard burials and the expansion of private funereal interment took place, following larger structural changes in patterns of political order and industrialization. Deeply intertwined with Victorian urbanization and new foundations of capitalist production, privately run cemeteries emerged as commoditized terrains, in counterpoint to ecclesiastic cemeteries. These were, in a particularly emergent division and order, classed spaces legitimized but not necessarily administered by central government. And they were driven by a particular specter of that which they were not: a mass grave. Under this new logic of class, spatially delineated in earth, abandonment in death became an acute truth for the living. The undignified pauper's funeral attended and commemorated by no one drove sales in individual private cemetery plots (Laqueur, 2016). To be sent to a pit in a jumbled mess with tens of nameless others was a powerful motivation for an alternative, as was the dream of being buried in a private, high-class cemetery at a distance from the urban and living masses. The cemetery of disappearance—the pauper's grave, potter's field—was a powerful catalyst for paying in advance for a burial, with early forms of life insurance.

This cemetery of the "unidentified" and its uses are not finite. They change in direct relation to the governing logics of life. In Brazil, questions of cemeteries, burial, and disappearance take distinctive historical forms, even well before major industrialization. João Reis (2003) documents how the city of Salvador in colonial times had varied cemetery practices that revolved around the church, both spatially and morally. Burial worked through societies organized around and through the multitude of churches, which themselves worked through racial and social groupings. Spatially, being close to the altar was important, and those at some moral distance, including pagans, slaves, criminals, indigents, and those who died by suicide were buried elsewhere in a specific cemetery, the Campo da Pólvora. Christians were prohibited from being buried here, in a cemetery run by the city. The labor of bringing bodies to this cemetery was the same work as cleaning the city, and bodies were left in a condition that allowed them to be predated by hungry animals. As at the Cemitério dos Aflitos in eighteenth-century São Paulo, the hanging scaffold was adjacent to this cemetery, maintaining a linear relationship between deprecation, efforts to flee slavery, acts of criminality, and capital punishment.

Rio de Janeiro's heightened relationship with the slave trade in the eighteenth and nineteenth centuries meant that it had its own space of maligned burial, known as the Cemitério dos Pretos Novos, adjacent to the historic port area. Here, unbaptized or "new" African arrivals were buried in jumbled conditions in a space adjacent to the slave market, close to the port area. Pretos Novos was distinct in this case, existing apart from the everyday cemetery for the "unprivileged" which maintained a linked relationship to the church and the Santa Casa da Misericórdia hospital, which remains in the same location several hundred meters away. But at this time, Brazilian society was not predominantly urban.

The logics of medicalization and modernism were forceful in reshaping the spatial relationship between cemetery and city, even in Latin America. A new denomination of dead bodies as unhygienic brought with it centralized techniques of moving death outside the city, making it less visible and more spatially discrete. Reis's work on Salvador recalls an acute protest against this spatial transformation and privatization—which temporarily succeeded but was followed on, a handful of years later, by an acute crisis of urban cholera that might not have happened otherwise. This protest was to maintain death as a site of public commemoration, centered on the church within the city, working through the everyday festival and crucial sociality that vitalized the church and its forms of truth and belonging. The threat was that burial elsewhere would push all of this to the margins and invisibility—a move decisively shaped by the incipient truth of positivist science and enlightenment ways of knowing. Cemeteries, history tells us, are not static. They, too, are sites of political and social transformation, moving and shifting in kind.

But since then, nearly two hundred years ago, cemeteries appear to have not changed much, especially in the way that they push death to the edges of society. The cemetery for the poor retains a linear relationship between morality, violence, and defamation in burial, across time periods. It works categorically. In discussions of violence and democracy that surround post-Cold War Latin America, scholars often reference Brazil's 1992 Carandiru prison massacre. In a single incident, riot police killed 111 inmates—with machine guns, shotguns, knives, and bombs. This case has been theorized and historically situated as it relates to institutions, citizenship, and the development of Brazil's post-dictatorship democracy. But this massacre is nothing if not an instance in the historical arc of violence against marginal populations.

Where the bodies of those killed at Carandiru ended up further points to the historical congruence of the potter's field. They were sent to Vila Formosa, Latin America's largest cemetery. This place is vast—and unsettled, too. There are empty holes of red earth yawning everywhere. Remnants of past graves—broken portraits, granite plaques, pieces of clothing—scatter the fields, making it difficult to know what or who is buried where. The grounds are expansive—seven hundred eighty thousand square meters. In colloquial discussions, many have told me that there is only one larger; it is in China. An estimated 1.5 million people have been buried in Vila Formosa since it opened in 1949.

If death were the same kind of big business in Brazil that it is in the United States, things would be dramatically different still. In Brazil, though, state payments for health-related services go less systematically and fluidly to private third parties—old-age homes, caregivers, hospitals, and so on—that keep poor people alive, indebting them and turning their impending death into a commodity, until their death and an eventual payout. For the moment, everyone in São Paulo gets a free—if very sparse—burial. The city pays and manages most of the cemeteries. For now, they are public, open to all and made open for all. They have a clear everyday rhythm, even if there are pieces of coffin, bone, and plastic commemoration everywhere. Their management is utterly modest, succumbing to the demands of routine burial and disinterment.

In this social space, people find ways to commemorate despite the constraints. Just getting to the cemetery can entail serious effort. This place is in the eastern reaches of the city, a significant distance from metro and arterial bus lines. To get here is easiest for those who live in this part of the city, where, also, "quality of life" is of significantly less "quality" than in wealthy neighborhoods. People in wealthy neighborhoods bury their dead in places like Cemitério da Consolação, where tourists go to see the most ornate tombs, sculptures, and permanent funerary rites. This cemetery's walls are fortified with razor wire. Outside the walls, on a busy thoroughfare across from the medical school and University of São Paulo hospital, is a row of around fifty flower-vendor stalls. While they now also sell to those stopping by in cars, these vendors are historically rooted in the creation and display of bouquets to commemorate death. They compete for a lively market.

This is far from Vila Formosa. Here, commemoration works through small granite plaques, spinney wheels, and plastic flowers and figurines. Disinterred gravesites reveal something about these commemorations too. Fragments of solid wood—pine or similar—remain in some. In most others, bits of medium-density fiberboard blend into the earth around, leaving only bits of shiny faux-wood laminate behind.

On one visit a cold wind blew through the trees. The night prior had dropped to four degrees Celsius in the city. For São Paulo, this is very cold. On the way to the cemetery the taxi driver told me that a six-year-old boy who was living with his parents on the street had died of hypothermia. We conjectured that he, too, might be going to Vila Formosa, the place where many of the urban poor—those left to die—are buried today. This happens in an incessant routine. Rows of pre-dug graves wait, inevitable. Around them, disinterred graves of those buried three years prior dot the terrain.

This is the place where most of the dead from the Carandiru massacre were buried—eighty-seven of them (Rezende, n.d.). This momentous massacre early in Brazil's re-liberalization is often seen as evidence of the shift in categories of state violence away from the killing of real or suspected political insurgents and toward those—criminals, the poor—who might usurp economic prosperity. Most of the eighty-seven that were buried here have long since been disinterred.

This disinterment happens from 9 a.m. to 12 p.m. every morning, carried out manually by a shovel-bearing crew. But there is no time to collect everything in the coffins. In exhumations the big bones usually come up, as do what is left of larger remnants—clothing, shoes, or plastic items.[2] Those go in overflowing dumpsters. Most of the coffin stays in the ground. Much of the body does, too. Forget about any small bones—fingers, hands, feet. Or even big bones. The next one will go on top. This is not a disinterment of reclamation or reconciliation. Writ large, it is a disinterment of disposal.

Vila Formosa is historically significant. The beginning of its significant history starts with Brazil's Cold War government. Brazil's dictatorship in 1964 brought with it a wave of state violence. In 1968, the state's counter-insurgency accelerated with the signing of an "Institutional Act" (AI-5) that abolished habeas corpus, established media censorship, and closed the National Congress and state assemblies. In addition, this act effectively centralized power in the federal government under the pretense of national security, resulting in a highly coordinated campaign against real or perceived political dissidents. The result was an explosion of political killings and disappearances.

In São Paulo, a number of those killed by police and "communist-hunting" extermination groups ended up in the ground at Vila Formosa. There, they were buried as nameless indigents or with false names. Much more rarely, they were released to family members. An extensive 1995 report by the group Tortura Nunca Mais ("Torture Never More"), details the fate of fourteen such insurgents at Vila Formosa, drawing direct lines from their political activity to state repression and subsequent effort to make the individuals disappear. One such case is reported as follows:

> Hamilton Fernando Cunha, Militant of the Popular Revolutionary Vanguard (VPR). Born in Florianopolis in 1941, son of Fernando Manoel Cunha and Filomena M. Rosa. Killed by machine gun on February 11, 1969, while resisting arrest, as police from the Department of Social and Political Order attempted to capture him at his workplace. The police version of the repressive event states that Hamilton had been shot by a revolutionary companheiro, who escaped unidentified, when police announced he was under arrest. He was buried as an indigent at Vila Formosa Cemetery in São Paulo. (Torture Never More, 1995: n.p.)

Also among these known burials was the country's most prominent leftist revolutionary—Carlos Marighella, leader of Ação Libertadora Nacional (National Liberation Action, ALN), a group known for their kidnapping of the US ambassador in 1969. His action as a Marxist became internationally famous with his writing of the *Mini-Manual of the Urban Guerilla* (Marighella, 1969). Marighella was perhaps the most publicly known person ever buried at Vila Formosa, defying the insignificance of the place otherwise.

In 1969, the police were themselves looking to make bodies disappear unwatched. The terrorist must be made silent in death, must be uncommemorable. With the killing of political insurgents on the upswing under new federal powers, political leaders sought to make their own repressive violence entirely invisible. Vila Formosa was too busy. This potter's field was too expansive and not invisible enough. It could help make people disappear—but not without a trace.

On March 2, 1971, the state consecrated Dom Bosco, the cemetery that Débora speaks of, on the far northern reaches of the city adjacent to a neighborhood called Perus. Surrounded by steep hillsides and green forests, and only reasonably accessible by car, this remote cemetery was purportedly the city's first burial ground exclusively for indigents and the unknown. But much more was underfoot. The government contracted a British firm named Dowson and Mason to build an industrial-grade cremation furnace. This company found it startling that a cremation furnace was necessary, given the design of the cemetery, and the purpose. They wrote a note to raise their concern:

> It seems this project has no funeral hall, and has some things, frankly, that we cannot understand—even though we have been incorporated and working for 15 years on cremation projects around the world.... We would like to know the reasons why two enormous entrances to the cremation room, where the actual cremations take place, are necessary given that this is usually a discrete place where some people only ask to be. It would be especially disturbing for these doorways to remain open all the time for the general public or anyone to see inside. (cited in Bobadilla, n.d.)

Like the military furnaces turning the disappeared into ash in Peru, Dom Bosco wasn't meant to be a public place.[3] No one was supposed to see the bodies going in. By design, it was a closed factory that would allow a high flow of bodies to disappear in no-nonsense ways. At the height of a political moment where the Brazilian government was being increasingly and internationally implicated in tortures and disappearances, such an inhumane design was frightening to the contractors. Dowson and Mason did not build the cremation furnace. In some ways, this was irrelevant. Dom Bosco remained a cemetery for indigents, drawing little attention in a political moment where congregation in public and organized political activities of any kind were prohibited.

It was under this guise that Dom Bosco came to be a site for the disposal of political insurrection. Twenty years later, in September 1990, with the support of Erundina, São Paulo's first female mayor, human-rights workers and forensic anthropologists excavated a thirty-meter-long trench—Débora's *vala*—at the site, revealing a mass grave with 1,049 bags of bones, and another 525 bodies. Dom Bosco became the focal point of a national discussion and contested reconciliation with the violence of the dictatorship period. International forensic and human rights experts visited and wrote reports, and the case made headlines globally. Years later, investigations are ongoing. Political involvement with the process, including meddling in the universities responsible for the remains, stalled advances. Revitalized in 2014, the search to identify political dissidents had gained new momentum—having opened 151 of 1,049 boxes and analyzed 144 sets of bones. Of the bones cataloged, eighty-one were male and twenty-four female (Nuzzi, 2015). But who are they all?

The discussion about democracy, disappearance, and reconciliation around Dom Bosco is really the only reason this cemetery is well acknowledged. In that sense, the cemetery *is* the mass grave within it. There is no interest in the indigent bodies that surround it, or the unknown bodies that are jumbled with political dissidents. And yet the paradoxes are very striking: the total number of deaths and disappearances from the dictatorship, across the whole country of 180 million people, and indeed beyond, is known to be 434.

At Dom Bosco, in the mass grave, the number of suspected Cold War political dissidents is believed to be six at most. The rest—virtually all of them—are nameless individuals of the potter's field, or in other words, the politically threatening potential subjects of communist insurrection, whose disappearance was never publicly attributed to the state. The process of searching and identifying bodies—the manual sifting, categorical filtering, and assertive naming—a process of enlightening, creates dramatic silences. These ongoing constructions of knowledges about the past, and the silences that are created around *past tenses*, reveal important characteristics about the ongoing construction of political silences—and especially about banal disappearance in present tense.

If less than half of 1 percent of the bodies in the mass grave are political dissidents, the other 99.95 percent play almost no part in the national narrative about political disappearance. Little is publicly spoken of the victims of the extermination squads that patrolled the poor and informally urbanizing spaces of São Paulo and Rio de Janeiro in the same period, where men with "afro" hair, those without ID, and anyone assembling in groups of three or more during the day, but especially at night, were singled out and stolen off to police stations. National Intelligence Service documents from the time richly detail the military's fear that the Black population might be radicalized, influenced by the contiguous emancipatory politics of the American Black Panther Movement and Black Power ideas more generally. The logic of these organizations, written through international socialist solidarity with all oppressed peoples fighting for self-determination, was an affront to Brazil's historic regime.

These populations, especially urban Black populations, were repressed by the state and extermination groups through the dictatorship period. In Rio, where race is distinctively spatialized, Thula Pires (2018) writes that between 1938 and 1969 the city saw a rapid increase in the prison population from 3,866 to 28,538. In the late 1960s, after the coup, there was a sharp turn toward violence (and disappearance) as a means of repression, where some have noted that "nonstate" violence took on particular patterns. Using police files from the time, José Claudio Alves (2003; 2007) has shown that, from 1967 onward, there was an escalation in homicides with characteristics of summary executions in the lowland suburbs of Rio. Here, his analysis of police files showed that many homicides had particular characteristics: bullet wounds moving from the top down, happening at short range and with victims having bruising and marks on their wrists, indicating the use of handcuffs or restraints. While there were only six such cases between 1956 and 1962, between 1963 and 1975 there were a total of 654 of the same kind.[4] Such numbers can only be an underrepresentation, not capturing anything other than cases that were formally registered and written into the bureaucracy.

Nor is the effect of this kind of violence well captured by enumeration. It worked within a moment that Black individuals of the time speak of as being replete with fear and arbitrary detention. Rio de Janeiro's State Truth Commission, whose report was released in 2015, gathered a series of testimonials that traced the way the Black population was the subject of targeted repression. In a particular section, "The Dictatorship in Rio de Janeiro's Favelas," the report speaks through race, noting that efforts to repress the favela came in terms of both favela bulldozing and direct policing. Demolitions were part of an effort to move the Black population to the margins of growing cities, while direct repression through various means sought to silence incipient Black consciousness, organization, and leaders. Some Black leaders, such as Abdias Nascimento (2002), a pan-Africanist, fled the country and continued to fight for an internationalist Black freedom through written work and political organizing. Influential from there, Nascimento mobilized a powerful critique of both the dictatorship and Marxist orthodoxy, which objectified the slave as akin to capitalist figurations like "machines, credit, etc." (Marx, cited in Nascimento, 2002: 228).

In the 1960s, "anti-communism marked most favela policies," writes Brodwyn Fischer (2014: 3), where "the need to 'go up the hill before the Communists descend from it' had become a tenet of middle-class common sense." Favelas were directly and routinely policed, with disappearance for days at a time becoming banal. Such a strategy came from the highest parts of the military regime. The report notes an order, from the intelligence sector of the military in 1971, to "intensify the hits on the favelas, doing them on the order of three or four per week." These *batidas* ("hits"), colloquially called "blitzes," were moments of police going up the hill, and coming down with trains of Black men bound together, materially reestablishing a linear relationship with chains. As Xavante, a Black leader put it:

> Back then the *blitzes* . . . we called them the blitz, here in the community, you would be sleeping at home, and these guys burst in, there was nothing like a warrant, nothing at all. They'd bash [on the door] and if you didn't open up they'd put their foot to the door. They'd come in and if you were lying down they'd say "get up, criminal." They would tie you up and take you away, understand? This was the way they acted. They'd bring us down all tied up from up at the top. They put us in the "mother's heart," which was that car, a bus totally full of bars and from there we would go to the police station. And we'd stay there. . . .
>
> In the community here, when the guys came in it would be with that look, like: "everyone here is a *bandido*." And I remember that I was working on a renovation once, a renovation job in Botafogo, and I'd eat my lunch at the bus stop, for number 547. . . . So I would be getting the bus, and they would come by and just stop, look me in the face among the others that were there and arrest me. And so then I'd be in jail for, man, at least a week and a half.[5]

Such a condition left families in sheer terror. Some would return, reappearing from detention. Others wouldn't. And because the condition was sweeping and arbitrary, both directed in operations upon the hill and ongoing and persistent within the city itself, there was no way to know who might have taken someone—the military, police, or someone else. This social silencing and the acute repression of such voiceless individuals, those who didn't reappear, has proved easy to obscure in the category and soil of the *indigente*. They haven't been made to reappear in processes of exhumation and truth either, except in fleeting glimpses like those presented in this section of Rio's own Truth Commission.

In a material place like Dom Bosco, the indigent commingled with the reclaimable political dead are shrouded in silence, obscured beneath a much larger historical and national narrative about Cold War mass-grave redemption. But, more crucially, the sheer number of nameless people tells an important story about the generalized political silence around disappearance—especially for the poor and Black population.

Michel-Rolph Trouillot (1995) writes of the ways that silences are made in the production of history. For Trouillot, historical silences are made alongside knowledge. This happens in four ways: (1) in the making of fact creation, or *sources*; (2) in the moment of fact assembly, or *archives*; (3) in the moment of fact retrieval, or the making of narratives; and (4) in the instance of retrospective significance, or the production of popular history.

The *vala* at Dom Bosco is crucial to the production and contestation of political history, striking across each of Trouillot's suppositions. In Brazil especially, the idea of disappearance has been historically constructed around the notion of dictatorship and dictators, whether in the Estado Novo of Getulio Vargas (1937–1945) or in the Cold War military regime (1964–1985). Under these conditions, it is a historical fact that the military dictatorship disappeared "political dissidents." This has given rise to, and informed, the production of an archive at the heart of a national process of truth and reconciliation. Such a process has codified a narrative, though contested, about torture and disappearance "never more" as a categorical metric of Brazil's experience with democracy.[6] These historic missing bodies, and their found remains, have, like other remains, become useful "to tell particular stories," say Sarah Wagner and Adam Rosenblatt (2017: 238), "that stick to a set of remains and thus continue to circulate among the public, decades or even generations later." The stories they have come to tell are stories about what democracy should and shouldn't look like, and who it is and isn't for.

This is true in more than metaphor. Those who were repressed, who were tortured but not disappeared, have become central to political life. Two of them, Luis Inácio 'Lula' da Silva and Dilma Rousseff, rode straight into the Brazilian presidency, leading from 2002 to 2016 on the back of this historical narrative. Dilma's creation of a National Truth Commission draws on this legitimation, centering the history of political claims and their repression in the ongoing construction of liberal democracy.

Their suitability, redemption, is often crafted through their black-and-white images as dictatorship detainees, which brings sharp contrast between a wrongful then and an enlightened now.[7] The mugshots of these two former presidents are out of place, products of a different time and under a different, and ethically wayward, regime. The images are cast in a time when the mugshot was equivalent to direct political repression. The very strength of the historical narrative about the problem of disappearance and political redemption rests in the ethical inversion of the mugshot as a political frame, with the two being wrongfully cast.

This powerful narrative about political redemption informs liberal democracy's argument for post–Cold War democratic consolidation, which pits liberalism and citizenship against militarized government and the centralized authority of dictatorship but without ever contesting its own ethical underpinnings. The framing works as such: Lula and Dilma shouldn't have been in mugshots. Their mugshots have become a means of political sifting, fortifying a historical narrative and further reifying silences about who belongs in an image of criminality. For Lula and Dilma to have shed any justification for being represented in a mugshot has meant allocating the mugshot to its rightful place, to a person deserving. Mugshots are for other people, the process implies, for "real criminals"—like Xavante, who, though a leader, is Black and poor.

The National Truth Commission creates such silences. "In Brazil," the Comissão wrote in 2015, "forced disappearance was the result of a systematic politics of the military regime against political opposition. . . . Forced disappearance targeted both revolutionaries and leaders and managers of political parties, a majority of whom were men (89% of cases), students or young professionals." In assembling an archive of the missing, the commission relates the names and political party or movement affiliation, moving to make certain and "truthful" claims about its composition and circumstances. The commission's assertions center on disappearance as something scrupulously targeted and discrete, as though disappearance was for no one except the political opposition.

This was indeed a deliberate choice, made around being able to firmly establish the involvement of the state, and to assign responsibility. Or, as the document put it relative to forming the terms of engagement of the commission, at least 118 cases brought forward by families were "deferred because of legal parameters, whether because of the impossibility to characterize the [person's] participation or accusation of participation in political activities, or whether for formal questions of timeframe and legitimacy."

These delineations of fact assert a silence that shrouds other disappearances. Where the missing have been found, alongside hundreds of other unknown people, is a new assertion of which lives matter, and who is not *political enough* to have their disappearance discussed in national processes of truth and reconciliation. These unknown others are, in theory, the urban poor, ominous menaces of socialism, political insurgency and revolution in that same moment. But their political exposure is spectral, not in party affiliation or active agency. Indeed, though the urban poor have often been seen as having great potential (or threat) for socialist revolution, they were the subject of absent or misguided recognition from the Left. Through the contentious late twentieth century, the organized Left and communist intellectuals privileged industrialization, anti-imperialism, and the extinction of Brazil's antiquated feudal social relations over real attention to the urban poor and their politics. "While they may have sympathized with *favelados* or used their plight to illustrate Brazil's dramatic inequalities, the Communists' political vision did not prioritize a lumpenproletariat chiefly concerned with territorial rights, water pipes, and paved roads" (Fischer, 2014: 10). The political demands of the poor did not inform the foundations of leftist political organization. To the contrary, efforts by the poor to make political gains in the form of material goods and services revealed deep fissures and frictions in political mobilization that indeed shaped how and why some favelas were removed, and others were not.[8]

But when it came to the material disappearance of people by the state and shadow groups, both the specter of revolutionary urban-poor politics and party politics were a target. And yet only one of those two has been recognized and propped up as "real" in the national narrative. The Truth Commission's focus was on those who tried to organize the "popular classes," those who tried to sign them up to political parties, while sidelining the distinctive violence and repression faced by these populations. And in so doing, the commission further codified a historical narrative that

bypasses long-standing and ongoing violence against these classes themselves, both directly and indirectly. That these bodies are also important
and repressed—and at a scale incomparable to the White and middle-class
population being retrieved—seems entirely lost on historical factualness.

Such a focus on particular bodies, and the creation of historical knowledge surrounding it, follows a similar paradigm across global cases of disappearance. This is central to efforts to reclaim lives from death, requiring
reassertions about deservedness and which lives cannot be disappeared
and about what kind of disappearance gets a search, at what pace, or if at
all. As Jenny Edkins (2011) has written, the search for the missing in the
aftermath of the 2005 London bus bombings was immediately about two
different kinds of manhunts to identify missing people and bodies. These
two efforts were trained on a particular concern: to sift and discretely
separate the victims from the terrorists, both materially and morally. The
material remains of the terrorists had to be separated from those of the
victims, allowing for a discrete moral tag to be affixed on each, making
the distinction definitively political. And in the aftermath of 9/11, who
could be found was already dependent on who could legally be in the Twin
Towers. Beneath the search for fallen Americans, which fueled a new and
never-finished global regime of rendition and disappearance, were what
she calls the "doubly disappeared"—bodies that weren't documented in the
first place, could never get federal aid as a result, and who would not be
claimed by loved ones whose own existence was precarious.[9]

In Brazil, things have become even more complicated. While the search
for the dictatorship disappeared has, until just recently, undergirded dominant affirmations of what democracy cannot be, in the spirit of liberal
capitalism, countervailing forces have emerged. This historic narrative
of forced disappearance as unjust has reemerged as a contentious field,
bringing the specter of military disappearance and torture back to the
fore. Whether politically dissident bodies should continue to be exhumed,
identified, made political in the name of post–Cold War democracy, or
left in the earth, uncommemorated, is at the heart of Brazil's resurgent
neo-fascism.

In 2009, Brazil's current president, Jair Bolsonaro, was a national member of parliament. A major in the federal army reserves, Bolsonaro gained
particular notoriety for his voracious attacks on women, on the LGBTQ+

population, and on the urban poor. "Gun down Rocinha," he tweeted about Rio's largest favela. "Gun the Worker's Party down," he shouted to revelers in a public speech, referring to Lula and Dilma's political party.

Bolsonaro's rhetoric, through the 2018 presidential election and ongoing, hinges on a defense of the "traditional family" and the "Brazilian nation" against those that would—he claims—undermine it. White nationalist in tone if not in full spirit, Bolsonaro's comments are far-reaching and unapologetically violent, generating a sharp rupture with liberal democratic tropes of rights, citizenship, and nonviolence in public. And while many Brazilians find this odious, others do not. Bolsonaro has always been an advocate for militarized (or outright military) intervention, including suspending the rule of law to preserve "order," promoting the prospect of stability in response to what Brazilians have experienced since the end of the Cold War—exceptional levels of everyday violence. A vocal opponent of the National Truth Commission, Bolsonaro has eagerly waded into a long-standing national discussion about political disappearances, both as a polemicist and in substantively leveraging it to craft a narrative about the "threat of communism."

Even before he was elected president, Bolsonaro was outspoken about disappearance. A prominent but crude poster was affixed to the door of Bolsonaro's senate office. On white paper with exaggerated font and clip-art-type images is a picture of a cartoon dog with a bone in its mouth. Over the dog's head is a thought bubble containing a bone. Above the dog are two different phrases, one referring to disappeared people from an antigovernment guerrilla battle in the 1970s.[10] The other is a statement about the image, and what it means for those who seek to reclaim the bodies of the missing:

THE DISAPPEARED OF ARAGUAIA
Those who search for [a bone]
are
[a dog with bone]

Only dogs go looking for bones. Those who go searching for bones, who root through the soil of mass graves to find remains, are canine, subhuman. Bolsonaro's effort to dehumanize those who seek to reclaim the Cold War missing has never been masked. And while his target is Dilma and the narrative of liberal democracy derived in opposition to dictatorship, Bolsonaro's affirmations seek to extend far beyond. He doesn't name women like Débora and Neide, exactly. But they are just as included in the dehumanization.

On April 22, 2019, after little more than one hundred days of being president, Bolsonaro canceled all funding for work being carried out to identify the remains found in the mass graves at Dom Bosco and Araguaia, a site of Cold War guerrilla conflict. All of this does ever greater layered work in reinforcing a historical silence about disappearance. To reclaim the bodies of dissidents or not, at Dom Bosco this narrative and its field of contestation rests on efforts to reclaim fewer than twenty bodies from a mass grave of more than one thousand. The rest are silent. What of this vastly larger proportion of disappeared? Here, there are no facts, no archive—a narrative about the arc of disappearance is absent. Such bodies do not yet exist in the production of public history.

This same story can be said of other institutional spaces where political dissidents were made to disappear. Where they didn't torture, kill, and bury people in police stations or safe houses, the military regime also took political dissidents to the dungeon-like spaces of the prison system and to state asylums for the "criminally insane" like that at Juquery in São Paulo. As Maria Izabel Sanches Costa (2017) writes, at Juquery, amid an interned population of up to eighteen hundred that was subjected to medical and "curative" tests, at least four political dissidents were alternately held for things described as "suicidal tendencies" and "schizophrenia" in the 1960s and '70s. Others died the same day that they arrived, being buried "irregularly" in the asylum's cemetery—a space said to contain thirty-three thousand bodies. The silence that surrounds both the extent of the use of the asylum, and the other bodies, was also well produced by a particularly eventful fact: a fire in 1978 that incinerated almost all of the institution's files and personnel documentation.[11]

The silence at Dom Bosco, and less so at Juquery, is recognized by some as a vital terrain of politics and future-oriented contestation. At Dom Bosco, a commemorative wall, painted red with white script, was erected after the discovery of the *vala*. Amid the ongoing making of unmarked grassy mounds in the foreground, jumbled headstones, and wooden stakes identified only by numbers written in black marker, the red wall stands inert. It reads:

Here the dictators tried to hide the politically disappeared, victims of hunger, of the violence of a police state, of the death squads and above all of the rights of poor citizens of the city of São Paulo. Be it registered that these crimes against freedom will always be discovered.

Subscribing the text is the name of the city mayor at the time, Luiza Erundina. The wall at Dom Bosco, driven into material existence by Erundina, speaks to the historical silence of "other" disappearances and their longitudinal and incessant nature. While it is a testament to the egregious violence of Cold War political torture and rendition, the commemorative wall does not center it. Instead, there is an effort to craft a new set of facts and a different narrative about disappearance, from within the cemetery itself: Disappearance is systemic. The silence that surrounds the one thousand bodies that must be filtered out as "not subversives," and therefore not noteworthy, is that of a kind of disappearance that is mundane, working incessantly upon bodies that are not worth a public accounting. The bodies in this mass grave are axiomatic, ignoring the reality that they, too, are accompanied by a long-standing terrain of searching, political subjectivity, and suffering.

The words that flow across the red paint aren't so interested in disappearance as a historical moment. Instead, and though in past tense, the text points to the way that disappearance is systemically political, long-standing, and not tethered to a politics of state protagonist–citizen victim. The words contest the politics of Bolsonaro, *and* they contest the politics of liberal capitalist redemption.

This mass grave is the site of a battle over history and its ongoing construction. Socialists, like Erundina, who want to reclaim every last body, and who "dream of another world," connect all kinds of disappearance.[12] They include those that populate the ochre earth in the foreground, a few meters away from the wall, yesterday and today. The ongoing assembly of different forms of knowledge toward these different politics of life and death, of conditions of burial, helps to reveal how disappearance has always mattered, and why it might carry distinctive significance now. In the high-profile efforts to reclaim the missing, and their recent pseudo-fascist counter-valence to keep them in that place, "these high-profile examples speak to, and . . . speak *over*, the other missing and unknowns . . . the 'anonymous,' as opposed to the iconic, dead" (Wagner and Rosenblatt, 2017: 238, emphasis in the original).

And in this way the wall is transcendent, always timely, and always hopeful. It speaks to a problem that remains in the narratives that surround disappearance and their subsequent discovery, especially in mass graves, where the euphoria of discovery is quickly accompanied by the need to "disaggregate" who matters. And it stands, solemnly in the background of a politically produced and now forgotten field where a dramatic number of young men, many nameless, many of them Black, and many between the ages of fifteen and thirty, are buried—every day. There is historical silence. But that silence is definitively material and infrastructural.

5 The Usefulness of Capricious Knowledge

I meet Viviane near the hospital after lunch one day. She moves around the city while collecting information for her cases. Sometimes she's able to stay in one place for a few days to look at a set of files or to investigate particular concerns. But the problem with disappearance—in addition to everything affective and violent about it—is that there are few "edges." Where does disappearance begin and where does it end, especially in the institutional condition where investigation might take root?

To investigate or be jurisprudentially concerned with disappearance means understanding and interrogating its correlates. Many things emerge alongside it: suicide, prison, other homicides, organized crime activities, police violence, mundane mass graves, and indigent burial. It can also mean being attentive to the political economy of disappeared bodies, being attuned to the ways that disappearance isn't just happenstance—it is useful.

One of the most important places for those searching for the disappeared is the Instituto Médico Legal (IML), the criminal examiner's office. In this city there are seven, each of which carries out autopsies on bodies where violence is suspected as a cause of death. These seven units are aggregation points for all of the bodies that are discovered and that may have come to a premature death. These are the bodies of police killings, bodies of homicidal violence, bodies of *mortes suspeitas* (suspicious deaths), *ossadas* (found bones), and bodies of any other variety, even bodies that come from car accidents where *homicidio culposo* (manslaughter) is a potential charge.

Originally created in 1885, the IML offices are distinctive in at least two ways. They tell a story of process, and they tell a story of concentration. For those who have someone to find, they are a stop in the endless peregrination. They are an unavoidable institutional concentration point in a processual flow of bodies, bureaucracy, and decision-making, tracing difficult and obscured lineages of bodies that go missing. Decisions about whether a body is identifiable, worth identifying, or to be the subject of rigorous investigation (by DNA or otherwise) is often done here, taking into account police reports and other details. As a result, the IML is where unknown bodies and those looking for unknown bodies should meet. Here there is a waiting room on one side and an examination and storage room on the other, separated by an officious granite countertop.

Seen as concentration, the IML offices are places where the many layers of disappearance rest on top of each other. Paper on top of paper, where each sheet beneath the last seems to hold a different kind of horror. Here, what "made someone disappear" is less evident. Instead, what is visible is the political condition that surrounds and informs what disappearance means and how it advances in plodding self-denial, atomized to individuals. And those who remove and replace the paperweights that keep the sheets, the layers of disappearance, held together with expanding rubber bands and bulging paper folders, are acutely aware of the violence at their fingertips. Bringing a piece of paper between their fingers means dealing with a horror analogous to the last one, but with a different face to tell it to.

The IML is supposed to *know* bodies, to make them knowable via paperwork and codification. Yet the institution's practices reveal an inconclusive kind of selectivity, a capricious knowledge that illuminates how bureaucracies of life and death are part and parcel of a disaggregation of some lives-in-death at the expense of others, in a constant comparative exercise. From here, too, this selective knowledge is critical for understanding where bodies go, how they are used, and what their trajectories are through the state—which can eminently obfuscate the search for life.

On one particular day, Maria, an office worker, carries a particularly heavy weight on her shoulders for a conversation that she has to have. On this day and the next, she fields calls from mothers and family members who are looking for loved ones. From where she sits, in an uncomfortable office chair and constrained space of compassion, they can be demanding. They are unstable, unhinged, and unpredictable. They shout. They cry. They are angry, and they don't always know where to direct it. Maria gets it hard. She has been speaking to Angela, who is looking for her son, Lucas, who went missing many months prior. Angela has been back in touch, again. She has always been a regular caller, asking if new bones could be Lucas and pushing for them to be tested.

On this occasion, Maria has news for Angela. On the one hand, it is good news. There is a bag of bones. They have been definitively identified as Lucas. Maria knows that this will certainly send Angela off the deep end of despair. But it isn't even that straightforward. The bag of bones is incomplete. Not all of the bones are there. Maria has no information about where they might be. It is just a bag of bones, with no real information about where they came from or if some might have been left behind. She doesn't even know where that "behind" is. Worse still, not only is the bag of bones incomplete, but it also contains some other, unidentified, human bones. Big ones. The bag doesn't just have Lucas in it. It has someone else, or *some others*. With a kind of ongoing exasperation, the humanness behind one particular cog in a systemic bureaucracy of disappearance, Maria exclaims, "Now how am I going to tell her that?"

The IML is supposed to be the kind of place where evidence aligns with authoritative medical knowledge and reason, linking together cause and effect, victim and protagonist, in the positivism that many understand to be the pith of the state's knowledge-power. It is supposed to be a lynchpin in understanding the real reason why lives become death and how, in the case of the disappeared, unknown bodies become known. Medical evidence, DNA, and cause-effect are the irrefutable rationality of this scientific truthwork, and supposedly the bedrock of this institution. But the IML appears, instead, to be a space of both the capricious disclosure of knowledge and its selective dissolution.

The first time I visited the IML one of the senior figures took me for a tour down its corridors, into its lab-like rooms for DNA sampling, bone reassembly, and special techniques like forensic odontology, the "criminological science" of teeth placement and dental impressions. The odontology room is pristine, well organized, with lab equipment in place. Our discussions circulated around the difficulty of doing diligent work in a cash-strapped context. With all of this violence and all of these bodies, how can we possibly keep up?

We open a door and step into a new hallway. When we do, we nearly bump into a man. Startled, he shouts "Polícia!" into a door ajar across the hall. The man is a plainclothes police officer, likely from the Civil Police, an investigative police agency that manages case files, prison transfers, and the aggregation of evidence. He has made a partner on the other side of the door aware of interlopers. "Beware!" he says in code. Behind the ajar door, which is pushed open by my guide for me to see, are two other police officers and three detainees—all Black men—who are in the process of the *corpo de delito* (a mandatory body exam carried out after arrest) to document and verify the injuries of a detained person or dead body to ensure, ostensibly, that they are not the product of abuse or torture by the police. The body exam takes acute deformation of the body as evidence. Bruises, cuts, and broken bones are potential evidence of mistreatment. Damage to the affective condition—terror, fear, psychosocial trauma—made through the use of plastic bags on heads, claps over the ears—do not register.

We leave the gruff and discomfited police officers and prisoners behind, and they push the door fully closed this time. My guide points to a chip in the floor, noting in a casual but revealing aside, "Look, this is a gunshot from when an armed group came to break out some prisoners."

We move through one door, and then another. In front of us now, an examination room: white walls, stainless steel, three bodies on gurneys and an overwhelming smell of decomposition. A handful of people move about the room. The two of us are not noteworthy, either way, among them. It isn't a space I want to spend much time in. It is unnerving, sensorially overwhelming, blindingly bright through sun-facing windows. There is an odd contrast between the dull brightness of the whites, the sheen of stainless steel, and the heaviness of the smell that I can't tether to a particular thing. It feels everywhere.

In her living room on the south side of the city, Neide tells me that she has never been inside this examination room. But she feels like she has seen, heard, and smelled it all before. Perhaps she heard it from Maria, upstairs, herself, but she doesn't know. For Neide, the IML is a story of missed opportunity, of opaque intervention and obscurity, a story she tells about Felipe and the IML.

Early in her searching for Felipe, Neide was actively canvassing around the city. The IML was one of the places that she visited most frequently. But Neide has never gone there alone. She says it is too unnerving; she lacks the courage. The last time that Neide went was during *Semana Santa* (Easter week), years ago. She and her husband had gone downtown to a wholesale market, and they decided to stop by and see if they might find something out. And indeed, they did. There was a photo of a young man who had been found many years earlier, not far from Neide's house, but who had been buried as an unidentified indigent in a city cemetery. Neide was convinced it was Felipe. Convinced. "It is the only time I've ever believed that he is actually dead," she recounts. His legs were the same, the head and ears were the same. But the face was puffy and swollen. Neide was as close to certain as she could ever be, looking at photos of the body from before it was buried.

It was a Thursday. The attendant at the granite counter, who had been helpful, told Neide that she needed to speak with another staff person, who was already off for the Easter holiday. She wouldn't be back until after the weekend, on Monday. In the meantime, Neide was told to collect a DNA sample and prepare to bring it in. On Monday they would commence proceedings to get the bones and attempt a match. Neide waited through the weekend with bated breath. Was this finally it? Had she finally found him?

But before she could even make it back to the IML, the phone rang. It was late on Sunday night, almost midnight on Easter Sunday she recalls, and well after hours. The person called to report that, in fact, the body had already been identified as someone else. Neide was incredulous. "But I'd just seen the file three days earlier and it was marked as unidentified," she said. "How is it possible now that it has been identified since then?" The staff member was assertive that there was a complete match already. The body in fact had an associated national ID number, its identity was known. There was no way that it was Felipe, they said. Don't bother coming back in to look at this case. This file is closed.

This incident happened around six years after Felipe disappeared, many years after the body would have been buried as unknown and at least three years after disinterment from Dom Bosco or a place like it. This made no sense to Neide. The body had gone unidentified for years. And though it was a body of an unidentified young man, around the same age as Felipe, and with the same skin color, found in a place near where Felipe disappeared, roughly matching the date, Neide was never made aware. As a result, to her, the file—and body—had sat abandoned to disinterest for years. But then, all of a sudden, within two days of her finding it, and only after her inquiry, the body was deemed identified, the case resolved, and the file tightly shut with the finality of a trite goodbye and the sound of a phone line going dead. Neide's retelling of the story exudes doubt, suspicion, and mistrust that a body that was disposed of without an effort to find its next of kin could be ignored for years before abruptly being identified over a holiday weekend.

Recounting this story, the murky doubt about how they came to assert such certain knowledge of the body so quickly, even on an extended holiday weekend, revives the uncomfortable sense that she's always being watched. Someone doesn't want her to know. She briefly digresses into a story about a man that she's seen outside and around her house, who once followed her onto a city bus. He's a "normally dressed" person who, when she once confronted him for following her, abruptly departed—but not before making a gun out of his thumb and pointer finger, directing it at her while mouthing the word "*Pá*" ("Pow"). Neide surmises that he might be a police officer, but finds it hard to settle on this idea.

There is also nothing ahistorical about Neide's ambiguous interactions with the IML or the doubts that overlay it. The IML is well located in a historical arc of the politics of dead bodies, the politics of missing bodies and the "flexible" use of medical authority to obscure political violence. Between 1964 and 1985, this IML unit received the tortured and lifeless bodies of those who were politically disappeared by the military dictatorship, shrouding their identities and battered bodies beneath medicalized terminologies and certifications. Before they proceeded to nameless graves, misnamed graves, or other unknown interment, these acutely political bodies required some kind of testimony, archival existence. Tracing this "disappearance machine," at the height of the dictatorship's repression, Marcia Hattori and her coauthors (2014) found that 2,892 "unknown" people came through the IML's internal bureaucratic registers between

1971 and 1975. In these registers, more than half of the autopsy documents do not state the place of death, and many register the identity of the person as "unknown"—even, in some cases, where the body was found in their own residence.

Around the time that Neide was at the IML inquiring and holding out hope for the identification of Felipe's body, the public was being reintroduced to the IML's place in past political disappearances through the National Truth Commission project. Such discussion was often tethered to names and cases, with journalists evoking individuals and their fates.

Helber José Gomes Goulart ended up at the IML. He was born in 1944 in Mariana, Minas Gerais, a small town founded in the seventeenth century by colonial settlers known as *bandeirantes*, who were hunter-capturers of Indigenous peoples.[1] In his early years Helber worked as a newspaper boy and later as a typist for the town, but, like hundreds of thousands of others in the second half of the twentieth century, he left home to move to rapidly growing São Paulo for better work. Like his father, a card-carrying member of the Brazilian Communist Party, Helber was active in working-class politics, stridently opposed to labor exploitation and poor working conditions. In 1964, immediately following the coup, Helber was tried by a regional military court and sent to an industrial project on the western edge of São Paulo state, where the construction of a new hydroelectric dam had just begun. Amid exploitative conditions, Helber fled. Soon after he joined a clandestine political group, the ALN, Ação Libertadora Nacional.

When police first abducted Helber in São Paulo is not exactly known. The official version of events eventually describes Helber's death in 1973 as a result of a shoot-out with police. "Dangerous subversive killed in shoot-out," a newspaper headline around the time read. "Armed with a 38-caliber Taurus revolver, Helber fired on agents as they approached, beginning a shoot-out that resulted in his own death."[2] Seventeen years later Helber's body was discovered in a shallow trough close to the mass grave at Dom Bosco. He was one of the first three to be identified by forensic anthropologists from the University of Campinas.[3] He had been buried nameless, as an indigent, among thousands of others who remain unknown.

In 2014, in the background of Neide's search, Helber's body was being politically unearthed, becoming part of a meshwork of public discussion about reconciliation, torture, medicalized legal authority, and disappearance. At the heart of the matter was the conclusion of the National Truth Commission. In 2014 the final report was publicly released, engendering widespread discussion of people like Helber and other killed political dissidents. It was lauded internationally for doing so. "This truth commission stands out," Sikkink and Marchesi (2015) wrote soon after, "in terms of its thoroughness, its willingness to name names, and its call for prosecutions, the commission has done exemplary work."[4]

As with Helber, the commission did name names, and it did result in attempted prosecutions. The report helped to link Helber to a particularly important figure, Harry Shibata, the director of the IML from 1976 to 1983 and, previous to that, a coroner working on autopsies and criminal cases. Shibata had spoken publicly about the political nature of his work, having already been reprimanded by the São Paulo Medical Council. As a cog in the medical machinery, Shibata had falsified causes of death, writing medical fictions about the bodies of the dead, including Helber. Now, with this new political fuel and some momentum, the public prosecutors charged that he had engaged in a deliberate and widespread campaign of falsification of medical examination records. Records of autopsies signed by Shibata at the IML regularly did not recognize marks, bruises, and other evidence of violence on bodies, leading to fictitious and illogical conclusions, such as suicide, that shielded the state from national and international scrutiny.

Shibata's role and work came under particular fire in 1975 with the murder of journalist and University of São Paulo professor Vladimir Herzog. Herzog had come to a military office voluntarily for questioning. Three hours later, he would commit suicide—but only after journalists heard him being tortured (Godoy 2014). The related medical records, signed by Shibata, declared his death a suicide. The report was accompanied by photographs, blatantly staged, a fallacious narrative for the media, and a generalized disinformation campaign. And yet the truth was well understood, far beyond the absurdities of the medical certificate. Herzog was Jewish and the rabbi responsible for preparing his body, Henry Sobel, recognized and understood the many marks of torture on his body. In an act of "cemetery activism," Sobel had Herzog buried at the center of the Jewish cemetery, and not at its edges—in Judaism, the space typical for those who have committed suicide. The case is often seen as a turning point, a counter-political illumination of the arbitrary use of violence by the military regime, and an instance in a larger shift in sensibility against the dictatorship.

In 2016, following the National Truth Commission report, federal prosecutors charged that Shibata's work obscured the fact that Helber had been arrested, tortured, and subsequently killed while being held by the state. The accusation documents key details, including that the original request for him to be examined occurred hours after the time he was declared dead in Shibata's report. Moreover, Shibata's declaration that Helber's cause of death was the result of a hemorrhagic shock occurring after a perforating wound to the lower lobe of the lungs, did not acknowledge the trajectory of the wound. Later examinations found that Helber had been shot from a position above him, the bullet moving downward and from left to right, as though he was kneeling or on the ground. Moreover, an additional wound on his right forearm had punctured from the outside in—a "defensive wound" consistent with an arm being held in front of the body in an effort to protect from a gunshot.[5] Shibata, the declaration and legal process held, was one of many who deliberately overlooked evidence of torture and assassination in a specific effort to "alter the truth" about the death of Helber, and others. Shibata, they continue to argue, should have his pension sequestered.

None of this ongoing history of the IML is lost on Neide, nor on Viviane. The political nature of the IML, then as now, is axiomatic and barely needs mentioning. While the process of searching for the contemporary disappeared is ongoing and current, the legal process speaks about disappearance in the past tense. Neither instill confidence in medical efforts to identify bodies. Maybe Neide was misunderstanding the circumstances, and there had been a miraculous and rather spontaneous identification of this one body. Still, inexplicable ambiguities of misidentification and false identification like this are not an anomaly at the IML.

Today, Eliana Carneiro and Patrícia Gennari (2016) argue, the IML is a central node in what they call "redisappearance." These authors describe how common it is that bodies arrive with full identification and pass through the system as autopsied and known but the family is never notified of the location of the body, nor of its burial. Such a circumstance means that many bodies go "unnecessarily unclaimed," leaving them to be buried as indigents in a city cemetery within seventy-two hours of being found. This kind of process is akin to what Flavia Medeiros (2016) calls "killing the dead," the process of removing the identity from the dead through the very process of bureaucratization that is intended to assert knowledge. Viviane, for her part, has already successfully sued the state for burying people nameless, winning compensation for those families that are able to discover that it actually happened to them.

The process of redisappearing and killing the dead continues. For authorities, one important way to frame this is in terms of costs. There are too many bodies to be attentive to and, amid the thousands that must be accounted for, some are bound to be misidentified, to have their ID mixed up or lost. The solution is a question of capacity: More resources, greater training, more refined science, and better knowledge of best practices will help to consolidate medical-legal rationalization and level out questions of lost and misplaced bodies.

Families of the disappeared see a much different pattern—one of indifference and deliberate obfuscation, where particular bodies are institutionally assigned a fate of being unknown, or unclaimable. There is a deliberate will to not search for knowledge. This is especially the case for young Black men, disappeared, killed by the police, or otherwise, around whom supposition about the deservedness of an indigent burial is fitting. This, especially, since a body in a city cemetery can go from discovered at a scene to buried nameless and unclaimed within seventy-two hours— high efficiency indeed. Though costs might be high, the pace is quick and disturbingly efficient. The difference between being nameless and being unclaimed, and how the two work together, is written, in part, through magnitude, resignation, and multitudes of antecedent cases that come in the form of incomplete bags of bones of different people, jumbled together.

There is some bureaucratic recognition of how bad the problem of unclaimed bodies has become. In an effort to help people find their missing or dead loved ones, in April 2014 the city of São Paulo created and updated a municipal webpage that provides the details and characteristics of indigents sent to the potter's fields for free burial. Originally updated every Saturday, and since 2018 updated only every four months, the webpage lists thousands of cases—some named, some unnamed—of people sent by the IML for a pauper's burial. Many suffered deaths from treatable "let die" health complications, such as pneumonia or septic shock, that occurred in places such as a public thoroughfare. Many other listings cite violence and trauma as the cause of death.

Take one example surrounding a police killing: Police shot and killed Marcelo Sabino dos Santos following a vehicle chase down a major highway. Unclaimed at the morgue, he was sent to Dom Bosco. A newspaper report recounts what happened:

> A police chase on Wednesday afternoon ended with a shoot-out, one dead and one wounded on Pinheiros Ring Road near the Eusebio Matos Bridge. The incident caused the lanes toward Interlagos to be totally obstructed between 1 p.m. and 2 p.m., creating seven kilometers of backup. Around 2:15 p.m. the lanes at the incident and the express lanes were opened up.
>
> It all began when two armed thugs accosted businessman Mauricio Menezes, 46, at a gas station at Ponte Bandeiras, on Tiete Ring Road at around 12:50 p.m. The thieves forced him to get out of his car and drove off. "All I could hear was them shouting: 'You lose! You lose!' Then I got out of the car." Menezes managed to stop a military police car, which began the chase.
>
> Near the Remédios Bridge, the thugs collided with a number of cars and hit a motorcyclist. Rescue was called and the victim taken to hospital.
>
> Further along on Pinheiros Ring Road the robbers ran the car into an abutment and skidded across the lanes. Immediately after, the shoot-out with police began. One of the robbers was killed and the other injured. The police helicopter assisted in the work. "When the shoot-out began I could only think of saving my car and the death of the two thugs," affirmed Menezes.
>
> After five hours of traffic paralysis the Pinheiros Ring Road was clear for motorists. The body is with analysts. It will then be sent to the coroner [IML]. No identity information is yet available for the dead man. (*Veja*, 2014)

The article's emphasis on how this incident interrupted urban life for a specific few, and its characterization of the individuals as "*bandidos*" who deserved to die, is striking. That the first sentence about a police killing immediately shifts to a second sentence about traffic consequences speaks volumes about what is implied. The robbed man's open desire to see them dead, while distinctive in this story, is a common trope among large segments of society, and it also defines many aspects of policing.

Subsequent media reports identified the dead "thug" as Marcelo. The entry on the municipal potter's field webpage makes a transparent connection to the incident: "Marcelo dos Santos, 26, born 21/09/1987, died 21/05/2014, son of Antonio dos Santos and Maria dos Santos, Police Report 392/14, 51º Precinct, place of incident Pinheiros Ring Road, 6800, Interlagos, multiple bullet wounds, sent by IML for free burial at Dom Bosco Cemetery in Perus" (Prefeitura, n.d.).

I was unable to find Marcelo's grave at Dom Bosco in 2016 when I first learned of his condition. Other aspects of the case are equally elusive: whether his parents could not afford to collect him, were afraid of being accosted in the process, if he was estranged, or, perhaps, it all happened so quickly that his family never knew where he was. Maybe they are searching for him.

For all that the IML contains in both process and concentration, telling varied and enlaced stories about the edges of disappearance, that isn't why Viviane has been coming to look at files. Rather, Viviane is concerned that the IML is also not able to do its job well based on the bodies it is given. As the institution responsible for examining bodies for criminal investigation, the IML should receive all bodies intact or with all their associated parts. Anything less prejudices proper investigative work. This includes any unidentified bodies, which are to be treated as criminally suspicious until examined and proven otherwise, and any bodies where there is a possibility of violence. The only bodies that should not come to the IML are those where the person has died of natural causes and is identified.

Part of the problem is that there is sawdust. And, sometimes, the sawdust exists where organs should be. Before bodies arrive at the IML for a criminal autopsy they come through the Serviço de Verificação de Óbitos (Death Verification Service, SVO)—just down the street. While the IML is an organ of the Public Security Secretary, the SVO, which provides the medical basis for death certificates to be issued, is a public unit associated with an adjacent state university. Bodies go first to the SVO, and sometimes then to the IML, with the public health examination, which is used to provide a death certificate, occurring before (and empirically superseding) criminal autopsies. This creates a paradox, where death can be verified, legally, before any criminal examination has even taken place, making any criminal concerns structurally secondary.

The problem, it seems, is similar to what others have recognized in another part of the state: bodies are transferred from one to the other (and sometimes back again) without obvious reasons or due justifica-tion. But in this case, the concern is deeper; it is about what might also be happening to these bodies as they are shifted between spaces of law, bureaucracy, and their ambiguities. Sometimes, organs go missing; they don't accompany the body. Instead, sawdust fills the cavities where they were. Indeed, the IML has found that sometimes bodies arrive with duplicates—two hearts, or "mis-matches," a pancreas where a kidney should be. For Viviane, there are so many questions. And some of them, for law, are primary: How is it even possible to do an autopsy to establish whether someone was murdered if the body doesn't have all of its vital organs? Worse, where are they?

In various moments in history, the body and its parts have been used for the production of knowledge and science. The 1832 Anatomy Act in England allowed for pauper bodies to be dissected for medical investiga-tion before their final burial in a mass grave. This new law made an implied practice normal. Previously, this treatment had been reserved for hanged felons or racialized "criminals." Under this certification the trade in pauper bodies redrew the normative categories of the living, with science as justi-fication. Elizabeth Hurren (2004) shows how this political effort to create medical knowledge was intertwined with both early Victorian Poor Laws and expanded government anti-welfare policies—which facilitated the provision of bodies. One clear beneficiary was the Cambridge Anatomical School at the university's Downing College. Cambridge received bodies from around the region, leveraging the political moment of disposable bodies to advance its dominant position in health-science research. The same pattern of pauper body trafficking was crucial to the creation of medical knowledge in the United States (Blakely and Harrington, 1997; Sappol, 2002). At that time, the body could be preserved well enough for medical study and public examinations in "theaters," giving ever more life to the enlightenment.

A need for bodies has never really changed. Medical schools aren't healthy without death. Such schools draw on bodies that acquiesced in life and others that were too poor to speak for their rights after death.[6] In this city, that means drawing on a difficult recent history. Until the 1980s, São Paulo's medical schools were bursting with bodies for study. There was, indeed, a pipeline. As in Rio de Janeiro and Belo Horizonte, medi-cal schools were a vital beneficiary of the state-run insane asylums. São

Paulo's now-shuttered Juquery asylum breathed life into medical study. "Every day three or four bodies would arrive in hearses," recounts a full professor from the medical school. "Those were the days when research was widely done."[7] Those bodies would allow for exceptional hands-on medical learning, and acceleration of knowledge. But these bodies were the edifice of a professionalism that is evermore enwrapped in accumulation, growing a privileged and racialized sphere of knowledge and wealth.

Brazil's redemocratization in the 1980s brought with it a new legal and ethical regime for the state's treatment of bodies. Juquery was renamed in 1988, just as a new regime of rights was installed through the constitution and in the public sphere. This renaming provided a different kind of veiling, directly linking knowledge, medicalization, and power, through the learned namesake of the institution's first head. Juquery, which is now known as the Professor André Teixeira Lima Prison Hospital for Psychiatric Treatment, has a jumbled cemetery of its own, believed to contain at least thirty-three thousand bodies.[8]

The withdrawal of the state from the provision of bodies for medical research shifted the paradigm, delinking the supply chain of bodies for medicine. Brazil doesn't have a "culture of organ donation," as a medical professor has put it. For one reason or another, few willingly allow the use of their body for study or medical research after death. Those who need bodies now struggle to fill the need, leaving medical schools and the government to actively advocate for more.[9] Not only is there a demand for bodies to study and learn from, but there is now, too, a growing demand for bodies that can provide live organs for transplants. Medical knowledge and practice, and the politics that surrounds it, doesn't just use bodies to create knowledge that can give life. The relationship is more direct: it uses bodies to give life, moving the materially vital, a beating heart, from one and providing to another. Such a demand is increasingly fueled by private medicine, requiring guises and discursive construction of a public good (Scheper-Hughes 2001). Or, as a public health secretary put it, further clamoring for more transplants, "The fight to expand donation must never stop. With the full support of the population, we are going to break a new record for transplants this year."[10]

A concern with bodies and their uses can be seen in terms of supply and demand. That bodies must now sustain other bodies is self-evident. And it is not just in the egregiousness of organ "repurposing." Blood flows more mundanely. Otávio's wife would not have survived if their friends and colleagues had not rolled up their sleeves. Her death was put off materially by taking life, vitality, from others. That was done through social bonds, willingness, emotional repair. Amid inequality, where the poor are forced to draw blood or plasma to save themselves (or else), there is a constitutive moral system where blood is most often exchanged as a commodity, remunerated in menial kind, giving days, years, to a soul that pays for it. The public health system can't get enough of it. The demand, and thus the cost, is too high. For dollars, one doesn't have to scavenge for the blood of friends and family as Otávio did. Giving of your own marrow is the only means to survive. There is a stark paradox when one's own blood is worth more than what the public system is willing to do to keep you alive.

Julio was a twenty-four-year-old university student in São Paulo who worked as a server in a restaurant while attending university. Over a period of time he accumulated a series of traffic fines for skirting the rules of the "*rodizio*," a municipal traffic management law requiring cars to stay off city roads on a given day. For one reason or another, on a few days, Julio didn't take public transport and instead drove to get to work or school, getting caught by traffic cameras when he shouldn't have been driving. He now owed more than R$510 (around US$120) in fines. If he were ever pulled over by the police, his car would be immediately impounded. For at least this reason, Julio was terrified of the police, and especially of the spontaneous police roadblocks called "*blitzes*," which would pop up especially in neighborhoods like his especially.

Julio was driving late at night, alone, in June 2016, when he came across a *blitz*. As reports put it, he accelerated, trying to speed away from the police, reaching 120km/h. Police gave chase, and began firing at the car. A bullet hit Julio in the head. Sixteen bullets perforated the car. According to the police report, the story was more complicated than this. They saw *um clarão* (a flash of light). In giving chase, as the car sped, they were fired upon. When the car came to a rest, they found a gun and a "white substance" inside. Julio died when the bullet pierced his brain, causing brain death.

The case was polemic. For many, Julio was a university student, working to pay his way through. Money was tight, and he made acceptable mistakes. He didn't come from a wealthy family, but he was White, had no criminal history, and was formally employed. His condition traced something quite normal, perhaps idealized for the working class in Brazilian society: a young man who was both working and studying. He had a trajectory, a good one, and couldn't really be framed as a threat to society. The "white substance" and idea of him shooting while speeding away seemed an absurd post-facto justification for his death. On television a school friend called his death "an assassination."[11] The police ombudsman, who has the capacity to call for investigation but not to make arrests, followed a similar line: "There are concerns that this was an execution. Many shots were fired. . . . We're surprised by this, especially since the suspect is a university student, apparently without any criminal history."

Like many victims of police violence, Julio's body was young and strong. His parents opted to donate various parts of his body for organ transplantation. Doctors removed his two kidneys, his pancreas, his liver and both corneas later that same morning. "We are going to share our pain with the happiness of others surviving," his mother said on television.

This case was exceptionally public and controversial, at least in part because of the circumstances of the victim—or "suspect," for some. And while there is no reason to believe that the violent death by the state was motivated by a need for organs, the case underpins a larger condition. This condition, where violence and the production of bodies is consistently high—indeed *constant*—but the supply of organs and cadavers is consistently low, creates perverse incentives. Irrespective of Julio's innocence, or, for police, his "legally committed" death, Julio's parents had a choice of whether or not to have his organs removed and donated.

In early 2019, a newly elected federal parliamentarian, Daniel Silveira, tabled two new national laws that would make what happened to Julio's body after death obligatory. Less than forty-five days into his mandate, Silveira, who is a former police officer from Rio de Janeiro and member of President Bolsonaro's political party, framed his proposal in terms of "human compensation." As he argued on various occasions and in different media outlets, "Those who are seen to have threatened the lives of some, should have their own bodies used as a means to compensate the public for their violence." The laws, 727/2019 and 729/2019, take this plainly, cornea for cornea:

727/2019
Article 1:
This law establishes the compulsory provision of organs and tissues, cells and parts of the human body for transplant or graft that are derived from an individual who, in clear and proven criminal conduct, endangers the life of public security agents, having been in confrontation with them and/or of others, results in brain death.[12]

By contrast, and in addition, proposal 729/2019 works as an amendment to existing organ donation laws, dating to 1997. And not insignificantly. The existing law stipulates a particular legal requirement for family members to authorize any donation:

Article 4:
The removal of tissues, organs and body parts of deceased persons for transplantation or other therapeutic purpose, will depend on the authorization of the spouse or relative, of age, obeying the succession line, straight or collateral, up to and including in the second degree, signed by two witnesses present at the verification of death.

But Silveira's proposed law added one last paragraph to this, transforming its meaning: "In the event that the body shows evidence of death as a result of criminal acts, the removal of tissues, organs and body parts for transplantation or other therapeutic purposes will take the form of compulsory assignment, i.e. without the obligation of obtaining express family authorization."[13] As it is, organ donation can only take place after brain death and with a process of legal and family authorization. Silveira's laws would mean taking organs from young men like Julio automatically, without any means of recompense or protest on the part of family members. For Silveira, Julio's parents wouldn't deserve a choice. Julio's apparent sins would require social reparations.

Such a law would collapse two temporalities into one. The horizon for organs to be useful would become the same as the time to determine criminal guilt. In the hours after brain death, criminal guilt would be fully consolidated. With organ extraction would necessarily come guilt, following in a straight line how police killing currently works to implicate the dead as an aggressor who resisted arrest.[14] In Silveira's Rio de Janeiro, where police killed an average of five people per day, almost all young men—1,249 in an eight-month period in 2019—a maximum of 12,490 organs would have been made available just in this eight-month period.[15]

Silveira's proposal gave a startling new scale and transparency to the relationship between violence and organ donation. It did so, too, within a historic pattern of the production of dead bodies that give life to the living. With all of the horror that they evoke, Silveira's proposed laws failed to get through parliament, quashed by vocal human rights advocates and other lawmakers who argued that any such law would be both unconstitutional and highly immoral.

At the moment, Viviane and others know that the law requires that a public prosecutor must authorize any transfer of organs. It also stipulates that no body that has been killed, by police or others, or was the subject of violence, can be used for medical or organ donation. They also know that exceptions to the legal word define legal practice. Julio, killed by police, should not legally have had his organs used. And yet his story could be told publicly, in newspapers and on television, without legal consequence.

Still, while the failure of Silveira's law is good for the hundreds of families that grieve like Julio's every year, it exposes the banality of violence and its uses on other bodies, and especially those that cannot contest their condition as police state it: "criminal". Beneath the ombudsman's defense of Julio, as "a university student, apparently without any criminal history," is an acknowledgment of a discrete ethical space for a 'real criminal'. If Julio had not been a student, or if he had committed a crime, the demand for his organs wouldn't have been less.

There is a din of whispers among mothers of young men killed by the police, a group that grows by several hundred more every year. This din contains many tales, yet to be publicly told, and not to be told here, of organs being removed without authorization. The critical mass of dead young men has given life to organizations of mothers who, increasingly vociferously, speak out against a pattern of political order that routinely and unapologetically takes young Black lives, and what they offer to life.[16] Assembling collective knowledge around this, of what it means as a collective fact that unites a disparate family, allowing for public voice, has not reached a critical mass.

For someone who is killed by police but never claimed by family, the body and its organs become useful under a different paradigm. There are few who might even whisper. These two temporalities are already collapsed into one, where the end of a life declared criminal means immediate new usefulness for the body. The incentives push away from burying the body as a whole, as is the case for the usefulness of any body that is not identified, or becomes unidentified, by family. An unnamed body without family to adjudicate over it is discretionary terrain. It is for this reason that most of the bodies used in medical research are those who have been slowly killed, predated in through rough-sleeping on the street, sepsis-suffering ways. These are, as one medical student puts it, "the Black bodies that train White medical students."[17]

And so, back in the IML, Viviane sees sawdust. Sawdust where organs used to be. Amid the jumbling, the missing organs and the duplicates, Viviane has noticed many different patterns. The poor are prominent, and so are young Black men. And yet in the files that she has gathered, with the help of Maria and others, other patterns have emerged. One of these is that many brains are missing. They can't be properly accounted for. They are missing from the bodies of the elderly sent to the IML for a criminal autopsy. With their body comes a question: *Did they die violently?* But ancillary questions arrive: *What violence happened after they died?* It happens, though, that the adjacent university has a globally famous brain bank. In an era and a political condition where bodies for research are said to be hard to come by, and where particular bodies provide, 1,602 brains were collected from this space in a twenty-one-month period—a pace of 2.5 per day (Grinberg et al. 2007).

6 The Disappearable Subject

I meet Samira on the West Side of the city. We're off to the other side of the urban outskirts. The streets are quiet and it takes us hardly any time to get there. We're going to a prison unlike almost any other in the world. It is a prison solely for wayward police. The sharp edge of disappearance and containment, or so one might think.

We park the car in a sheltered space under tall trees. Acacias, I think, their canopies seem to both cast shadows and make a light breeze that is out of place in the city. To enter the prison we walk past an unmanned and makeshift stall where prisoners sell things that they've made or produced—honey, lettuce, fruit. All attractive, and a bit like a petite bourgeoisie farmer's market. It is cheap, too. We enter the prison, passing through a metal detector. It beeps. No one takes particular notice. After we register, providing ID and stowing our bags in a tin locker, we walk from this white building to another, where the administration is housed.

Sometime later, after formalities with the administration, we walk beneath an arched pergola draped with passionfruit vines. The ripening fruit hangs in suspended drops almost ready to fall. "Everything happens for a reason," Luis tells us. Luis is a military police officer walking the grounds with the two of us, introducing us to people. In the distance, gunfire crackles in occasional bursts from a police training ground behind a grove of trees. "He killed eight people," Luis says. "All while off duty." Luis is speaking of someone that he thinks has turned his life around. "He isn't one of those people, you know, the corrupt kind. . . . He was taking justice into his own hands, you know?" His eyes seek recognition. Pedro is a good person, *right*?

Pedro, also a military police officer, later shows us around the apiary. "I got lost in the emotion," he says. Pedro goes on to tell us, again, about how he ended up here twelve years ago. Sentenced to more than one hundred years in prison, he had been on a killing spree. Off the job, and over the course of a year, he described how he "cleaned" a poor neighborhood on the south side of the city. Unable to control the thrill of killing, he misstepped, getting in trouble for letting people notice.

Pedro fits in a historic and shifting line of twilight state violence, where current or former state agents continue to "work" after they are off the job. Some of this is generally accepted. Many police do this as security guards, bodyguards, and money deliverers "because they need to pay the bills" and make ends meet given that police salaries are only a few hundred dollars a month. Doing this twilight work is accepted, even valued, until it strikes into public discussion, becoming too visible. On the clock, violence is work for legitimate pay, survival, protection of the public good. Off it, violence is work for illegitimate pay: "justice," protection of "society," racial superiority. The boundary between them is nebulous. The latter kind of work has gone from open and publicly celebrated through the 1980s—indeed the subject of adulation and celebrity production—to quiet and ongoing but shrouded. Where people like Cabo Bruno, a fired police officer who confessed to killing more than fifty "*bandidos*," once graced the cover of glossy weekly news magazines in the 1980s, they must now either work quietly and in groups— or learn to be measured and controlled killers on the job.

Pedro ended up here because he fell through these cracks. His killings drew too much attention and couldn't be camouflaged or obscured. Or perhaps his killings were chosen not to be obscured. He was egregiously violent. His acts were individual, but he shares social and historical space—the off-duty "*justiceiro*" ("justice maker")—with celebrities of violence like Cabo Bruno, who have now come and gone, their ferocity fading into old age, curtailed by a short stint in prison, or ended by a run-in with an assassin.[1] Where this violence used to be publicly displayed, and bodies were left with signed letters, it must now occur more surreptitiously.

"Try my honey," Pedro says. "Everything in it is natural. The sugar for the hives comes from cane. The starter beeswax, I order. The pollen . . . is pollen." The honey is really good, and Pedro is very personable. As he shows us a dead queen bee with its wing squeezed delicately between tweezers and then stings himself twice with bees from a hive, explaining that doing so regularly strengthens the immune system, it is easy to be lulled into acceptance. It is hard to believe that this person—affectionate, gentle, good with words—sent tens of young Black men to the cemetery for someone like Otávio to bury and disinter, or to be buried as an indigent like Marcelo. Especially in a prison environment like this, adjacent to a pond full of tilapia, a greenhouse with rows of lettuce, and groves of tangerine trees, Pedro doesn't seem so bad.

We are interrupted by two kids who run up, panting from scampering freely around the lush grounds. "Do you have honey?" they ask Pedro, between gasps. "In the jar and the basin, guys," he says, pointing to the shed. "And close the door behind you." Luis, seeing the incredulity that must be displayed on our faces, interjects, "They are the boss's kids." How bad can Pedro be if the prison boss leaves kids in his care?

There is, of course, an important conceptual connection between prisons, racialized urban spaces, and the cemetery. The cemetery hovers in the empirics of what Loïc Wacquant (2002) calls those "peculiar institutions" of policing in the afterlife of slavery. Indeed, empirical and material registers of this archipelago there are remarkably transparent, existing in actual geomorphic islands, as in New York City, where this archipelago includes both Riker's Island and Hart Island. Prisoners at the former are made to bury prisoners and indigents at the latter for fifteen cents per hour.

Many have drawn conceptual lines between urban ghettoization and prisons, noting the symbiotic spatial relationship that binds them together through the processes and political economy of historic policy and practice to contain Black life. In recent times, under the War on Drugs, this historical relationship has taken the form of criminalization and incarceration, with a fluidity of movement between these analogous spaces of containment in materially different forms and spatial locations. The near seamless movement of young Black and ethnic-minority men in this penal archipelago underpins the reinvention of the city from post-industrial "wasteland" to gentrifying techno-utopia.

To borrow a turn of phrase from Manuel Castells (1989), there is a "space of flows" in the penal archipelago too, through which Black people are corralled, always the subject of containment. Indeed, Castells's use of the "space of flows" to capture the reorganization of space, time, and politics in the global information and communications technology economy must be located in raucous concert with the constantly ongoing spaces and practices of containment that securitize globalized flows, "value chains," and privilege, necessarily producing what Neil Smith (1996) once called the "space of vulnerability." The uninterrupted space of flows, where some people, money, and high-value goods must flow, requires security, a similarly seamless removal of threats in global terms; a "space of detention," as Elena Zilberg (2011) puts it. The attention to the value of things and people that should move means disaffection for those that shouldn't. The space of vulnerability is fed by segregation, incarceration, and failing cemeteries. To that we must now also add deportation centers and disappearance, especially from North to South. It should be no surprise that this is especially obvious in major global cities, where dramatic wealth is so closely adjacent to violent poverty.

In this global condition of containment, firms and governments increasingly seek to level their costs with the labor they contain. In the United Kingdom, detainees in deportation centers work for £1 per hour or much less, taking at least £1.5 million in service expenditure off the shoulders of the private security firm that runs any one center (Bales and Mayblin 2018). As the reader will eventually see, in the United States, where deportation has become a prolific political economy, cash-strapped local counties reap windfall revenues bound up in the operations of private migrant detention centers contracted to ICE. Here, detention centers do not hire kitchen workers, cleaners, or other administrative staff. Instead, detainees like Matias—a young man in flight who will be introduced to you in the final chapter—are compelled to take part in a "voluntary work program" for one to four dollars per day. It is the only way to pay for "basic necessities like food, toothpaste, toilet paper, and soap—and contact with loved ones."[2]

Having people and conditions like this is good for profit. Tanya Golash-Boza (2016) and others document how deportees, having gained some

English-language skills, become useful for work in call centers and other low-paying international circuitries. Met at the airport by employment recruiters, their removal from a country with a high concentration of global wealth but a tiny proportion of global population asks them to both disappear and to be useful as they do.[3] Deportees can also become entrapped in prison and criminalization, shapeshifted back into urban violence, as an outcome of what Amina Zarrugh (2020) calls the United States' "logics of disappearance."

Some—those who search for a way out, who flee as migrants and asylum claimants—must make themselves dead or killable in a process that Gilberto Rosas (2019) terms "necro-subjection." This shaping of subjectivity is a kind of reconjuring of personhood, through submission, into a category of deserving supplicant to be saved by "the inner solidarity of Western liberalism and the enduring presence of colonialist relations" (304). To be, in other words, saved from the inside as a means of pointing to the exception of the outside, as evidence of deservedness and valuable life that should be saved.

Pedro's place as an imprisoned police officer in all of this seems obvious, if not well theorized by scholarship so far. Though he took it too far, he worked for the maintenance of this "carceral archipelago" of "mobility control" on the streets of this Global City, sending poor and Black men from the urban margins to prison during the day, and to the cemetery in the twilight.[4] He maintains and enforces this archipelago of global inequality, which must be understood as an expansive space of securitized flows between locales like prisons, processes like deportation, logics of organized abandonment like urban deprivation, and state-enshrined materiality like the cemetery.

But, on the other hand, this particular prison doesn't make linear sense according to the archipelago logic. Why contain those who work to maintain capitalism and advance a world of discrete "global value chains"? Why should there even be a prison for those who defend it?

Latin America's prisons, as the prisons of the United States and elsewhere, are roundly described by scholars as spaces of disposable life. They are decrepit places where a throw-them-in-and-shut-the-door politics prevails, while the contained and depressed labor is held as exploitable: to fight ever greater wildfires, to build furniture for the California State University system, or to bury the dead at Hart Island.

Otávio wouldn't have a job if he were in New York or California. Prisoners would do it. As Angela Davis has put it, US prisons are "a source of cheap labor that attracts corporate capitalism in a way that parallels the attraction unorganized labor in Third World countries exerts."[5] Such prisons are sites of exploitation, where entrapped indefensible labor exists in conditions ripe for incontestable use. Here, the relationship between disorganized and submissive labor, maintained morally elsewhere, is created through an institutionalized process of containment. In the United States, Black life is held and used in different valences. In the "Third World," labor is similarly held—restrained—at a distance from solidarity and personhood. This is to say little of those who are not subject to the labor organization that does exist. Spatially, whether in the United States, Britain, or the Global South, such a logic of containment exists in the prison, is lived in spaces of urban segregation, and is reproduced in the cemetery. Someone like Pedro is typically its guardian, paid to maintain its peace.

A confluence of containment, extraction, and race define much of this condition. Indeed, in Latin America, the presiding paradigm for criminalized populations is lock the door and forget them. In the absence of the most minimal provision of goods and protection, this has led to all sorts of egregious problems. A rapidly developing body of incisive work on Latin American prisons laments the bleakness of these spaces—sexual violence, massacres, and fires that consume hundreds of lives. Prisons are sites of acute degradation, overcrowding, and extensive violence, strongly evoking a presence of political will through its absence.[6]

A remarkable and similarly contrasting pattern has emerged across the region. Many prisons are regularly "self-governed" as a result. Behind the walls built evermore by states, prison groups of different varieties manage everything from distribution of food, rooms, and beds to security and cleaning. Under the mitigated authority of a handful of guards who rarely enter, rich and complex political economies drive patterns of survival and meaning. As Jon Carter (2014: 475–76) has put it, such spaces become "gothic," structured by a kind of absent power that is nonetheless "haunted by crypts of its own lawlessness."

Such a crypt has a counterpoint, a sharpened paradox. None of these problems and practices are present in the police prison. There are no "gangs," and there is no substantive sexual or other violence. The prisoners don't carry out their own tribunals and in-house punishments. There is no concern for high walls and fortifications. Guards walk the grounds, strolling with prisoners. Administrators walk unaccompanied. This prison is widely celebrated as a model. Unlike perhaps any other prison in Latin America, its managers commemorate and invest in its distinction. The International Standards Association, a global reference for quality management under capitalist logics, has certified this prison for maintaining key principles like "customer focus," "leadership," "evidence-based decision-making" and "relationship management," for a "quality that is consistently improved."

It is hard to imagine a more distinctive and stiff departure from the global prison condition than the lush green lawns and market stalls of this terrain. Perhaps this outlier case is a throwaway. But, on the other hand, exceptional cases have important analytic potential. These kinds of studies in contrast evoke the content of political will, underscoring how the inverse of political withdrawal reveals the content and conditionality of political power.

Ivan Ermakoff (2014) has argued that exceptional cases like this allow for heuristic interpolation of well-entrenched patterns and assumptions; in this case, about who is banally constructed as the logical beneficiary of "the dignified serving of one's time"—and who is not. This kind of frame places that divergence in real material and spatial terms. One contains a police officer who killed in the double digits while off duty but ends up tending bees in an apiary. The other contains Black men, upwards of 40 percent of whom are pre-trial and a majority of whom dealt small-time drugs, living without toothpaste and toilet paper. Exceptional cases are important because, as Ermakoff puts it, they stand at odds with some "general model of causal relations." This one is egregiously different; it saves, shelters and fosters. It is reparative. Its materiality, its orderliness and its very existence make it clear that almost all prisons—but not this one—are terrible and tortuous for a reason.

But if the use of violence to maintain racial order is this linear, why should those who work on behalf of power be subject to punishment? That this prison exists at all, especially under these conditions, is an empirical and conceptual puzzle of its own. One reason might be that there are police prisons around the world but we don't see them—they are obscured from view, both mitigating an interest in them and constraining access to researchers. Only in a country like Brazil are police so violent and "extra-legal" as to require a prison of their own. A second possibility is that there is really no good reason for such a unique prison to exist; wayward police would typically be placed in a prison for the general population, perhaps in a particular wing. In other words, there may be peculiar institutional and historical reasons such a prison should exist at all. A third explanation might be that such an instance isn't really exceptional at all, being, instead, the product of different "cultures" or moments of punishment in which Brazil sees punishment of police as a kind of cultural imperative, or a product of a distinctive political or government crackdown on police violence.

In Brazil, everyday "beat cops," who are the most numerous, most public, and most central, interface with citizens on the street, operating under a separate system of justice administered through a military hierarchy. Any street-level police officer is a military police officer and a reservist in the national military. They are not subject to ordinary legal procedures but instead to military jurisprudence. Other smaller and more institutionally distinct police institutions, civil ones, do indeed send their wayward police through "normal" penal channels. When convicted, these civilian police end up in the regular prison system, albeit usually in a small wing specifically maintained for police, the university-educated, and politicians.

And so the question that matters in these citrus groves is, amid the reliable arbitrariness of law, where the "unrule of law" is axiomatic, what kind of violence is not acceptable for work on behalf of orderliness? Police violence, in post-dictatorship times, runs on. But it is subject to new kinds of voice, incipient demands in liberal terms. Police must be seen to be punished. There is pageantry and performance here. But beneath it all, this prison seems to justify Carl Schmitt's (2010) argument about power: that sovereign power, political will, is legible in the exception. Power, violence as order, is inscribed in every ripening passionfruit and in each of the drips of honey from Pedro's comb.

Police in this city killed 3,287 people in the span of three recent years, 2013–2016. Of those, 66 percent were Black, almost all of whom were men. Such is the logic of the banal police killing, where the death of a person at the hands of police is bureaucratically and morally inscribed as victim caused: "resisting arrest followed by death." This condition, where the dead caused their own death, places the onus on the dead for their own emancipation, a logical impossibility.[7] At the heart of this matter is the preordained subject of police violence, the *"bandido,"* a discursive but deadly real category deployed socially and politically to justify all kinds of state violence, death, and, recently, a transparent rhetoric of "at war" nationalism. To see this logic from the street, from newspapers or on social media is one thing. But to see it from inside the police prison, where on-the-job violence is only temporarily contained, is another. Here, police speak of what kind of police violence is actually scrutinized—what violence is the real subject of punishment—and what is not.

Carlos was a long-serving police officer. He likes to talk about what the public knows of policing. There is an important distinction to be made between what is presented to the public, he says, and what occurs on an everyday basis. To be a police officer is to know and act in a different reality—as this special prison shows. As he puts it, "When a guy enters the police force, he comes to live in a fictional world emulating a stage of war. The people around him induce him to think that he is in a war and that this war is legitimate. This is not 'the police' but some of the important people who represent the institution."

Carlos's analysis distinguishes between "the police" as a formal entity, and the shared sensibility that exists, as a set of assumptions and practices, within it. While police trumpet and publicly perform respect for human rights, the everyday understanding of police work, behind the stage, is much different; it is a "stage of war," of violence. For Carlos, the idea of being a soldier in the war is a feeling present throughout life as a police person. Far from diminishing this desire, police work condenses and legitimates this logic. As he puts it, until the early 1990s, "the death of *bandidos* was a practice institutionalized by the police, with the understanding of all." If an incident "really happened" in the course of a criminal act, or if it was *forjado* (contrived) after the fact, it didn't really matter. No one would have understood it any differently. "What mattered," he says, "was the end result." Carlos believes things are no longer this way.

But Carlos didn't end up in prison for any of this kind of violence, or for the on-the-job violence that he speaks of openly. Carlos is in prison for something much different, quite despite his nostalgia for a kind of police work that he speaks of in past tense, which could openly exalt lethality. He has been convicted, twice, of murdering sex workers off the job.

If there is a divergence between how Carlos talks about the violence that courses through policing and what makes him a resident of this prison. Like him, prisoners routinely speak of what they idealize about policing's relationship with order maintenance. And as in Carlos's case, the values of policing emerge in stark relief to the actual historical and legal condition of their containment in this prison.

Pedro claims that the police have always supported the use of lethal force, as long as it was done in a "slow way." A former beat cop, he speaks of having "snapped" following a personal experience with crime: the sound of his car being stolen outside his house. As he put it, "I started to go crazy off duty . . . and suddenly had eighteen police reports on my back." The new killing spree he describes, of at least eighteen men, was off duty, but it targeted the same kinds of people that he'd already been killing on the job. He recalls blithely that after finishing his shifts he used to pick up his car and go out "hunting" in the low-wage neighborhood where he lived, picking up clues and tips from local merchants. He sums it up in his own terms: "I only killed delinquents."

Until nearly the year 2000, police officers commonly and publicly received medals after what became known as on the job "resisting arrest followed by death" cases. These "death medals" operated as an archetypal and public benchmark for the success of an officer's career. The linear and public relationship between death and commendation has been pushed underground since the Cold War. The symbolism of such medals and commendation has a front stage and a back stage; what they mean to a police officer is different from how they are presented to the public. Crucially, receiving a medal was an affirmation of leadership and bravery. Even today it allows a police person to claim an esteemed social category—"the billy" (Bueno and Denyer Willis 2019), a brave, effective and deadly efficient police officer. Today medals are divided into five grades. The first three are given by a local commander, and the next is given by a regional commander. The highest degree is bestowed by the commander general of the military police. It is very difficult for a police officer to receive all five commendations.

Another prisoner, José, boasted that he had received the five medals, describing in detail the "white medal"—a first-degree honor given to him after a killing. For José, medals were official commemorations of valued everyday police practices. The most common of these was to mark the butt of the service weapon with white paint for each killing—an informal commemoration. "The more stripes, the more billy," said José, who could not disguise his pride of having a "zebra gun." José speaks openly of killing sixteen people throughout his career as a police officer. He was, however, convicted of the murder of his ex-wife and of three attempted homicides, one of which was against a girlfriend.

Younger police officers often complain that today no medals or public commendations are awarded after killings, nor do they get away with dressing up an execution. "There is no honor in death," said Paulo, evoking the disappearance of public exaltation. He was frustrated that he'd not won a medal when he broke up a bank robbery and killed two criminals. Before ending up in prison for what he called "high-risk incidents," Paulo was a police officer in a regional tactical unit akin to a low-level SWAT squad.

Paulo served for eight years in one of these specialized units before being arrested for killing a man in a shopping mall, whose death, he says, was paid for by a foreign mafia. Being violent on the job wasn't enough. He'd been killing for years, "without any financial benefit, just out of job satisfaction." He decided to make a living, taking money from others to go on doing what he'd been doing on the job anyway. Paulo sees his own passage into "billy status" clearly: "The tactical unit man is baptized and no longer an ordinary man. He feels different, he's different, he's not a regular cop or an ordinary human being." For Paulo there is a key distinction in being *the* police and being *of* a particular unit—placed systemically above all others. There are hierarchies within the police, too, of erudition and trust with a transparent kind of violence. Here, the ability to use violence on the job, to deploy it with little worry, exists in a higher order of superhumans.

This concern with hierarchies in policing closely follows the ways that police talk about their fondness for on-the-job violence and the sought-after social categories that operate within it. Where elite units are professionally sought after, better resourced, and enabled to carry out violence with impunity, incentive structures and desirability follow. Policing is a collective enterprise, with police advancing, every day, a set of assumptions about how to protect "good" populations from those who would do them harm.

The same logic appears in José's words when he speaks of the killings he carried out: "For us police officers, you feel satisfaction, you feel more satisfaction than when you arrest. For some cops, killing becomes an addiction; when you cannot kill you feel like your service has not been done properly. You feel that you can solve the problems of society, and you want at any cost to do it." But transgressing these limits creates practical political problems for others, who are otherwise following correct protocol.

Such violence has a distinctive and clear history in Brazil, with some individuals gaining public and unabashed fame in the national press for cleaning the streets. While this violence was more transparent in a different historical moment, for which these police have nostalgia, they describe how this violence remains but in transformed ways. What matters now is that it needs to be maintained in more secretive ways. It wears a shroud. Luis's explanation mixes personal satisfaction with professional recognition. According to him, the reason he ended up in prison is that he took it too far. As he put it, "That [killing] was ostentatiousness, I was feeling like superman, being recognized on the side of good.... Everyone knew, my superiors knew, my colleagues knew.... Although I did harm to many, I did very well for others."

"In my view I was doing the right thing," a prisoner named Joseph recalled. Joseph was convicted for killing sixteen people off the job. "By eliminating the enemy and protecting good people; society wants you to do this, but it crucifies you when you do." Indeed, the process of being remanded, publicly shredded, and held in this prison feels like punishment for police like Joseph. They have a sense of being thrown under the bus—which might indeed be true given how banal violence is in institutional practice.

Victor sighs before discussing a cornerstone of his past, and of fitting in. He describes having killed at least thirty people as a police officer. "What the police taught me," he says, "is that I was different. I am a born follower. I've always wanted this, to do it perfectly. There is no way to take the blame and be caught out; you just have to assume who you are and do it exactly like everyone else." Victor was eventually caught after veering into different territory. He killed a man, in the midst of a fight, who he alleges had murdered a friend of his.

Not all the police that are here see the wrongs of the violence they were punished for directly or indirectly in opposition to the violence they carried out on the job. Around five years ago, Jorge was a police officer working the day shift in the police prison. It was a Sunday, and he had worked all day tending to prisoners and other duties. He left the prison and went home. Arriving there, his wife confronted him. She wanted to separate. As he put it, she had cheated on him previously, and he had forgiven her. But this time, she seemed to be laughing in his face—or so he saw it. He felt hurt, his honor deflated, a "lesser man." He wouldn't accept a separation. Jorge shot and killed her. She should have known the risk this time, he said. He ended up as a prisoner in the place where he once worked.

Jorge's case is symptomatic in other regards. First, the egregious murder of his wife is what police describe as a "crime of passion"—a gendered socio-legal category of violence that typically involves men murdering women. And while the category itself contains a mechanism for normatively diminishing or justifying the act—passion—new laws for batterers and discussion of femicide have raised public scrutiny of what gender actually gets killed amid "passion." According to administrators, 18 percent of the population is held for "crimes of passion." Jorge's act, which he proudly and unrepentantly owns as the result of an affront to his masculinity, is the subject of new public concerns.

Second, like every other police officer we spoke to, Jorge is now posttrial. He is a convicted murderer serving out his sentence, following the letter of the law, as laid down by a judge. He spends his days in the general population. Much of his time is spent circulating around the prison and its lush green grounds. Not all prisoners live together, however. This is defining in other ways: convicted rapists are held in their cells, though administrators deny this is a formal practice. Convicted thieves and those found guilty of corruption are not seen outside their quarters either. Those that killed off duty walk the grounds. And those that killed on duty are, simply, not here.

This exceptional prison can tell us crucial things about policing and the use of violence. Three are preeminent. First, in this city, one in four violent deaths is the result of police action. But even in a city where at least 25 percent of all formally registered violent deaths are committed by on-duty military police, virtually none of these are sentenced and punished.

This won't come as much surprise to those who study Brazil. Much work attests to the feeble or nonexistent judicial responses to police violence that result in few police being arrested, brought to trial, or found guilty.[8] Policing is, after all, about what must be done to keep things as they are.

Particularly striking, given the racial inequality of Brazil and the patterns evident in statistics of police violence, is that race appears only as a pseudonym in how police speak about their violence. Police almost never use racial terminologies to locate their violence. Instead, they used myriad color-blind synonyms: "wolf," "bad people," "*bandidos*," "prey," "delinquents," "fringe elements" or "bad fruit." These constructs, under symbol and pseudonym, produce and rely on wider assumptions of an "evil" and threatening figure that must be combatted at all costs and with all available means. In the version of liberal capitalism practiced in this country, a country that solicited and received the most chattel slaves from the transatlantic trade, order maintenance and threat are centrally about race. But under democracy, where many still profess "racial democracy," such an enemy is rarely explicitly defined as the young Black or ethnic man. In Brazil, as elsewhere, color-blind narratives have been fastened together in the years since the end of the Cold War. Implied in these whitening euphemisms is what Jaime Alves (2014) calls the "blackpolis"—the city built on policing Black life.

Second, there are mechanisms for obscuring how unhindered this violence actually is. In an era of supposed democratic accountability, rights, and the rhetoric of justice reform, the political sphere must defend itself. "Participatory security," citizen councils, and public oversight are some of the ways. Similarly, this prison is a foil, casting a façade of police accountability through a peculiar performance and pageantry of punishment. Many police arrive in this prison, but few become long-term residents. Most are held for the duration of their trial and judgment before being released. Only one prisoner that we spoke with, a man named Francisco, was in this prison after being found guilty of killing a young Black man on the job in a city favela. (Francisco describes police officers as specially trained "hunting dogs" that need to go through a "beefing-up process.") Under these conditions, this prison operates as a kind of temporary insulation, contained away from public scrutiny at a physical and moral distance, evoked in news reports after spectacular and egregious events, effectively deflecting criticism under the hopefulness of institutional justice-in-process. Politicians and pundits can claim that accountability and oversight is coming, implying that justice is about iterative gains, a long arc, and the making of citizenship. But, inevitably, public outrage blows over, consumed by the next case, unable to sustain its attention to individual cases in the flood of others. Many months on, news quietly leaks out that police have been *inocentado* (cleared) for their killing, and by now, they are flying well below the public-outrage radar.

Third, this institutional and material aberration reveals the dissonance between law on the books and law in practice. These walls serve a logic of containment different from what is widely surmised of prisons. To speak of police violence as "unjust" doesn't make sense if law is the reference point; it flows through the law in everyday terms. Each of the police officers we met participated in many "resistance killings," but were never held "responsible" for them. Instead, they were arrested for crossing other fungible but observable lines between what permissible violence, and permissible subjects of violence. What emerges from the evidence is that police who fail to kill in the appropriate manner, to kill the right people, at the right time, on the clock, to kill with the approved justifications and with appropriate self-control, are subject to punishment. Don't be wayward. You can't kill your wife and not repent. Don't take money to kill. Don't kill too many people too quickly. Don't kill again after you've been punished.

A contrast emerges here: learn to kill on the job. You will almost never be held to account for it. When it comes to holding police violence to account, politics itself goes missing. This is especially true when mothers and fathers come searching for answers to their dead and missing sons and daughters—last seen with or near police.

7 From Disappearance, Presence

In the prison just for police, Carlos describes pulling the trigger in a historic prison massacre, an event for which he was also never punished. Now confined to a prison, it was once the other way around—with him as part of a police unit storming into a prison and shooting those within. More than one hundred inmates died in that incident in the early 1990s. For Carlos, the killings were justified. They had to shoot them all, and should have shot more, because there was a riot; the prisoners were out of control. There was no other option. His reasoning traces a banal kind of everyday sensibility, where because urban poor populations can't control themselves and not rebel when they are thrown in prison they require lethal repression. Those who suffer this kind of state violence are made to be "both victims and the agents of their own violation"—as were slaves (Aidoo, 2018: 49)—in a process meant to both pacify and contain into subhuman disappearability. To contest this subhuman condition can mean deadly violence from people like Carlos. To live within it means mundane disappearance. And yet, as I will show here, collective recognition of this condition, in the dense surrounds of prison, enables a search for a different appreciation of life, and an assertion of this appreciation through violence on counter-ethical terms.

Alongside policing, prisons have become the most banal technique of order maintenance by states in the contemporary world, having had a dramatic expansion across the globe over the latter half of the twentieth century. This technique of containment represents a simplistic best practice, carrying with it powerful incentives for governments to align it with good developmental economics. Prisons are built to contain "criminals," but they also create jobs, offer easy state investments, deliver excellent "pork" for constituencies and political allies, and create ample opportunities for graft, pay-back schemes, and partial outsourcing. With their depressed and rights-devoid labor, prisons are also employed to solve other problems—like fighting the upsurge of wildfires in California due to climate change. In São Paulo, some conditional-release prisons for women provide "employment experience" to prisoners by allowing them to package toilet seals and assemble brake-light harnesses for cars, among other things. And yet, for all that prisons do to contain so-called criminals and depress labor, they do it in a moment when crime rates are in decline—belying the idea that they are actually a response to crime and suggesting that criminals are hardly more than a sociopolitical construction.

In the United States, the explosion of prison construction through the 1980s was part of a shift toward a penal political economy, emergent from a shifting mode of production and post-Fordist change in social and political relations. With capital flight in search of cheaper and deregulated labor, companies uprooted skilled and unskilled jobs and took them elsewhere, removing them from cities—and the country. With the making of surplus labor, prisons became fashioned as a novel solution, providing new jobs for some while addressing the problem of lack of jobs for others, allowing investors a reliable return and politicians to demonstrate action. As Ruth Wilson Gilmore (2007) writes, states like California not only embarked on explosive new efforts to expand the use of the prison by issuing bonds, but they also created new ways of financing them through particular kinds of sleight-of-hand debt that kept the full scope of state expenditure on punishment out of the public eye as it grew to upwards of 15 percent of the public budget—avoiding confrontations with voters through referenda or propositions on spending. This debt-financed mass incarceration similarly built new means of making money into the everyday functioning of the prison—with spin-offs, subcontracts, reliable interest rates on bond debt—while creating dramatic new incentives to find criminals to fill them. Amid a raging but politically fabricated "war on drugs," the existence of more prison spaces begot more criminals, the majority under either superficial discretionary categories at the disposal of police—like loitering or small-time possession—or under mandatory sentencing, such as "three strikes" laws, that codified and fortified the pipeline between city street and prison cell. In vast globalizing ways, as both a technique of governance and a material space, the prison is a mode of disappearance that steals people from their social relations, from families and friends, and from the possibility of being political as voters. And this kind of disappearance makes money. It isn't happenstance.

In Brazil, the prison boom arrived late, following the end of the Cold War, and in a different kind of configuration and political economy. Since the 1980s, hundreds of millions of dollars have been invested to build new prisons through public budgets. This has been fragmented across its states and deliberately advanced by the national government—even under the so-called "pink tide"—including as part of major infrastructural investments. Most recently, the Brazilian National Development Bank—much lauded in South–South development-policy scholarship—is developing a policy to help Brazilian states finance prison construction by issuing social impact bonds to help *global* investors feel good about where they put their money.

São Paulo state's prison system has seen an especially dramatic expansion in prison construction as a result. In 1983, there were fourteen prisons in the state, housing 9,972 detainees (Salla 2007). In 2011, with 148 prison units already in service, Governor Geraldo Alckmin, who would run for president (twice) and fail (twice), announced a renewed investment of R$1.1 billion (US$650 million) to create forty-six new prisons.[1] Since 2011 the state has built seventy new prisons, which together contain more than 240,000 people. The prison boom is now in full swing and growing stronger.

And yet the massive expansion of prisons masks the actual moral logic of imprisonment, and its everyday practice. The incentive to build more spaces to respond to overcrowding and so-called "demand" is not met with improved conditions within. Brazilian prisons have long operated under the logic of material containment but lack of everyday provisions to those on the inside, including some of the most basic human necessities such as basic toiletries and hygiene products, clothing, food, and security. While prisons elsewhere have a rich political economy rooted in private contracts for food, supplies, commissary, clothing, and uniforms, Brazilian inmates must rely on social ties, family, or other relations, to ensure their survival and security. They line up at the gates to do so. Out of this bleak space of non-provision, and a prevailing notion that prisoners should disappear from state interest once inside—since their outward threat is neutralized—other logics and contestations have forcefully emerged in a search to reassert belonging. All too commonly, however, these logics and contestations play out via a recurrent script: the prison massacre.

A closer look at the massacre as an event is revelatory. Carlos's recollection of his massacre reminds me of an image that circulated widely after a 1992 massacre at Carandiru, a penal complex in São Paulo. In response to what was described as a riot, police flooded into the prison, taking aim at prisoners with guns, knives, and explosives. The bloody aftermath was colored by a kind of foreshadowing of the politics of responsibility, materialized in a photo. One photo depicted naked prisoners lugging the dead out of their cells and into the halls, wading through blood on the floor. The iconic image, taken from behind one prisoner, who clasps a body wheelbarrow-style by the feet, now seems cast in an archaic, analogue time. The white colors look yellowish, the blues are faded, and the graininess of the picture, lit by a brutalist flash in the foreground, says "then."

This image, which was published in the glossy newsweekly *Veja*, is now coded in these historical terms, as depicting something terrible that happened once but is unlikely to again because police and policing have become more democratic, legitimate, and responsible.[2] While the massacre has not faded from public consciousness—far from it, indeed—it is typically situated in past tense, an exceptional moment of acute police violence and repression indicative of the disorder of an "immature democracy" suffering through a crucial juncture in post-authoritarian politics.

In this way, that photograph, each now-digitized pixel, makes sense in a globalized turn toward liberal democracy and individual self-determination and responsibility, where past egregiousness in different historical moments, or in the shuffle immediately after, becomes the ethical means to assert the goodness of the cause. Disappearance, massacres, these kinds of things happened then, as vestiges of an illiberal moment and its extinguishing legacy, and they will be snuffed out by the freedoms of contemporary political democracy. Such democracy, it is said, will remove the state's ability to be so violent, will require the state to take greater responsibility for its actions, and allow more authority to citizens to constrain it.

Such a framing now seems absurd and disingenuous, a dubious sleight of hand; naively presentist. This circumstance, like disappearance, should not be seen within the narrow historical frame of post–Cold War democracy or its hoped-for political trajectory. Instead, both should be reframed by the long-standing and enduring rationality and ethics of responsibility that they trace: Let the poor manage the outcomes of their violence, of their death, of the squalid urban and prison conditions that *they* create.

Here violence is allowed and made to move from and upon some bodies, in some spaces, and, logically, from the state as an arbiter of optimism and rational justice onto populations situated as threatening or disorderly. Locating the massacre in these terms, of political power dislocating responsibility for violence and its aftermath to individuals, means having to ask if such a condition has actually changed over time. How far back does the political condition of blaming the victim go? Since when has it been reasonable to let the "disorderly" kill the disorderly? And if it stretches as far back as manumission, how far does it promise to go forward? Carlos's massacre is not the product of a neophyte democracy. Framing it as such helps to maintain "the good" of a state that presided over racialized inequality, allowing Carlos to wash his hands clean.

This condition that underpins a massacre event endures. In January 2017, a prison in the far North suffered a massacre. In a regional agricultural penitentiary near the city of Boa Vista, wedged in an area between Guyana and Venezuela, thirty-three people were killed. The next day, January 7, Brazil's largest newspaper, the *Folha de São Paulo*, placed a photo of the aftermath on the front page, above the fold—for the nation to see. The image centers five surviving prisoners, stripped to their underwear, lugging bodies on a trolley to a coroner's truck as officials look on. Their bodies glisten with sweat, necks and arms straining as they prepare to lift and slot a bagged body into the back of the truck. The work, the emotional labor and the blood of these prisoners fill the carriage of the state. A man's fingers protrude from a body bag as though trying to get out. The news-paper gives this image full view.[3]

These prison massacres, twenty-five years apart, seem different in distinct ways. The first was carried out by Carlos and his colleagues, employed by the state and deployed into a prison that had "become disorderly." The massacre happened in a moment of particular hope, in the glow of a brave new end of history, complete with a constitution. It also happened in São Paulo, a city that had been central to dictatorial repression. The riot that required police to intervene centers the state as protagonist: it was *state violence*. Political leaders had to deny responsibility in the aftermath, desperately trying to frame the event as caused by pathological prisoners and their violent and disorderly nature.

The second massacre was carried out by prisoners themselves, upon other prisoners. It happened in a backland state, in a region often described as less developed, and many decades removed from dictatorship. It came in the midst of a moment of national political doubt, teetering on neo-fascism. The state seems absent from the acts of direct violence, providing only the walls and the truck to take the bodies away. The prisoners killed each other, and the massacre came direct and unfiltered to the population via WhatsApp videos and macabre photographs captured on the inside, and during the event.

And yet these two massacres are not discrete. They are tied together in at least two ways. The first is in a political logic of containment structured by affective terrains of active and passive control, working through a dialectic of state absence and presence. The state has been diligent in holding these bodies in this material space, in ever greater numbers, and yet it is passive in its provision of goods, rules, and security once bodies arrive. The second is in how such passiveness, especially in the aftermath of the first massacre, shaped the way that prisons took on a life of their own. The state's violence in the first set in motion the conditions for the second—a massacre that has been repeated in mirror-like fashion all around the country since.

For those in the PCC, a self-defined organized crime group, the first massacre is Genesis, an origin story.[4] Within months of the event, a written statute emerged from survivors, scripting the moral terrain of an organization that would grow exponentially in space, power, and membership over the next decades. These early-days members, part of what would become an *irmanidade* (brotherhood), traced a new and prescriptive paradigm for prison life, where rules and coexistence would reshape the banality of violence, from both the state and among the prison population itself. "We must remain united and organized," they wrote, "to avoid a similar or worse massacre as that of October 2, 1992, when 111 prisoners were cowardly murdered in a massacre that will never be forgotten in Brazilian consciousness." In the midst of a nascent national re-democratization, these prisoners saw violence and politics in a long arc, and not from a position of demands on the state. "We the Command will change carceral practice, its inhumanity, brimming with injustice, oppression, torture and prison massacres." They would do it themselves, out of the terrain of state violence, leveraging the capacious lived experience of being left to die, maintaining themselves as a credible and legitimate body under widespread logics of political withdrawal and resignation. The prisoner who carries a dead inmate isn't just moving flesh and bone, he is shouldering the burden of a historical condition where his own place amid violence can only be his responsibility.

Since 1992, the PCC has become a colonial force, not just expanding to monopolize almost all of São Paulo's prison system, implementing what scholars euphemistically call "self-governance," but also leapfrogging to other states. In the years after that massacre, the PCC would embark upon a ruthless policy of pacification of the prison system, moving from one prison to the next and overtaking rivals under the guise of coordinated riots. It would do so while shaping what Camila Nunes Dias and Sacha Darke (2016) call the "social figuration" of almost every prison, restructuring practices of punishment, predictability, and justice from behind bars. In doing so, it achieved a near perfect hegemony over time, with the help of various governors.[5] But its logic, then and now, does not only rely on violence to instill its paradigm of order, which Biondi (2016) describes as non-hierarchical, diffuse, and "rhizomatic." Its notions of *proceder* (process) and *justiça* (justice) move faster and further in space than the membership itself, meaning that locations "dominated" by the PCC—visitor lines leading in on family day, some prisons, urban neighborhoods—may have no baptized members. Such a logic of moral order is also prominent in prisons where the PCC is anticipated but not present in institutional form, meaning that by the time a baptized member finally arrives, he is often already there.[6]

In some ways, the advance of the PCC through São Paulo and then far beyond has been like a chronicle foretold. This chronicle has repeated itself in varied chapters of peaks and troughs of violence, often accompanied by assassinations of street-level bureaucrats or outright violence in urban spaces.[7] From south to north in the country, these chapters seem to follow a steady expansion roughly outward from São Paulo, stretching toward the farthest reaches of the country, and indeed beyond. It happens within a distinctive local context, working through acute frictions, regional politics, identity, and impacts with local gangs or existing violent organizations.

This chronicle foretold is the script for the second massacre. Most speak of the dead at the agricultural prison as being rivals of the PCC, wiped out amid a riot as the organization continued to further expand its reach. But, in fact, this second massacre happened in the immediate aftermath of another, just days earlier, near the city of Manaus on the Amazon River, where fifty-six were killed. There, the opposite happened: a rival group known as the Família do Norte ("Northern Family," FDN) set out to kill PCC members that had begun to establish themselves in the penitentiary. Terrified that they, otherwise, would be exterminated by the PCC, as others had been in many Brazilian cities, the FDN is believed to have preempted the PCC's action. Said to be allied with the Comando Vermelho ("Red Command"), one of Rio de Janeiro's primary organized crime groups, the FDN used explosives to break down a wall separating the wings controlled by the different groups, allowing them to attack, and for tens of prisoners to flee the prison into the surrounding jungle as well.

The prisons of the 1992 massacre and this 2017 massacre might be 4,630 kilometers, two ferry rides and twenty-five years removed from each other, but politically they are right next door. It matters not that "nonstate" actors carried out the latter and not the former. The violence is adjacent, contiguous, enabled by a logic of incarceration and disappearance that fills prisons with bodies and leaves them to die. This logic allows—requires—other violent actors to emerge, utilizing them to maintain order in a terrain otherwise governed through disorder. The logic of Carandiru, and what it breathed life into, makes successive violence rational and virtually necessary, the shroud of prison violence past continuing to inform and produce prison violence present.

Unlike the first massacre, though, these recent massacres don't stick to a politics of democratic accountability. The state played no obvious part in the violence. In fact, some guards were taken hostage in the process, creating a sense of the *state as victim*, as itself violated by violence. A Supreme Court judge, formerly the minister of justice in São Paulo, argued that the blame belonged to the third-party security company responsible for managing this and five other prisons in the region. In another facet, other politicians were quick and transparent to praise the rioters for eliminating other undesirables. It was, after all, just a gory scene of Black and Indigenous prisoners murdering other Black and Indigenous prisoners. "More should be dead," wrote the National Secretary for Youth, a presidential appointee at the time. "There should be a massacre every week," he added.[8] There was no innocence to be lost. An elected federal representative, himself a former police officer, made headlines by speaking of a scoreboard of the dead, which he used to "cheer on" prisoners in other prisons to raise the score.[9]

Massacres and their logic are a fixture of a prison experience defined by both acute intervention and non-provision. This violence is a socially and organizationally informed response to Brazil's ongoing experience with mass incarceration, which works through a dialectic of active and passive. Alongside its vertiginous levels of police killing, between 1995 and 2010 Brazil had the fastest-growing prison population in the world per capita, behind only Indonesia. The growth of the prison population means major overcrowding, with capacity at 161 percent. Today, Brazil has the world's third-largest prison population per capita. Between 1990 and 2014 the prison population in the country went from 90,000 to 607,000, an increase of 575 percent.[10]

But the expansion of the prison project was not done by a conservative state government. The idea that prisons are overloaded and inhumane has been understood politically as a problem to be dealt with by building more prisons and not by decreasing the numbers of people being arrested for menial crimes, held with little evidence, or kept for months or years before trial. The language of "humanizing" the system has been useful, too, perhaps especially, for apparently leftist leaders, and in spite of the systemic dehumanization that prisons do. In the early 2000s, a new federal prison system was invented and created under the Workers' Party administration of Lula, hinting at the real shade of Brazil's "pink tide" experience in carceral terms. Six new federal maximum-security prisons now dot the country. And while these prisons house only a few hundred prisoners, and mostly those whose high-profile presence in state prisons is seen as risky or destabilizing, their hyper-modern and new facilities are intended to be orderly and well managed in comparison to the violent and gang-ruled state prison systems. They augment, not replace.

In 2011, then president Dilma Rousseff announced the Plano Nacional de Apoio ao Sistema Prisional (National Prison Support Plan). This initiative sought to "expand and modernize" prisons around the country, creating more beds and better spaces for detainees. Backed with US$650 million, the plan allowed for states and municipalities to draw on federal funds also as a means of "local development" that would create prison-related jobs. The plan would make the prison system safer by reducing overcrowding and it would pump money into infrastructure construction, creating a kind of developmental win-win. The plan promised to create 42,500 new spaces, making an important dent in the crisis of "*superlotação*" ("overcrowding"). By January of 2017, ninety-two prisons had been approved as funded under the plan. And yet, in the aftermath of a political crisis and so-called "impeachment" that stripped Dilma of her presidency, and financial crisis with an imploding economy, more than half of the construction projects were stuck in the mud or embroiled in graft.[11] Even under these conditions of economic austerity and accompanying efforts to pare back public pensions, the Temer government introduced a brand-new R$1.2 billion (US$375 million) "build and modernize" prison package.

The manifold growth of the Brazilian prison system since the early 1990s is a multiparty effort. The consensus across politics, and even among many "progressive" scholars in and out of the country, is that prison construction and greater infrastructure investment are the logical means to address violence and disorder, somehow emergent from "too many people per room." Such a position doubles down on adequate prison space as a solution, where more spaces always beget more bodies. This pattern of intervention, containment and disappearance as public policy has done little except build walls, augment a system controlled by variegated organized crime, and enable its expansion in near lockstep with the step-changes in the number of prisons.

The rhetoric of humanizing the prison system by expanding it is a fallacy. Seen from within prison walls, and through the prison experience of families, such a foil obscures the real work of material containment, violence, and systemic racism. As prisons have expanded with major investments, the underwhelming internal provision of goods and services feeds its own "self-help" political economy. Order and everyday coexistence are mediated by groups like the PCC. Major cash infusions under "humanizing" or "modernizing" narratives very rarely, if ever, reshape mundane and basic problems of security and provision of adequate food or other necessities. Day-to-day costs don't count. The long-standing lived status quo is a system where families and prisoners must provide goods, food, and simple hygienic materials for their loved ones on the inside. With the substantial demand for such goods to flow into prisons, the cost being borne by prisoners and their families, have come new kinds of supply—online businesses that promise to deliver packages themselves. Otherwise, families must travel hundreds of kilometers, or move closer to the prison, to lug things in. The inside is so dependent on the outside that the organization itself routinely pays for transport for family members to come and visit.

The Brazilian prison system advances as a regime of disappearance, of both a political and an empirical nature. Prisoners are contained and entrapped, held at a distance from society, while their families are consumed by the manifold burdens of maintaining households, paying bills, and scraping by on an everyday basis. This comes in addition to finding ways to provide anyone who is in prison with the ability to survive, stay clothed, and maintain basic hygiene.

And yet it is also common for family members to not be able to find their loved ones. Prisons are also places where people actually, materially, disappear—scarcely to be found by families, legal representation, and others. Under the nebulous knowledge of absent bureaucratic ordering on the part of the state, people arrested by police and sent to prison can disappear within. In the system of prisoner transfers that happen between initial jail lockup and the network of prisons subsequently connected, people's documented location isn't always what it seems. Someone arrested on the street—especially if not witnessed by others—can functionally vanish, with one of the only mitigating conditions being a phone call to family or others, if it is actually allowed by police. Families commonly speak of knowing that someone has been arrested or picked up by police by word of mouth but then not being able to find them within the state. Araújo (2012) writes lucidly of one such case, of a group of mothers whose sons were taken into a police armored personnel carrier and disappeared in the state bureaucracy. Subsequently they somehow were released into the hands of an armed group—who tortured and murdered them.

Even with the PCC providing some semblance of order within the prison system, people disappear within this vast depository. The PCC's own records describe the illegibility of order within it, especially when it comes to knowing where people are, tracing their movements within and between prisons, and figuring out their whereabouts. "When he arrived home he was shaken down by the police and arrested," reads one internal record of a member, "He's now inside but we haven't yet found out where he is." Says another, "He's on the inside and the last penitentiary he was in was the one in Black Creek." Others put it more plainly in a simple statement. "He's deprived of liberty—location unknown."

From these structural circumstances of an expanding system of material incarceration, police violence, and everyday containment, a sphere of sociality and social life is fortified, fashioning legitimacy from a search to assert life on new terms. Anything that can make life a bit more bearable is very compelling, even if that means violence. Care, and the use of violence to define who deserves it, is the new terrain of the prison system— tendentiously humanized from within, but with a difficult new underside.

For those who live amid the PCC in the prison system and outside, this paradigm is obliquely stated, written and reiterated in *salves* ("shout-outs")—sent to all and shared among them. These remind the population of what this care for their condition looks like, how far it goes, amid the organization's rapid expansion across the country. As one shout-out from 2014 put it:

Awareness Shout-Out

Awareness communication from the disciplinary group
On this day 05/08/2014 we send a strong and loyal embrace to all
    Through this communication the disciplinary group informs all of the importance for everyone to participate in the work of the organization. We have permanent objectives for the income gathered from this work *where this money is re-given in benefits to the less fortunate and those who find themselves in federal and state lockup.* Today the organization works to strengthen the brothers and affiliates that keep coming, we choose to financially strengthen, with lawyers, tickets for visitation, basic baskets of food, clothing for the cold, medical assistance, cases for support, medicine, and

funerals for those who lose their lives. All of this is only possible if brothers and affiliates are punctual and responsible with their payments for the raffle, dues, cocaine, and marijuana, indeed to all of the work of the organization in and out of the prison system.

Many times we come across brothers asking: *where is the support?* But we ask whether these brothers as our affiliates are taking their difficulties to the leadership in their state [*geral do estado*]. Has the state leadership done reports and put out a request to the group or is it suggesting jobs?

We are a chain where our brothers strengthen the organization by partici- pating in our work responsibly and with dedication and the organization strengthens those who need it according to precise individual needs. Today we are dealing with many states that need help and it is of extreme impor- tance that the organization's membership within the state analyzes the needs of affiliates and brothers so that we can strengthen them, remembering always that this strengthening is the fruit of the work of the organization.

This communication is to be passed by hand so that all will read and reflect on the *importance of the disciplinary and financial evolution* of the organization.

Once more, a strong embrace to all

P.S.: You can seek out your local leadership for clarification if you have any doubts.

SIGNED BY THE DISCIPLINARY GROUP[12]

Out of a search to assert the importance of life within prison, the PCC now speaks and acts forcefully of taking care of its own. It differentiates between who belongs and who does not by codifying who joins the col- lective search to safeguard life, taking care of others by paying fees and work back into the organization, joining it in a rapid process of national expansion throughout a national prison system where the assumption, otherwise, is disappearance.

This logic advances rapidly within Brazil's carceral system as a historic and ongoing political economy of organized disappearance. Such a condi- tion reproduces itself and has become predictable, understood, and logical for those susceptible to it, even as it is written through violence and ambi- guity. There is a response to the politics of disappearance and it comes as a means to redefine the terms of life and death, and with new violent means, as part of an empirical search to revalue "criminal lives" that are otherwise subject to ritual killing at the hands of police, or disappearance and slow death in a prison system growing manifold.

8 Muted Martyrdom

The graves are in linear rows in Otávio's cemetery. One day, in 2018, I walked between them. In one row all the graves had been recently disinterred. Three years had passed, and it was time for these remains to leave the earth. The process left a jarring topography of dirt, casket fragments, clothing, and bones spilling out from holes in the ground. But amid this terrain of disordered fragments, three graves were untouched, elevated above the line of unnerving voids where humans used to be.

I approach to more closely examine them. Each of the three had a granite tablet with name, date of birth, date of death, and an oval button photo. They still had adornments. The grass on them was well trimmed. All three were young men in their twenties and thirties. And the three shared a common date of death in late May 2012.

The day is significant. It was a day when a military police operation in this part of the city ended in the killing of six men allegedly associated with the PCC. As the newspapers had it, the men had gathered at a car wash to plan a prison break when the police broke in, guns blazing. During previous fieldwork, I had accompanied the homicide detectives in their attention to this massacre.[1] Five men were killed on the spot in what was later portrayed as a "shoot-out" by police press relations. No police cars were hit. One man was taken away alive by police, only to be killed during a circuitous trip through the city that ended up at a regional hospital. According to a witness who related the incident over the phone in real time, the man was executed on the side of a highway.

This revelation, after some handwringing in the station, and with the hard evidence of the witness testimony, led to the internal affairs division of the military police arresting three police officers. These officers were remanded to the exceptional prison where Pedro, José, Carlos, and the others were locked up. But unlike them, the officers involved in the massacre were ultimately found not guilty. They were set free, able to return to duty.

While the event was major and public, its repercussions seemed even bigger. Shrouded in extrajudicial intrigue and manifest injustice, it was widely spoken of as the incendiary for a half-year-long "blood feud" between the PCC and police, punctuated by a series of further massacres whose trajectories led, similarly, to the cemetery as a material space. Eventually, the PCC was said to have sent out a *salve* to all members that eye-for-eye violence was to be enacted; for every member killed with *covardia* (cowardice) by police, two or three police would need to fall.

At the graveside, I was struck by the paradox between yet another police action toward the ritual obliteration of the racialized poor and this definitive assertion of their memory in a powerful but circumscribed way. Were these men the subjects of that violence, and that defining moment? Long after the police massacre, these bodies—now, surely, bones—were being held aloft in the cemetery, supported by hands that I could not see. And so the question I had on that day was, whose hands were these, protecting their dignity? What did that signify? What was the politics of dead bodies at play here, within these acute conditions of cemetery apartheid? This memorial was not a granite mausoleum adorned with a copper spire and a pearl-faced angel with wings—but it spoke just as loud in this topography of disappearance.

Perhaps this condition of being held aloft was made more visible by the eventfulness and materiality of a massacre. Multiple graves, maintained past their time, make this condition more visible in the cemetery landscape—a material status quo ante, in multiple. Perhaps these men were indeed the victims of police assassination, their burial and non-disinterment paid for by the organization and others as a result. Maybe this is why these bones, and not others, were not subject to the state-provided indignity of disinterment.

A reading of the massacre—this one, those previous, and those to come—from the cemetery moves beyond the temporality of moral outrage. As in prison, the eventfulness of massacres—their visibility, rupture, moral insurgence—can obscure the banality of everyday logics that circumscribe and work unexceptionally. These men, and indeed others like them, are made alive in their death. Their burial and the maintenance and recognition of who they were in life, through the event of their death, become the basis for an organization like the PCC to reassert its meaning and justification. In the violence and death of its members and community, it regenerates by asserting the importance of life. Like many social groups around the world, past and present, the PCC turns the vulnerability of death into a search for strength in life, crafting a moment of disappearance into an assertation of presence and collective power.

Commemoration of death is not just a question of massacres, of course. Sometime in the latter half of 2012, a man affectionately named "Teo" worked a job on the outskirts of the city. One day at work he was shot and severely wounded by police, sending him to the hospital for a number of days. Costs accumulated quickly, encumbering his family with a new kind of burden. Teo died not long after, leaving behind the cost of a dignified burial as well as the futures of his loved ones. He was one of 655 people killed by police that year, seven in ten of whom were Black.

Teo had been a PCC member. The job was a means to make money to pay, at least in part, the monthly membership dues that were used to care for those on the inside—in the certainty that he too would be there soon enough. In the PCC's own bureaucratic documents and accounting for expenditures, a bookkeeper writes of giving Teo's "people" US$2,700 before and after his death, as a means of comfort and cost abatement. This is no paltry sum, amounting to around nine times the value of one minimum monthly salary and more than twenty-two times the maximum monthly amount Brazil's famed conditional cash transfer, the *bolsa família*, gave to the very poorest.

Whether in prison or on the streets, the PCC operates as a form of "life and death insurance," made necessary and attractive by abject and predictable conditions of violence and death, then as now. It maintains its significance by speaking through the horrors of premature death and what it creates—worlds of suffering, debt, broken family relationships, and anger. The PCC not only provides "life insurance" to its people and their loved ones when they die, but they also ensure, by their very organizational logic, that those who belong are not forgotten. It has found footing, a social rationality, in the ways that it marginally mitigates the conditions of death and disappearance that gave rise to it: police violence, squalid prison conditions, and racialized precarity. It does so both by commemorating those who belong, immortalizing them, and by denying commemoration to those that do not, emphasizing their forgettability by burying them elsewhere, in mundane mass graves, hiding their bodies and shrouding them in derision. These people should be forgotten, be made ungrieveable. They should disappear.

Teo's case, which happened within months of the massacre, is one example of a thoroughgoing logic. One of the most foundational concerns of the PCC is to ensure that its members and relatives have a dignified burial. It has come to occupy a space from a position where such a thing was not possible, where life and death and its conditions of burial were made to reinforce the disposability of lives. Paying membership dues to the organization, or being associated with someone that does, means being part of a sphere of "life insurance" that emphasizes how the PCC operates as a burial society, motivated by the persistent threat of violence and death.

There is perhaps nothing distinctive about the PCC's use of disappearable subjects to craft a new sensibility and belonging. Indeed, existing scholarship focuses on how lives came to be biopolitical, saved from premature death, stressing the importance of the body, medicalization, and the project of industrialization. New and dense concentrations of people in cities—and the concordant spatial remaking of cemeteries—demarcated new logics of burial, increasingly divided between public and private cemeteries, that made invisible the obliteration of individuals through the burial process, in space.

This logic has distinctive historical providence in rapid industrialization and the subsequent globalization of its cemetery logics and spatiality. In the eighteenth and nineteenth centuries, amid a great amount of death, the event became a vital occasion to differentiate the value of bodies, and to celebrate social status. In doing so, the lives of some in the death of others could be exalted. In the social life of Liverpool at that time, and in those "classic slums" like Salford, described by Robert Roberts (1990), and in adjacent cities like Manchester, the specter of death was heavy. The shadow of death, the possibility of being buried in a pauper's pit with others, was the ultimate form of shame, reframing the worth of life in ignominious death.

At the heart of the matter was a comparative exercise that worked through two kinds of logics. The first was how burial operated upon the poor, reinforcing the vital importance of getting paid through the experience and specter of burial in a pit. The rationale for getting a job and keeping that job was not necessarily just to put food on the table; it was also to be able to save for a dignified burial. And in highly gendered ways. "What did a woman work for," recalls Laqueur (1983: 110) of a member of an early burial society, "but in hopes she should be put out of the world in a tidy way." Amid new scales of economic production, and unprecedented uses of labor and disposability in urban space, death "on the parish," in a pit, was violently symbolic—and productive.

Julie-Marie Strange (2003) describes how a pauper's burial in this late Victorian period was especially abhorrent because it denied rites and mourning customs even where the dead did have family. Burial "on the parish" meant not anonymity (necessarily), but acute central government control over the impossibility of commemoration—a plain pine box was afforded, with no individual markings or space for mourning. This ultimate disgrace was catalyzing, and led to new kin efforts to get people out, even years after their "disgraceful" burial. Some families applied to exhume bodies from communal graves once they had the money to pay for a proper burial. Such was the logic of the *workfare* New Poor Laws, where the evisceration of poor lives-in-death was a powerful governing technique for driving economically productive life.

It worked pedagogically, serving as a novel kind of necro-incentive, and not just for those who might be most subject to it. "The pauper funeral became a symbol of great power even to those in no danger of ever being subject to it," Laqueur (1983: 109) writes. It served as an incipient rationale to "earn wealth"; to be part of a social group, and to buy into membership that might ensure this would never happen. "For the rich and successful, for those with social ties," wrote Laqueur, "the funeral could be anticipated with equanimity. Not so for the poor and friendless; it haunted them as the specter of failure." The ability to ensure a dignified burial was *the* incentive for the urban poor to save money. Insofar as they saved for anything, Laqueur argues, they saved for a dignified burial.

The second was the way that death in society became a comparative exercise in a new capitalized order. To denote that the poor belonged on the edge of a common pit, or inside it, to be buried in a sparse pine box, could now be seen alongside a material and symbolic counterpoint. Now moving apart from piety and connection to the parish and church(yard), death became a marketplace, liberally "democratized," driving differentiation both in the varied hallmarks of burial—tombs, statutes, ornate gravestones—and in its spatial location—the ability to be buried in classed space away from the dirtiness of the city, and as a means of not making the city dirty. Such a logic always implied a real antithesis and an ongoing potential.

Cemeteries and funerals are not for the dead, of course. Their audience is the living; death matters most to those left behind, opening a window onto the actual value of life beyond the rhetoric of social ties and affective legitimations of worth. The same is true for the absence of funerals, and how they hang and are spoken of through ignominy. Industrialization drove a new wedge in historic burial practices, creating new and opulent terrains of commemoration alongside new means of disposal. New private cemeteries made such differentiation spatially discrete, reinforcing and reterritorializing justifications for segregation in life through death. There was no such thing as a pit grave in a new private cemetery; it had to be elsewhere.

The unprecedented emergence of life insurance in the early nineteenth century is rooted in the growing ignominy of death amid industrialization and the rupturing of social ties. Laqueur (2016: 315) describes the dramatic growth of commodified indemnification for death:

By 1874 two and a quarter million people, mostly men, belonged to friendly societies that provided both death and sickness benefits; millions more, their spouses, were insured for a funeral only. Six hundred and fifty thousand men and women belonged to local burial societies registered with the government and hundreds of thousands more must have belonged to the many thousand small burial clubs which remained unregistered. In addition more than a million belonged to so-called collection societies, commercial ventures which were founded to insure primarily women and children not covered in other ways.

From its earliest days in the United Kingdom, life insurance was made necessary by the industrial excessiveness of death and a vertiginous Victorian commodification of burial conditions. Together, these gave the problem of a breadwinner's death a new kind of undertow. The incipient life-insurance sector was very alive under this condition, speaking through the working-class male breadwinner, the man—often from the colonies—who left behind a family, a "Scottish Widow."

Of course, the commodity widely known as "life insurance" is really nothing of the sort. Being derived from a process of mitigating death, it is, truth be told, death insurance: A fantastically profitable way to benefit from how the global capitalist economy in a particularly explosive historical moment went to work on bodies. Life insurance, the commodity, allowed the relationship between death and the relative value of bodies to be dulled, making the experience of death sufferable, manageable, and not so voracious as to consume those left behind.

Life insurance became possible for the working class in Britain, while continuing to generate strength from the possibility of a bad death. Such a comparison was not just local to the city, or to the country. It was also forged internationally, through the logics of the commodity and system that made death so violent in places like Liverpool. Saving for death and/ or contributing to it in anticipatory ways was possible where money could be accumulated—even if only in marginal terms. For this to be possible, bodies had to have some control over themselves. While this was the case in the British corner of the triangle trade in cotton, it was not the case for the enslaved bodies that harvested the cotton woven in the factories of Britain—allowing, eventually, for bodies to be indemnified.

The triangle trade of cotton as a commodity gave rise to great cities and great new orders of death in Britain. But it did elsewhere, too. This trade linked sub-Saharan Africa with the Americas and Britain through chattel slavery, cotton plantations, and cotton textile factories, where textiles were then traded for more slaves, sometimes on par.[2] The triangle trade cast new materiality into being, where the uses and death of the Black body provided the capital for brick-and-mortar mills, factory walls, and urbanization especially around Liverpool. "Liverpool sailings," writes Williams (1973: 103), "accounted for 1,099 slave voyages out of a total of 1,283 such voyages undertaken from British ports in the ten years from 1795 to 1804." At the same time, between 1791 and 1802, a crucial period of growth and industrialization, 40 percent of the cotton used in Liverpool came from Brazil (Pereira 2018). The triangle trade drove Victorian urbanization, which was itself driven by the uses and disposal of Black bodies in Brazilian and American slavery. Brazil's especially insidious slavery was further fueled by a South–South trade exclusively between Southern Africa and Brazil.

This relationship between death mitigation and life insurance was only possible for some, and specifically those who could accumulate, develop class mobility, and benefit from labor organization in some parts of the world. Others were denied. "We the Black-African were the victims of the capitalist process," wrote Abdias Nascimento (2002: 229), "and we were newly victimized by those who supposedly combatted capitalism in the industrialised space of Euro-North America." Black bodies of primitive accumulation were a foundation stone for lives in Britain to be indemnified, that possibility premised on an antecedent. This precondition, that some lives became able to pay for insurance against death, and Black and Indigenous others elsewhere made it possible, was the systemic undergirding of "life insurance" as it is widely spoken of today; the pre-purchased and publicly traded ability to care for one's loved ones, and oneself, after death. Life insurance was always for some bodies, in some parts of the world, and premised on bodies antecedent in the global supply chain of life and death. "And when the European workers had their life conditions rise," elaborated Nascimento further, "it brought with it expanded costs for the enslavement, oppression and destitution of Africans."

Outside of Europe, repression and slavery meant that commemoration and life-in-death sociality worked in other ways. While slave owners relied on opulent displays of wealth in death—statues, memorial gardens, white granite mausoleums—slaves were denied control over their own bodies and engineered to the brink. Slaves were only occasionally given space to commemorate their own kin's dead bodies (Jamieson 1995). Such commemorations struggled to take place on their own terms, or in spaces explicitly delineated to burial—especially in Brazil. The history of spaces of Black burial or disposal is written and reproduced in White and Black. Through oral histories and intergenerational testimonies, Black populations have kept them alive, beneath historical silences that surround denigrated death, until they are "discovered" and brought into a public telling of history.

The persistent but unequal relationship between the slave, the slave owner, and death generated its own distinctive "mortuary politics." Written through slave relations, Vincent Brown (2008) writes that this politics of life and death "mediated group cohesion, property relations, struggles to give public influence a sacred dimension, contests over the colonial moral order, and efforts to politicize legal geography and history" (11).

Today, "forgotten" slave burial grounds are unearthed as new layers of capitalism, and its urban re-spatialization are laid down, digging deeper. The scraping away of earth, and sometimes existing buildings, to rebuild a revanchist city on top reveals dramatic slave burial spaces. In New York City, twenty thousand bodies were found and later relocated to make way for redevelopment, from what is now called the African Burial Ground.

In Rio de Janeiro, the redevelopment of the historic port space in the lead-up to the 2016 Olympics allowed for new but very limited excavations of the Cemitério dos Pretos Novos (New Black Cemetery), discovered in 1996. In what was called the Porto Maravilha ("The Marvelous Port"), the city's Olympic redevelopment scraped away the streets above to lay down a new light-rail transit system that would help to recast and revitalize this decayed part of the city as investment worthy. The cemetery beneath is a space of jumbled bodies of slaves that died during the unimaginably violent Middle Crossing, and before they could be "saved" by baptism into the Catholic Church. This cemetery, said to contain thirty thousand bodies of former slaves, functioned as a space of disposal between 1769 and 1830. Since its rediscovery by the family living in the house sitting on top of it, Pretos Novos has seen only piecemeal and patchwork efforts to commemorate or reclaim the intricate mixing of bodies within. Pretos Novos continues to exist inside a former family home, having been nearly forced to shutter on a number of occasions for lack of funding.

As the White working class of Liverpool and the United Kingdom were forging new social and economic relationships to insure against death, that condition of possibility rested on the sphere of violent production that preceded it—and created contemporaneous spaces of human disposal like Pretos Novos. Life-saving techniques were always only for some, requiring the conditions of others to trace the paradigm of what lives *not saved* look like. For those others, disposal on the parish or in Pretos Novos continues to shape powerful incentives for other forms of possibility.

In São Paulo, a historic Black church called the Capela dos Aflitos (Chapel of the Stricken) was adjacent to the first cemetery in the city for criminals, slaves, and the unbaptized. Here, next to the capital punishment stocks, bodies were disposed of as at Pretos Novos. Immediately nearby, in a historic space that Andrew Britt (forthcoming) describes as the "*zona do negro*," the Our Lady of Remedies church served the freed and quasi-free Black population, growing into a space of abolitionism where fleeing and freed slaves attempted to build a new political terrain at the end of the nineteenth century—including with a museum of slavery.[3] Recently rediscovered and now in the slow and halting process of archaeological reconstruction, Our Lady was demolished in the 1920s by a modernist urban-planning project that displaced the Black community from the city center and smothered its incipient post-chattel effort for political voice. Amid wide new avenues and planning as top-down statist progress, they called this new city neighborhood "Liberdade" ("Freedom"). Today, this same neighborhood, since the home of successive waves of immigrant populations, surrounds the Praça da Sé, the central church square that gives the Mães da Praça da Sé their name.

Once again, life insurance is at a crossroads. "The life-insurance industry needs new vigour," *The Economist* proclaimed in 2018. "Life insurers are struggling like never before," reads the sub-header. Life insurance is an old industry by now, whose margins aren't what they used to be. It needs to be "reinvigorated," to be made "lively anew." Why now? The project now, for many, is to "make live," and to marginalize death under guises of deservedness. In some parts of the world, death has become too predictable, too well quantified and sapped of value, the number of bodies it wants to save isn't growing. Everyone, it seems, is already on board.

The logic seems clear: as life insurance in *The Economist*'s part of the world has become ever more tapped out, "struggling like never before" in some parts of the world, violence is running amok elsewhere, globally, creating new justifications and modes of organization to keep people from being tossed in an undignified pit. Such populations, elsewhere, have never really been the subject of life insurance.

Even so, the everyday project of insuring people against ignominious death existed well before and outside of industrialization, in contexts where it couldn't become a commodity and through its denial to some lives as not deserving of it. And it continues to work as such, beneath the possibility of commodification.

Here insurance operates as a meshwork of social relations indemnifying populations from the everyday crisis that surrounds death on the doorstep. Such forms are visible especially in moments, spaces, and conditions where the commodity didn't exist, was always denied to some populations, or where the risk was "too high." Between the fear of death and the fear of social death, in the twilight of political and legal regimes, particular kinds of shared identity emerge near the graveside, reworking everyday justifications for violence upon some bodies into a logic of self-protection.

As with the life insurance industry, signing up for a society of this kind requires an ongoing fear of death, which must be read relative to the prohibitive and burdensome costs of life and the afterlife. The greater the specter of death, the larger the real or imagined cost of it falling upon you and those you would leave behind, the greater the incentive to find shelter from its deleterious effects.

Where the violence rate is high, and its costs are too, efforts to find shelter do not mean just paying into a collective pot for subsequent redistribution. Whereas the development of the life insurance industry out of Victorian times worked through the high mortality rate and its costs for laborers in the factory or on the precarious fringes of employment, today's death insurance mobilizations also work through those people who live, experience, and practice violence themselves. The rationale to pay, and the payment itself, is continually forged by the presence and possibility of violence, both as subject and protagonist. One pays to indemnify oneself from death and violence by using violence and, sometimes, death. Here, the possibility of being the subject of violence is linked to the likelihood of practicing violence against another, in a mutually reinforcing pattern.

The PCC is just one example of the social responses to violence, inequality, and death. It is an organization that protects some people from violence while wielding it upon others, one method to mitigate conditions of suffering. It is also another way that people carry a sense of the fear of death in everyday life, allocating it to particular kinds of bodies. The organization exists in a long historical logic of sociality motivated and legitimated through death. Newsboys in industrializing America buried their own (DiGirolamo 2002), cobbling together piecemeal sums to pay for a proper burial in a community made up of orphans. So, too, did "taxi mafias" in apartheid South Africa (Van Onselen 2000; Bank 1990), who, amid the terrain of violent relegation, came to protect and nurture their own through the process of death and commemoration. Similar instances are myriad and widespread, historically and globally, and especially in conditions where social ties are in the throes of transformation and violence. They are especially prominent where capitalist forces are reshaping how burial works upon individuals and identities, creating tensions that extract individuals from their social fabric. Death insurance becomes a means to sew some of that social fabric back together, in new ways.

The story of burial societies, established and made legal or unestablished and de facto, is in many ways a narrative of capitalist expansion and the expulsion and containment of populations—both voluntary and involuntary. The scales and logics of these circuitries are normatively and temporally global, while the sites of burial, death, and organization become materially local. Burial societies work through social groups that are seen not to belong, and they themselves can become institutionalized by reframing new categories of non-belonging or non-being.

Charles Van Onselen (2000) writes, for example, of the establishment of the Chevra Kadisha burial society by Ashkenazi Jews in turn-of-the-century Argentina, which, adapting to an influx of poorer Jews from Russian-Polish backgrounds working as pimps and prostitutes in the twilight economy, "took deliberate steps to exclude those moral offenders whom they had deemed to be 'unclean'" (111). This process repeated itself spatially in the sphere of Atlantic-world Jewish marginality at the end of the nineteenth century and the first part of the twentieth, where newly arrived "unclean" Jews were spurned because of their real or perceived association with criminal and twilight activities, in places like New York, Rio de Janeiro, and Johannesburg. The Zwi Migdal for Russian-Polish Jews in Argentina, the New York Independent Benevolent Association, the Sociedade Religiosa e Beneficient Israelita in São Paulo, and, briefly, the "Immorality Trust" in South Africa, were all created—and often inter-linked, in both their activities and their shared interest in life—in an ambivalent sphere of violence, degradation, and "immorality." All recast life through death, premising deliverance and cleanliness on relative jus-tifications of identity and belonging. These instances of life insurance outside of the United Kingdom, made through the movement of bodies and the global re-spatialization of Jewish life, further imply a relationship between populations that are the subject of violence and social organiza-tion amid transformation.

Perhaps some spheres of marginality and subjection have changed. Others, around Black and Indigenous life especially, have not. Blackness in Brazil, constructed through the maintenance of Whiteness, continues to shape the possibility of social belonging and being human. Members and affiliates of the PCC have no illusions of being part of society, where the labor that should have gone into making them human has forever been dis-placed elsewhere, to the subjects of security and the good life. Indeed, they describe their existence through a subjectivity made in opposition to the kind of good that Brazilian society valorizes and seeks to produce. It is their mothers and fathers who have been forced away from home, on thin and precarious employment threads, working to provide security and family sustenance for the rest. Jaime Alves (2016: 78–79) describes this condi-tion through the words of Eliseu, who carries out robberies on rich White boys—playboys—in the city as part of a historic sense of wrong, of *revolta*.

"For Eliseu," Alves writes, "putting a gun to the head of a playboy meant more than just stealing something from him (more than just the 'revolt of the belly'). . . . Eliseu explained it this way: 'Shit, this is for me and for the brothers in my *quebrada* [hood]. This is for *minha velha* [my old lady; mother], changing the playboy's diapers; that son of a bitch.'"

In this condition, which is recognized and understood as emergent from a space of historic and ongoing injustice, death and violence is not an anomaly, something that "just happens." Its everyday nature is no longer banal, apolitical, not worth weeping over. To the contrary, while Eliseu's mother was forced to work changing the diapers of White boys, Eliseu was out robbing supermarkets. Once he was caught, taken to the back room, and tortured by the security guards, ending up in prison. On release he managed to get a job at a hardware store, starting on a different trajectory.

But when his boss learned that he had a criminal record, he fired him on the spot. To complain about the firing, Eliseu checked in with the brothers, who gave him permission to do something more dramatic. They cornered his former boss as he was closing the store one day and cleaned out the safe. They later went to his house and cleaned it out too. The kinds of things that Eliseu has gone through are not seen as anomalous. They justify a response. Such a response is expected to be countered with violence, from police or otherwise. A death here is not suffered in vain; it is full of a difficult kind of aspiration. What the PCC did for Teo, it would also do for Eliseu—if he was killed.

This subjectivity circumscribes a kind of "death with weeping," centered on a social organization that specifically demarcates death as *requiring* commemoration.[4] What the PCC did for Teo, and would do for Eliseu, it also did for at least four others in a four-month period alone, a narrow window of documentation, and in just one part of São Paulo state in 2012.

When Marcos was shot and killed in 2010, a peer member in the organization wrote a short note to accompany the circumstances in a document titled "Deaths and Losses":

"Marcos was done in during an operation where he was hit and injured. He was in the hospital for a few days but died. The brothers from the city passed along that for a funeral to take place they need help because the family doesn't have the conditions to do a burial."

In a separate document, dated the following month, that accounts for the organization's drugs sales, costs, and expenditures, I find a line between "360.00 for cost of car to take family members back home from visit to W2 prison" and "700.00 for Fred's trip to the capital city." It reads: "1.900 re: payment of funeral for our oldest brother from Quarrytown" (Denyer Willis 2018). In this case, the R$1,900 they paid is roughly three times the monthly minimum wage, and R$1,600 more than the R$300 required to avoid ritual disinterment after three years. This notion of care means ensuring an appropriate mortuary ritual and a proper coffin in a city cemetery. It also means that the body will not be disposed of in the pit.

Poor, nasty, brutish, and short, but, contra Hobbes, not solitary. Life outside the social contract, the space of citizenship and dignity circumscribed by the state, is not necessarily unsocial or stricken with anomie. Even amid acute violence, in this space between the fear of death and the fear of social death, societies like the PCC find the means to compel and maintain belonging amid and through a subjectivity of violence. Composed of people who know they can expect premature death, sometimes ending acutely, death and belonging have become vital means for appreciating and bolstering the prospect of life.

"Gang members constantly talk about their loyal, honorable members who have fallen in the name of the gang," writes Martín Sánchez-Jankowski (1991: 140). "No one forgets who was killed where and for what purpose." Many scholars have written of the ways that the dead haunt the city, its street corners, murals, and its materiality—and indeed perhaps only in memory. Death matters not just as an event, a moment that begins and ends, but as a space of social signification that works through those surrounding it. The "loyal, honorable member" is aspirational, a figure who lives on beyond the nasty, brutish, and short. Sánchez-Jankowski sees this sphere, the commemoration, as a "measure of immortality" for the individual who has gone. But it is the way that those who surround the event of that person's death, raising it up, that codifies—in social terms—the importance that a death has for belonging in a world structured for belonging to never happen.

Belonging that is made at the graveside is not fanciful, fleeting, or folkloric. There is good reason to believe that the more attention to death commemoration that groups like the PCC have—which is a function, too, of how often death comes—the more they are able to endure as a social and institutional form. Such questions cut across larger engagements and research on the amorphous nexus of "drug traffickers, mafias, transnational organized crime and gangs"—and its own political economy. Where hierarchies are evident within armed sociality, with head honchos and "druglords" receiving grand attention, the terrain is morally inequitable. In Mexico, where Claudio Lomnitz (2019) describes how bosses are buried in their trucks in opulent displays of social signification amid a rise in drug-war tombs, a counterpoint is evident. Others, those who are put to work on the street by these bosses, are disposable; never commemorated.

"Instead of handing [their bodies] over to their families, what do you think [our chief] did?" Falko Ernst (2018), a scholar of Mexico, hears from "The Cricket," a former *sicário* (hitman) of the Knights Templar in Michoacán. The Cricket and other members had been fighting a nearly outright war, amid a distinctive terrain of fear. Here, Ernst describes, The Cricket was made to kill or be killed, to take a list of names or to become a name on a list. His work was reproductive of the violence in a kind of organizational hierarchy that eschewed any form of identity or belonging. There, The Cricket and others speak of "bosses," unknowable but known figures up above who run the show—and who treat death as nothing but a biological event, though uneventful, within a larger project. The death of some, like The Cricket, is axiomatic, uncommemorable. It means replacing those bodies with others. Describing his disillusionment, The Cricket says to Ernst, "*He* burned them and dumped them into the river. . . . We weren't worth anything. We were fighting without recognition, for a cause that nobody knew." Within six months The Cricket's name was crossed off a new list. He'd been demoralized by what he saw, turned toward drug use, and became the target.

The homogenizing influence that works through banal routine—urban relegation, violent policing, prison order—doesn't operate here. There is no sustained space of identity, where a collective understanding of what it means to be "the subject of wrongs," as Robert Samet (2019) puts it, can take root. Such a collective understanding can operate at different scales and in particular publics, or subjectivities. And if a sense of wrong can't take root, especially around common experiences with death, then there is no way to begin to craft a new understanding of what it means to be a subject of "rights"; of a set of moral rights, perhaps more inalienable than any codified today, that are derived in a linear relationship with chronic and ongoing lived experiences with death, punishment, and indifference.

And yet even the process of commemorating death can be the subject of state repression. In 2018, after two men were killed by police in Mato Grosso, a state on Brazil's western border, the organization they were associated with sent money for their funeral. A video of the funeral, which showed the bodies being buried by a crowd of onlookers in a modest cemetery, was posted online.[5] As the bodies are put in the ground, the group of people—too many to count—break into song. The song—"A Faixa de Gaza" ("The Gaza Strip")—is written by a hip-hop artist, MC Orelha, from Rio de Janeiro, and is an emotive anthem of the terrain of violence in the city and what it requires for survival. It evokes the cause of one of its primary organized crime groups, the Comando Vermelho, speaking through death. "How many brothers I've seen going to live with God in the Sky," the song says. "With no time to say goodbye, but playing their role."

After the video was posted online, police got wind of the event, which ruffled feathers. They carried out an investigation. "During the investigation we discovered that it was the leaders of the Comando Vermelho who paid for the burial and funeral of the two who died in a confrontation with the military police," said a police detective during a press conference. "They paid around R$10,000 for all of the event. We found out that the mother of one of the criminals didn't have money to pay for the funeral. Because of this the leaders sent resources so the mother could commemorate her son."

Annoyed that the event represented "an apology to organized crime," the police detective ordered those involved—singing a song at a funeral—to be arrested. Seven people and three minors were detained and questioned as to whether they were members of the organization, and whether they engaged in an "apology for violence." All denied it. Regardless, the seven who were arrested were detained and formally charged on those grounds, sent—ironically—to a prison controlled by the Comando Vermelho. The minors were released.

Commemoration of death, and especially death that comes at the hands of police or rivals, is a constituent part of life amid violence throughout Brazil. How it happens, how much money is given, and how public an event becomes vary a great deal. But whether an event becomes so public or not, the logics of such commemoration can never be completely repressed. Just as organized crime is strengthened by ever-greater repression—the more people sent to prison, the stronger it becomes—the more the commemoration is repressed, the stronger the need becomes to evoke the idea that death is indeed meaningful, important, and unjust. Repression of this kind, at the graveside and of death itself, gives an exceptionally powerful meaning to life.

If the PCC or the Comando Vermelho enact a powerful reason for belonging by making burial dignified for people like Teo and Marcos, the story is actually about those who will never join these organizations, or any other like it. Taking shelter in these organizations, within a sphere of acute repression and containment becomes logical—if not necessary. But for those who struggle on, who eschew violence and struggle to make ends meet amid precariousness and against the odds, without ever having any kind of insurance, are destined for undignified burial and disinterment for disposal. The space between being part of a group made necessary by violence, that commemorates the fallen, and having the money to pay to be buried permanently or in an opulent tomb is a space of disappearance. How and why bodies are claimed, symbolically and perhaps also with cash pay-outs, hearkens to martyrdom. The martyr is someone who gets claimed by a public, for memory and identity, where an incident of death is put into the service of a collective project. The martyr is made to have died—sacrificed themself—for a cause. The making of a martyr does not necessarily happen deliberately or willingly, typically entailing a postmortem social battle over the process of claiming someone as having sacrificed themself—and defining the "cause" in question. Indeed, how martyrdom is invoked often has very little to do with intention, where suicide or death happens deliberately as a means to mobilize a public.[6]

Martyrdom works where the circumstance of death forces the ethical tether between the expected—a population can be left to die, structurally repressed, or can be killed—and the unexpected—the terms of being left to die, structurally repressed, or of being killed—are ruptured. Martyrdom and a collective demand to claim a death is tied to affective conditions—surprise, shock, grief, outrage—that are definitively undergirded by mutually acknowledged but perhaps unspoken structural conditions of violence and disadvantage. Especially in the Middle East and North Africa, martyrdom is aligned with the language of protest, mobilization, and collective recognition of a loss akin to sacrifice, becoming especially dramatic in scale, and in the occupation of public space.

And yet the idea of the martyr or martyrdom tends to merge two cleavages, which blur together. The first is the difference between the concept of the martyr and the social practice of claiming a body as having sacrificed itself for a wider good. The second is the outward use and claiming of the term as deliberate political language for an individual or case. The claiming of the martyr as social practice looks inward to a population, reasserting it, perhaps especially through attention to conditions of burial and commemoration for the remaking of life. The making of the martyr emerges from the cauterization (and perhaps reification) of identity through a death that is taken by a collective.

The process of claiming the language of the martyr is outward looking, toward an audience of some kind. Here the deployment of the term is part of asserting the legitimacy and necessity of protest, and of claiming an injustice. The claiming of the language departs from the claiming of a death, working upward in scale and in a battle over public meaning and sensibility for a structural or transcendent claim outward, performatively.

The language of the martyr has specific religious connotations in Latin America and Brazil, with scripture delineating an ultimate martyr, Jesus, and a subsequent ecclesiastical history. In everyday terms, the language of the martyr is uncommon, perhaps because counterclaims to a powerful hegemony rarely follow theological frames. Rather, Brazil's recognized martyrs include a group of thirty Jesuits massacred in 1645 who were beatified in Rome by Pope John Paul II, and a group of forty "Brazilian" Jesuits—destined for Brazil but had never been there—massacred in the Canary Islands in 1570. Both groups were massacred by Calvinists, shaping the language of a sacrifice they made, defined postmortem, for the Catholic Church.

But that isn't the only kind of martyrdom, by any stretch. An attention to death and burial in contemporary Brazil, around groups like the PCC or the Comando Vermelho, reveals a very distinctive format of martyrdom, or of the ways that particular deaths are claimed by a collective toward the reaffirmation of that identity category. PCC belonging is reinforced at the graveside, both in the way bodies are allowed—better yet, afforded—commemoration and in the inward-looking language of sacrifice for a particular ethical project of justice in the midst of systemic injustice. "Our oldest brother," they write, is a means to both claim a death and to reiterate the conditions of life and death that make the organization necessary. And yet, at the same time, this language does not suggest an appropriation of the death, or of a process of *taking* death from those who would commemorate it—especially families. The PCC's claiming of some people in their death reveals important striations, apparent in the way that the organization affirms its identity in a death while leaving the body for the family.

Two crucial things seem absent. First, the organization does not appear to take death from grieving families. Instead, the organization affirms its importance by providing the funds for a death to be fully commemorated by those closest to it. A death seems to be taken by a collective, for its collective ends, but without removing that death from family to be carried, by others, through the streets.

The second is that the affirmation from these deaths of the importance of a particular kind of life, of the ways the fallen stand for the ethics of the organization, does not become laden with the language of protest or, typically, of dramatic and public performativity. It is muted, symbolically powerful, within a specific public and audience who come to know that the celebration of life—in death—by the family was made possible by the organization. This kind of martyrdom works below the radar, without the deployment of the language of martyrdom or a dramatic, escalating protest or claim for justice, from the state or the public sphere. And where it does not, as in the case of the Comando Vermelho, it becomes the subject of repression; a death that cannot be celebrated or commemorated as a means to assert a "criminal identity."

This paradigm of *muted martyrdom* is highly localized, interstitial, and concentrated. All at the same time, it must be hushed and transcendent, imperceptible, but discretely raucous. The cemetery, a distinctive place of suffering and of public omission withdrawn from society, is both the logical place for this symbolic claiming to happen *and* the very pith and rationale of its making and ongoing meaning.

9 Make Live, Make Disappear

One of the most distinctive things about the PCC is its penchant for documentation, process, and bureaucratic ordering. Its own bureaucracy traces a politics of disappearance, its internal machineries and of who must disappear. As a decentralized organization, morally centered and guided from the prison system but sustained by criminal jobs on the street, it works through an ability to rationalize rules across expansive territory and material and political boundaries like prison walls. The prospect of losing protection and welfare provided by the organization is a powerful incentive to comply with the rules when the likelihood of ending up back in prison is exceptionally high.

In São Paulo, the organization is internally subdivided by area code, with each region managing and reporting on local affairs. To do so it creates records in abundance, often in formats mirroring those that proliferate within the criminal justice system. Nearly all of its baptized members have been subject to a distinct and oppressively bureaucratic legal system, shaping their subjectivity about both what bureaucratic ordering does and how it should be done differently. Such documentation spans everything from organizational expenditure, drug disbursements, rolls of membership dues, payments, and inventory of guns and cars. Vital, too, are the "criminal

criminal records" that it maintains, which document in detail who has broken rules, which ones, whether it was the first time, and who was involved in deciding the punishment.[1] The documents also contain many other individual details about "losses," deaths, and the excommunicated. These documents tell a story about what the PCC is, what it is not, and how it exists within everyday conditions of disappearance. They also describe a condition of people on the run, who can't or won't pay back debt, or who broke rules, making disappearance not simply a question of life and death but also of people struggling to get out and searching for a life beyond. This reveals the relationship between systemic and material disappearance; someone is extorted by police, accumulates a debt from consignment goods they can't repay and might not be able to account for, and must then disappear.

Sumiu ("disappeared") is a prominent category in the PCC's own documentation. Of the sixty-three total reports of people not repaying debt, twenty-seven (42%) conclude with a statement that the person has, through synonym or pseudonym, "gone missing." This repeats itself across cases in patterned ways, as seen in the selection below.[2] Sometimes it is with a thick storyline and other times with an abrupt statement such as, "He's just gone." They are replete with detail:

> He is on the street, the man on the street passed along that since he's been in the city he hasn't come across him, the cat that is his godfather passed along that he went to his family's house to ask if he would show up and come to discuss because the reason is just to get [the money] but they've had nothing back he's on the street missing since 2010.

> He was on notice and on the day that expired the brothers from the city picked him up to discuss but when it was happening he dropped the phone and ran off, later the brothers came together to trade ideas and the police started showing up since then he's been missing.

> The brothers from the city brought him in he said that he didn't have the money . . . he was let go to get the money and after this the brothers from the city passed along word that his mom paid 200.00 which is now in the hands of the city but he has disappeared.

> He's been kicked out, is on the street working the brothers found out where he is living they went there but on that day only his wife was there, they came back on a different day and all the lights were out, he's been missing since 2010 and hasn't been seen since.

He was expelled because of the debt on [date] one month later the brother responsible for finance came across him he said he was going on a job and would be right back to settle the debt after these discussions he hasn't been seen.

He was expelled because he was smoking crack on [date] he is missing from the neighborhood and the brothers from regional finance didn't find him to give him the shout-out.

He was put on notice and on the day that we would trade ideas he got into the trunk of his friend's car that he was with and snuck off [. . .] from that day he has disappeared.

The brother from the city went to his family and the only news they have which isn't confirmed is that he left and has disappeared somewhere near the valley.

He's disappeared and the brothers went after him but his mom said that he is in [another state], but it isn't known what city and there is no more information.

He said [the murder plot] was a lie and that they would have to prove it he was let go to go and get the other person and disappeared.

He is missing from the neighborhood and his location is unknown.

He is on expired notice as a companheiro and until now is missing.

He's in prison, but where he is located hasn't been found.

He is missing without any word.

This one was kicked out on [date] because of overdue debt and lying he's on the inside, location unknown.

"Going missing" takes shape in the constitutive relationship between debt, suspension from membership, expulsion, and disappearance, where disappearance appears and a decision is made in difficult conditions. But making oneself missing from the organization can also come as a result of fear of being punished for having broken the rules, especially around the unauthorized use of violence. Such a decision to flee flows from the need to disappear from the prospect of the PCC's own criminal punishment *as well as* from the criminal justice system—leaving, potentially, family members and other loved ones behind.

The organization is at pains to keep its members paying debt, to ensure that its membership remains satisfied. The PCC, in this moment, is at pains to explain to members that debt repayment can be negotiated. And, in fact, the large number of members who are unable to repay compels it, it seems, to undertake a major one-time write-off of the debt—R$502,647.50—that cannot be retrieved.

At the same time, writing off debt is a necessary part of what the organization must do. Some debt can never be repaid, for reasons of the extreme violence that circumscribes its logic. This is at least in part because of the exceptionally severe violence that they are subjected to from police, and others. The PCC documents show that, in one part of the state and not including Greater São Paulo, at least two of its members were killed by police, one was "cowardly murdered by two unknown individuals in a Palio [Fiat],"[3] and a fourth died in a car accident. Together, these four left behind R$12,400 in unpaid debt—the equivalent of about ten months' pay at minimum wage.

Viviane is very familiar with the logics of indebtedness and the difficulty of flight for young men in or at the margins of the PCC. She tells a story about it: "I used to often say to them, 'How come you got involved again [in crime, after getting out]?' And they would say, '*pô, doutor*, I had debts to pay from back then.' The only way to pay those debts is to *entrar no corre* [go back into the game]." The ability to make enough money in a regular job to actually sever a connection with the organization is thin, even if another sphere of existence was either attractive or possible. Such a possibility of escape is further constrained where any other factors are layered on top—drug addiction, financial demands in the family, chronic imprisonment, temporary or repeated stays in rehab. While there is good evidence that the organization has been flexible with these constraints and repayment in the past, in some regions, at least, there is nothing universal or certain about renegotiation. Debt, too, can be "private"—between members—and not associated with something like a mutually recognized drug consignment. In all of this, debt functions like it does for most in the contemporary political economy—as a mode of enslavement in keeping with extreme individualization.[4] One of the only clear ways out, or so it may seem, is flight—disappearance.

Maybe Kaio is indeed out there, somewhere in Brazil or beyond, having chosen to make himself scarce in the face of something much more severe. In such a case, he might never want to be found—even by his own mother, Débora.

For the most part, though, the desire is to stay, to not flee and have to leave everything behind—family, neighborhood, friends, all of one's most meaningful affective tethers. As in capitalism generally, this means continuing to buy in, to take out and repay debt in different forms, and to live with it as an everyday but depoliticized mediator in social relations. In the ways that the "cruel optimism" of accumulation works, debt begets more debt. How one pays that debt—through the violence of reproducing capitalism by working for a firm, by paying into a pension fund invested in the stock market, or through violence on the street made necessary by the same—is in many ways irrelevant. Debt is violence in at least two ways: entrapment and enforcement.

Amid this terrain, to fall afoul of a regime with a real or de facto system of taxation and predation, such as a state, is a high crime. For the PCC, as for a state, nonpayment of debt often means nonpayment of tribute, tax. And nonpayment of tribute, for a state or for the PCC, means punishment. This moral regime circumscribes both why people might flee, and why disappearance is both attractive and possible. It also means what necessarily happens alongside: punishment for those who do not flee and are subject to consequences. Here disappearance contains two very different but nonetheless inseparable logics: a body that has disappeared itself and a body made to disappear. Under such banal conditions where disappearance is structure, disappearance also becomes agency.

The PCC is a system of care for some. But it is also a system of slaughter and violence. For the PCC, the adjudication of care versus violence works through particular rules and an ethical vision—what it calls "an ethic of crime." Under this perspective, the PCC purports to defend a collective interest, working along two broad lines: tribute is to be redistributed to the less fortunate, and there are rules—"moral" derivations—that matter. The rules are clear to all involved, having been written in the form of a statute like many other such statutes across time and space.[5] These rules make it clear that all violence must be approved or conform to understood guidelines—zero tolerance for sexual violence, no violence against children, no dishonesty or theft from the organization, no homosexuals to be admitted as members, among other things. For those who uphold this "ethic," paying tribute to it, care is possible. For those who do not, varied and escalated punishment—both symbolic and real—is in order: temporary and increasing expulsions for nonpayment of debt on the one hand, murder for harming others, stealing from the organization, or undermining its collective efforts on the other hand. Under these conditions, murder in the city of São Paulo has been greatly reduced—by at least six thousand people per year.

And yet, that the PCC is behind murders should surprise no one. Take this brief description of a homicide from a newspaper report in 2011:[6]

> A 27-year-old man was found dead the night before last in Campinhas. The body of laborer Ronaldo da Silva was located in a barren field on Miguel Santos Road, in Parque Sol. He was found by his family at 7 p.m.
>
> When police arrived, family members explained that he had been missing since Saturday afternoon. The incident was handled by detectives from the investigations unit.
>
> The family does not believe that Silva was killed to level a score, though he was an occasional drug user. The victim was a resident of Jardim das Flores. Police will continue to investigate the case.

A different interpretation of this same case exists, and it is in the hands of those responsible who decided whether Ronaldo da Silva should have been killed. The outcome of their decision is filed as one of the many PCC records of punishment, dated the same month as the newspaper report. It follows:

> Nama [*sic*]: Ronaldo da Silva
>
> Membership number: 999.999
>
> Nickname: Copperhead
>
> Neighborhood: Campinhas
>
> Place of baptism: CDP Pinheiros
>
> Godfathers: MC David, Little John, Néné
>
> Date of baptism: 28/10/2010
>
> Date of exit: 04/12/2010
>
> Position: Moneyman of Campinhas
>
> Date of death: [blank]

Motive: diverted funds, hand in the pot

Amount of debt: R$1,100 in crack cocaine, March 2011

Ronaldo's body was found by his family. He'd disappeared and did not come home. They went looking, searching the terrain to find him. And they did, in an abandoned field, the kind littered with peri-urban detritus. He wasn't buried. Or, perhaps he was. It isn't clear.

While the PCC has been able to shape a new terrain of relative nonviolence, its own existence is nonetheless predicated on the continued extraction of tribute, which comes, in effect, from criminal activity. A threat to that condition, committing a crime against crime, is a threat to the organization itself. The most acute threat is when someone acts against the organization's ethical logics. Whether Ronaldo did or didn't, he paid the price for others believing he put his hand in the collective pot.

Among the documents, which detail all punishments in most of the state of São Paulo but not the city itself, this is the one single case of murder implied as having been carried out by the organization itself, on a member, over a one-year period. It speaks too, though, of desiring it for others who have committed similar infractions but who are out of reach or can't be found. "He disappeared," they write, "taking R$6,500 from the finances and 800g of crack from the management he's now in the lockup at [place] in an unfavorable wing. *Abater* [Kill]."

The PCC is an effort to redraw which lives must be cared for, and which lives need not be. The latter can and must be forgotten to protect the integrity of the former, in a kind of violent work that operates socially. And not only are members and affiliates of the organization subject to its rules, but so are the communities where it is rooted. Here no one can use violence except the organization, which must give explicit approval. This creates a particular kind of logic, mirroring that of the state itself, and of bureaucratic order as war by other means: monopolization implies that only this party can kill others to reproduce its ethical regime. Violence, otherwise, should not exist. Where it does, it will be repressed, so long as it does not follow the logic of order.

This creates a distinctive dynamic that bifurcates what disappearance means, and how it happens. Not only might a person disappear because they are fleeing an unpayable debt, but they might also disappear—through punishment or flight—because they harmed someone else without prior authorization. Take one example, from the files, of a man pseudonymously named "Chubby":

> He was involved in a death in the city, the brothers in the city picked him up and took him to a discussion because he was denying it he was let go to bring the other involved person and since then has disappeared. Following the death there were witnesses that saw [his] car passing by and picking up the friend that was supposedly the person who killed the person that was the cousin of an in-law of [his] that went missing after going with his friend, according to witnesses [he] had her killed because she knew too much (that he was cheating on a brother, and this was to eliminate that story) [He] said that this was a lie and that they would have to prove it and he was let go to go and get the friend, and disappeared.

Because the use of violence is not possible without prior authorization, other efforts to use violence now must often evade investigation not just by the state, but also by the PCC—which is much more rigorous, relentless, and certain in its effectiveness and punishment. Chubby's effort, the files seem to describe, was to obscure his involvement in murdering someone that could tell a story that would harm him—that he had been involved with the partner of another man in the organization. The only way to avoid the situation would have been for Chubby to have the circumstance happen as a disappearance, where the person would vanish with no real evidence of violence or murder. Chubby's prod to the organization to "prove it" draws on the same unstable epistemic foundation of disappearance that undergirds the state itself: the absence of a body and of any knowledge that violence actually happened defies the ability of any authority to have conclusive and enlightened evidence. The absence of a body means the absence of the ability to know, whether the need to know is coming from the state, from the PCC, or from a mother.

Chubby, though, seemed to know that not having a body would not be enough for him to avoid scrutiny or punishment from the PCC for planning or being involved in the disappearance of someone. The PCC sees through the logic of disappearance under these conditions, writing of the incident as a "death" while at the same time saying the person "went missing." There were witnesses, others might corroborate, there was enough knowledge of a kind that was not about the body. He could be tortured into admitting the plan and divulging where the body was hidden. Knowing all of this, it seems, he chose to disappear too, to vanish.

But this is not just a question for members of the organization. Other disappearances, of people not explicitly associated with the organization, also seem to work through the logic of "unknowability." This exists in a larger condition where the PCC wants to know if someone has been murdered, but the state generally does not. After all, to count murders is not a great prerogative where high violence implies unstable conditions and insufficient political legitimacy. Let them disappear instead.

I met Mariana, a mother, through other mothers of missing people. Mariana lives somewhere past the switchbacks in the southwestern corner of the city of São Paulo. She lives a modest life. Her husband walked out and she now lives with a daughter, making ends meet as a seamstress to pay the bills. Mariana is forthright, frustrated, and stuck. Her struggle is written through the political condition where the state doesn't care about disappearance or the life of the poor, but others do. She recalls the difficulty of it all at her kitchen table over fresh lime juice with ice.

Mariana's daughter, Madalena, went missing a few years ago after leaving church one evening. Madalena had a son and a husband, whom she was in the process of leaving. Her husband was violent and had made Madalena's life miserable with both physical and emotional violence. Against great odds, Madalena had decided to go, to leave him, so that he would not be involved in raising her son. According to Mariana, she had clear plans in place. The next day she would move to a different region, taking her son with her, removing the two of them from a sphere of violence that had consumed their lives.

Madalena was never heard from again after being seen ambling away on the curb outside of her Pentecostal church that evening. Mariana has been searching everywhere—but with heavy suspicions about the involvement of Madalena's husband. He has been silent on the matter, suspiciously so, not expressing any recognizable concern for what is otherwise substantively missing from his life. He hasn't helped to find Madalena, and, to the contrary, he seems much prouder without her. Madalena's son's life has suffered exceptionally. Mariana paints a picture of her grandson, being held at arm's length now, that is heart-wrenching—he isn't being properly fed or clothed and goes to school soiled in feces. She speaks of him from a maternal place; he occupies her emotional state, shaping many of her most important decisions, like where to live, what to do, how to struggle on. There is little she can do for him now, but there might be in the future. In the meantime, her grandson's condition seems to echo Madalena's disappearance.

Like Neide and Débora, Mariana has exhausted almost all possibilities to find out about Madalena. But, in this case, there is one that still hangs open. "We are like any extended family," she says. "*Na nossa familia tem gente de todo tipo* [Our family has people of all stripes]." In a kin space written as much through social ties as biology, relations are variegated, paradoxical, contrasting. There was one way, a nearly sure way, to find a resolution to her nagging doubt about whether Madalena was taken by her husband, the man she intended to leave.

The boys up the street had offered to clear things up. They wanted to know what was going on, to give Mariana some of the certainty about Madalena that she longs for. She recounts it in a kind of metanarrative. "They came to me, and they asked, 'If you agree,'" she says, paraphrasing the men speaking to her, "'within twenty-four hours we'll know if he was involved. I guarantee you, Mariana, that if it was him, he'll say so. And if it wasn't, we'll leave him alone.'"

They were giving her the space to decide in a high-stakes game, to invite their intervention. Madalena's former husband would be questioned—the extent and acuteness of this interrogation unclear—and made to be straight about his involvement in Madalena's disappearance. Mariana was interested, and she knew she could perhaps arrive at the truth, at Madalena's whereabouts, this way. She could finally know.

As a devout Christian, however, she was worried. This would mean violence, the pain of disappearance could come again for someone else. And it would bring more uncertainty about her grandson, who might not fall to her. She was worried, too, about whether the certainty of this particular truth, an answer to "what happened," might also be a damaging and vicious fabrication of sorts, one that she did not want to be associated with.

"What if the next day, or the day after, we discover that it wasn't him?" she asked me rhetorically, about the result of an interrogation of Madalena's former husband. "What if they make him disappear, wrongly, and Madalena walks back in the door one day, returning from years in hiding?" She then returns to the metanarrative, speaking to the boys up the street: "And if it was him," she says, implying a confession, "will you bring him to me so I can take him to the police?" They wouldn't. That was not an option. The outcome of any discussion ends on its own terms, their terms. And Mariana knew, too, that the police weren't really a solution either. They never have been when she has needed them. The men would do away with the outcome themselves, following the kinds of material patterns that undergird the missing.

For all the allure of being able to know the truth, Mariana decided that she would keep searching on her own, holding out hope for a different resolution, distant and hard to conceive, in spite of it all. Mariana's choice, though, was also about not making someone else disappear, whether he "deserved" to or not. And while everyone around her, in the community, the neighborhood, knows all that she has said about Madalena's disappearance, this new potential disappearance would be different. It would happen in a condition that would never be reported to the state anyway, would never become one more added to the twenty-five thousand, much less counted into any formal tabulation or be indicative of a legalized representation of violence—except to all of those privy to what, probably, happened.

"I just hope that, before I die, we find out where all of these bodies are going," Neide says in a resigned tone near the end of one of our conversations. It has been almost a decade since Felipe vanished. She's speaking of it like there must be a space, somewhere definitive, that we might stumble upon one day that has this multitude of bodies. Perhaps she's imagining the mass graves of Mexico, spectacular in size and number, where family members of the disappeared just like her but more collectively organized find mundane mass graves in the landscape containing several hundred bodies jumbled beneath. At the same time, her doubt and longing to know not just where Felipe is but how tens of thousands of people can just disappear, never to be found again, should make more sense and be more obvious. How is it possible that this many bodies are never found? She doesn't know how to understand where they go—except that they *must* have gone somewhere. Of course, the nebulousness and unknowability contain the possibility that someone who has disappeared could be dead, on the lam, or on their way somewhere else in search of a life beyond the politics of indifference.

As it is, though, bodies of the disappeared are found all the time around the city. Most commonly this is in the form of *ossadas* ("found bones"), like those described in the stacks of papers that pile up for Maria on her desk at the IML, and in ways that imply that the very idea of bodies "out of place" is being reformatted and made banal. "Found bodies" often share a characteristic; they are often discovered because there is an inversion of the status quo of sorts. Someone stumbles across them, something alters how space is used, there is a change in what becomes publicly visible in new ways—a tip, an intervention. These spaces are not necessarily hidden or invisible, though; such cemeteries show up in places where the state is not expected to go, existing in a condition where the politically unseen becomes the means to materially obscure. Exceptionally rarely, though, are these incipient places of mass burial discovered by virtue of diligent investigation on the part of the state. Instead, their existence is reflected in the abiding condition of political indifference. Here, missing bodies actually appear exactly where we might expect, in the right place indeed: in spaces of political indifference. Here, in informally urbanized spaces where the state appears arbitrarily and selectively, people have had to find the means to get by. "Others" have come to rule.

Rio de Janeiro is a case in point. For decades, organized crime groups have controlled territory in the city, governing in spatially discrete ways, through real and armed force. Across the city, this distinctive territorial governance emergent from a politics of uncertainty exists within a patchwork of de facto politics. Here the actual political condition of government through indifference has been to leave such racialized territories out of the realm of political intervention—except in piecemeal form at election time and in acute and bloody police interventions. Such spaces of exclusion have become fortified, as a means to both defend territory from rival gangs and deter police from entering. And, for the most part, what has happened in terms of violence and order maintenance in these spaces has come to stay in these spaces. There is no good reason to dispose of a body where it might draw attention and violent intervention—at the interstices of de facto borders, or in public spaces, exposed—and create a rationale for a police operation.

When Rio de Janeiro won the Olympics in 2009 it embarked upon an ambitious policy to remake space in the city. The Pacification Police policy was an effort to invert this status quo of territorial governance, where lives left to die have taken on a life of their own. Previously left to their own devices, governed through a politics of urban abandonment since the end of the Cold War, these communities became the subject of policing in a new way. Police units, backed by the national military, rushed into these territories in a show of public spectacularity covered live on television. Many have written about the impacts of these efforts, and the difficult aftermath, especially after the policy imploded when the global Olympic gaze ended and the city fell into abysmal financial ruin.

And yet, beneath the spectacularity of the early days of interventions, much less noted was the significance of what police regularly found when they flooded into these spaces of political indifference. Most of these spaces, in their patterns of governance, hosted their own burial grounds, de facto spaces of routine and mundane interment that everyone there knew about but only spoke of in hushed terms. Newspapers were flooded with cases of "clandestine cemeteries" being discovered, locales where people that supposedly broke local rules were killed and disposed of. At least seven such cemeteries were discovered, with surely many more not making the news.

But these spaces should not be seen as a product of racialized hilltop "drug traffickers." Such cemeteries have also become common in areas controlled by para-state organizations, *milícias*, widely understood to be state violence workers operating in the twilight. In Rio de Janeiro, where territory and space are governed by long-standing practices of varied regimes of everyday taxation and protection, these groups rule through a particular paradigm of violence that is often highly conservative and patriarchal. In 2018, and again in 2019, police were tipped off to an especially egregious site on the outskirts of the city where fourteen bodies were found, requiring a backhoe to exhume. In this one community, where ninety-two people had been reported missing, the scale had reached a threshold, giving way to groups of families who organized and worked together in mutual recognition of who was responsible for the disappearances of their family members, why, and where they might be.

Elsewhere, throughout Brazil, mundane mass graves operate in the twilight of the public sphere—sometimes rupturing it violently. "Clandestine cemetery in Porto Alegre contains a hundred bodies, says public prosecutor," reads a 2019 headline.[7] "Police find clandestine cemetery used by extermination squad in Goias," reads another.[8] In a bizarre case in the South, prisoners cut a hole in a prison fence so they could go outside and carry out murders, bury the victims, and then go back inside.[9] The cases are geographically distant but entirely contiguous.

Such mundane mass graves at this scale, with such odd local context, or with a clear kind of spatial concentration, are eventful, drawing the public eye. In São Paulo, however, these graves work in fragmented and banal ways—without, necessarily, the same territorial governance and outright public violence. Here, the logics of disappearance work in an obvious outflow of publicly ungrievable life. Where bodies are found in mundane mass graves they come in smaller numbers, with questions about who the people were even less answerable, with little coherence to durable organization by family members, and without the shock and awe of dramatic headlines or exceptional cases. In other words, in this city, how people disappear is not always so obviously linked to spatial governance or parastate groups. Bodies appear in ways and places that defy easy explanation.

Some years ago, the homicide detectives I was accompanying were given a job. Acting on a tip, they went to a decertified private university in the city. There they found a mundane mass grave; a pit, dug in disorganized fashion adjacent to a footpath and building, where a jumble of bodies had been dumped and buried. In this pit fifteen bodies and parts of bodies of young, old, and fetuses had been tossed asunder communally with no identification. It seemed that when the university had closed, leaving its twenty-one hundred registered students in the lurch, it needed to get rid of this pedagogical material. For one reason or another, it didn't send the bodies through the right channels.

Sometime later the former rector of the university released a statement affirming that the bodies had, after all, been part of a study in the school's medical arm. She framed them as having benefitted science. With the university deactivated, she had ordered the bodies to be disposed of. And so they were, in a linear manner in a courtyard. There was no word of where each of these bodies had come from, who they were before they were used for science, nor a hint that it even mattered.

Even so, there is a spatial paradigm that accompanies these new burial terrains (Map 1). They are largely peri-urban, adjacent to or emergent

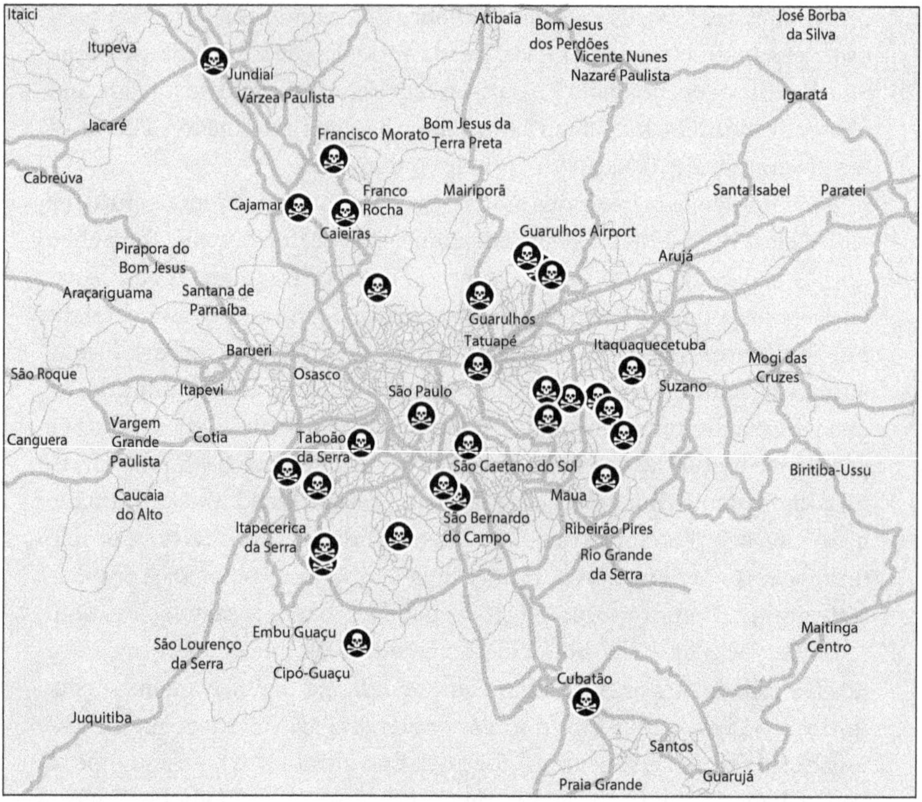

Map 1. Mundane mass graves in the greater São Paulo region (data and map by author).

from spaces where the state deigns to go, and they follow patterns of urban informality and lowland values—spaces of de facto deregulation. They are so banal, the presence of the state so empirically unlikely, that they can be used routinely over a period of months, even years. One news magazine did a crude tabulation: The twenty mundane mass graves found in São Paulo between 2005 and 2015 contained 89 bodies.[10] But that tendency, even, is accelerating. My own tabulation, based only on public media reports and descriptions of conditions, is that thirty-two mundane mass graves have been found around the city since 2007, containing at least 129 human remains. However, there is no legal category or definition for registering such a space, with any terminological deployment of *"cemitério clandestino"* determined by journalists and police in specific, newsworthy cases. Any count is bound to be a dramatic understatement.

Even so, a simple tabulation reveals startling characteristics. In only two of those thirty-six cases were police actively looking for burial sites. All of the rest were found following an unrelated investigation or arrest, an anonymous tip, or calls about "bad smells." The way that police have stumbled across mundane graves, with the graves finding them rather than vice versa, is revelatory of the larger political condition of indifference. Even when such a space is found and investigated, the condition does not change; the same circumstances that produce mass graves remain in place, creating more of them.

In a municipality not far from where Débora now lives, police found one such terrain near the outer highway rings. In 2018, police found three bodies there. Those three join a list of at least twelve bodies found *at this exact location* by police over the last five years. In 2013 they found five people here. Later they found four others. Even when police come and take away the bodies, this ground is filled back up again. And when police went back this time, they didn't just find these three latest bodies, where the other nine were previously, they also found three pre-dug graves. Someone had already done the work of preparing for the next round, entirely undeterred by the prospect that they might be discovered. This place has long since been known as a space of disappearance. But it just doesn't seem to matter.

There are many media reports of such clandestine cemeteries, including on YouTube and other social media platforms. These boneyards are sometimes large and well organized. One found in 2016 is said to have held thirty bodies. When found, journalists tie their existence to the outcome of PCC "tribunals," noting that bodies are sometimes buried facedown, in an act of negative commemoration and denial of memory.

Another field, located in the city's far south side, is striking for its material parallels and systemic position. Police were led there on a tip from a local community member who told them, "Have a look at the ground next to the cemetery, beside a fence." After searching through a densely wooded area they found an area of recently disturbed earth. Digging, they discovered a foot and, hours later, with many more people digging, three bodies. Eventually they found at least three others, with every indication that still more remained.

What makes this field noteworthy is not its existence per se, but that it existed and was used repeatedly, immediately adjacent to an opulent suburban cemetery. That cemetery has the same name as the informally urbanized community that surrounds it—Parque das Cerejeiras (Cherry Tree Park). Yet this is a private cemetery, consecrated and made legal by the state but not run by it. The owners declare on their website that it is made in the "American model," with expansive green space, grounds secured by twenty-four-hour private security, surveillance cameras, and gates manned via a fortified outpost. In an empirical materialization of funerary apartheid, its grounds are adorned with twenty-two landscape sculptures by a named artist, a pond with Asian carp, "ecological trails" and a viewing platform that looks out over a green vista that resembles a neatly manicured golf course. Steps away, bodies are jumbled, buried face-down.

The actual material separation between the two spaces is a feeble barbed wire fence that inscribes in earth a material distinction between the legal—the certified—and the illegal, through a notion of property. But is that difference what matters? In fact, this wall is irrelevant, at least in terms of political will. Cherry Tree Park and the uncertified cemetery are written through deregulation, allowing both to exist as by-products of state practices that normalize the PCC and similar groups. These two spaces are mutually constituted and intertwined, bound together in everyday practice and assumption.

The experience of mundane mass graves in São Paulo has global kin. In March 2017, Mexican police unearthed a burial pit outside of Vera Cruz in which they found the jumbled remains of at least 250 people. This case is important and enlightening in three ways. First, this enormous grave was discovered by family members searching, in defiance of the state's apathy, for missing loved ones believed to be buried in pits scattered across the Mexican countryside. Movements for this purpose, which are now commonplace across Mexico, practice a kind of citizenship to an indifferent state that is enabled by bake sales and raffles. Second, some of Mexico's mundane mass graves are exceptional in their scale. In the years since the country's violent explosion in 2007–2011, with tens of thousands missing, their size has grabbed public attention. To find one with 20 corpses is not noteworthy, but the discovery of one with 250 is.

Third, such a space encapsulates the obscured logics of the liberal violence of indifference. Though the state's institutions do not need to kill, they routinely do so in a way that displaces responsibility for their violence onto individuals or the violent groups that are made possible, perhaps necessary, under such a logic of behavior and personal choice. The mundane mass grave, while not a direct outcome of the state, becomes useful as a material invocation of responsibility for violence interred elsewhere. When these burial fields are made noteworthy—250 corpses!—a suite of rote questions floods in: How many were innocent? Who among them should be reclaimed? How much will this all cost to sort out? All of these questions confound the problem and deploy the same logic of value. Such notions of absent innocence and unproductive life that do not demand attention—letting disappear—is a precondition for the rise of the mundane mass grave as an outcome of governance that specifically *makes disappear*.

10 "I Just Want to Live"

On June 11, 2020, Matias de Souza left his room at an ICE detention center in Lumpkin, Georgia. After more than twelve months in this facility, owned and operated by CoreCivic, a private detention company listed on the New York Stock Exchange, Matias's time for his personal merits hearing before an American judge had come. This judge would determine his future, whether a nascent life in the United States, or involuntary removal back to Brazil. This day was something of a culmination; no longer would his detention make US$0.85 per day for the local county, add value to the stock price of CoreCivic—worth US$12.10 on that day—or help to create jobs for a county where 37 percent live in poverty despite having an unemployment rate of 3.5 percent. But no longer would he, either, have to live in medical isolation from other detainees because of his fear of large groups and the psychiatric problems he increasingly experienced while in detention. Hope of hopes, he would be given asylum. Down the hall, he entered one of the four courtrooms that have been built within the detention facility itself.

Two years earlier, a teenager of sixteen, Matias left Brazil. The best thing to do was to disappear. He just couldn't do it anymore. Everywhere he turned, people wanted to hurt him—and especially the police. At seventeen, he had almost committed suicide; wavering there on the edge of a bridge, nearly ready to vanish into the water below, as a friend living on the streets with him had recently done. And yet a stranger talked him down, soothed him into not doing it—convincing him that, as Matias put it later, "life one day would make me happy."

Matias was a boy, living and sleeping on the curbs of a big city in Brazil's Southeast. In between life and death, and living amid the politics of disappearance and indifference to his existence, Matias decided to change things: to find a life that he could actually live. It entailed a very uncertain journey beyond the world he knew as a Black boy in Brazil. As happens to so many, Matias could have faded away from memory and life itself, he could have joined an organization that might have propped up his life and provided a modicum of protection. His trajectory followed a different line than these, but hardly an isolated or exceptional one. Like tens of thousands of other Brazilians, he set out on a search for life beyond Brazil.

People have every reason to disappear as an active choice. Those choices are increasingly shaping responses from those charged with making decisions about who deserves to be given safety and who can instead be subject to death or disappearance. In so doing, they must engage with what Rosas (2019) calls a process of "necro-subjection", the process of demonstrating deservedness that takes shape in legal codification, moralistic posturing, and an unfailing dedication to the nation-state as the definitive moral actor. Here, collective inhumanity and inequality in life is sifted into individuals' ability to survive extreme violence, why some should and others shouldn't—reasserting the discursive position of some states in the world as preeminent guardians of the right to life.

Some time ago, an email arrived in my inbox. It was from the Immigration and Refugee Board in the country where I was born. "We're presently researching the PCC," they wrote. "We have people arriving that are fleeing." Their words described a condition that didn't make sense to them: "How can we, an agency of a nation-state, make sense of someone who is a victim or a witness of a 'PCC crime'? Would you help us understand what this means? Who do they harm, and why? How much can the Brazilian police or other state agencies protect them?"

But people are also fleeing the police. "His client was killed by police," read a different email written six months earlier, from a law firm in the

United Kingdom. "He's being extorted by those police now. Will he be safe in Brazil if he returns? Can we make a good case for him to stay here?" What does Brazil's witness protection program look like? *What is the likelihood that this person can effectively disappear within the country if he must go back?*

Flight from the PCC's mundane mass graves and the police's torture and killing is always bound up in the systemic politics of disappearance. Within, trajectories and life histories reveal why pulling apart a "causality of disappearance" is fraught with systemic obstructions related to the sinister politics of human inequality, especially as written through racial difference.

As an adolescent in school, Matias's schoolmates shamed him for being poor and Black, throwing things at him in class. When they were expelled after he told the principal, they attacked him outside the gymnasium, beating him relentlessly, shouting racial epithets. Eventually, and despite being a good and diligent student, he was kicked out by the school for causing all of the disorder and never welcomed back. When Matias's grandmother died in 2017, a woman who was his one piece of material and moral shelter, he was forced to the street. There he fought to survive for more than a year. He begged for food, slept on the sidewalk, ate out of the trash, and cobbled together some sociality with others in the same circumstances. He became devoutly religious, finding some meaning as a Pentecostal believer. But he was Black and poor and constantly under the watchful eye of everyone around him, seemingly both omnipresent as an imagined threat and systemically invisible as a person. People were constantly calling the police on him just, it seemed, for asking for food—the ability to subsist. In a year on the street, he had been nearly killed by the police three times and beaten by them many more times.

In 2019, now just a couple of weeks past eighteen years old and a year after nearly committing suicide, Matias materialized at the United States border near El Paso, Texas. After crossing around a wall, he walked for seven hours before coming across an ICE agent and surrendering himself. He sought something that he had heard of; the possibility of living a different life somewhere far from his own, in a place that people speak of as a land of justice and opportunity. He'd left because there was no other way to survive, and no other way out, except the vague hope of something else, somewhere else.

Figure 5. Sketching Halloween
(drawing by Matias).

While he waits, he sketches (figure 5).

At his hearing in the courtroom down the hall from his detention space, he did not have a lawyer. He spoke for himself, emerging from months of rights-less detention where officials had diagnosed him with psychiatric problems and chronic depression. Even so, he spoke passionately of the violence behind him in Brazil, including one incident in particular, that had pushed him to the bridge. But he spoke, too, of hope, which had finally compelled him eventually to flee. He did so before a judge appointed in 2010 by the Obama administration, barely a year after an election sloganized on *hope*. Through an interpreter, who complained that Matias's Portuguese was hard to understand because it had become inflected with Spanish verbs, he traced the world he left behind, and what he desperately wanted for himself now:

> On that day I went close to a shop where they would sell food, and I was feeling very hungry that day and I asked if they could give me food, and this person told me that he wouldn't give me any food, and when this person told me that she wouldn't give me any food, five or six people arrived in the place and started assaulting me. They started kicking me because I'm Black. And

they beat me until I passed, passed out. And when I woke up I was inside the police car. I had my hands, with my arms tied and I had my legs tied. And the police took me to a place that I didn't know where I was.

He continued.

They started assaulting me, they started kicking my stomach and they were kicking me all over and called me negro and other names that I couldn't understand because I was in so much pain that I couldn't understand what they were saying. And I was crying a lot because I couldn't understand why they were doing this. And they told me that that was life because I'm Black and I didn't have the right to be alive. And they kept beating me and beating me and my nose started bleeding, and they took me out of there and they threw me inside a hole that was about three yards deep. And my, and when I fell in the bottom of the hole, my arms were tied and I fell on top of my arm and my arm broke. It broke in two different places, on my wrist close to my hand and on my elbow. And the officers kept laughing at my face saying that I had to die, I had to die.

And they kept saying that I had to die, that I had to die and one of them grabbed his firearm and pointed at my head saying that he was going to kill me. And he end up shooting at me but at my direction, the bullet was one meter far from me. And I was begging, please, please, I want to live and I kept begging, please, please, I didn't do anything. And they stopped and they were thinking about what to do with me. They end up telling me that they were not going to shoot me, but they told me that if they saw me again they would give me, they would shoot me no matter where. They went down to the hole where I was, they cut the ties that I had on my head, on my hands and my feet and he grabbed me, and then he grabbed my hair and then he gave me, he slapped on my face and he said that if he saw me again he was going to kill me. And after that they left and I was left lying there with my arm broke. And I probably spend two hours lying there and I was in pain, a very strong pain that I couldn't talk.

Matias forged on.

And I end up being able to find people that lived on the streets and they asked me what happened. And I told them everything that had passed with me. And one of them, and one of them pulled my arm and they grabbed the shirt and they rolled my arm in that shirt very tight, here and here. And I couldn't move my arm for many days. I went to a hospital. I went to the hospital to tell them that I had my arm broken and they kicked me off the hospital because I'm Black. They told me that if I wanted to go to the hospital, I will have to pay,

I will have to pay a lot and if a doctor would accept to see me, he wouldn't see me inside the hospital, I had to be seen outside the hospital. And they told me that treatment was not available for people of my race. And after that I had to run away to the woods, where I had to hide there because I was afraid the police was going to find me again. And I was always hiding in the woods because there nobody could find me. Many people that lived on the streets would hide in the woods too because the same would happen to them.

As he concluded, Matias summarized his hopes, his search and aspirations, pointing back to all that had gone wrong.

I don't want to die, I don't want to die. I want to live where they accept me for, with my religion and with my color, in a place where I can go to the hospital and they will see me, where I can go and study and not be rejected because I'm Black. I just want to live.

Not long after, the judge left to review the case documents, to return with a decision.

Matias had put faith in the United States, and in the discourses of life, liberty, and prosperity that reproduce its moral superiority in the world. Under such a condition of apparent global primacy, often described as guided by rights, justice, and liberty, he understood that this place would protect him and that it would recognize the violence that he suffered in Brazil. They would listen to the struggles that he had faced and give him shelter. For these reasons, when he crossed the border, he turned himself in to a customs and border person at the first opportunity—for such a process of justice and rights-endowment to begin.

His faith in America moved him away from the option of crossing undocumented or seeking to test the deserts of the South and Southwest, which have been accurately described as a "land of open graves." He did not know that many people did choose that way, crossing a terrain that was deployed as an inhuman and highly lethal means of deterrence. They chose it as a constrained solution, a way of avoiding everything that comes with the asylum process, but one that holds only the slimmest chances of success. In surrendering himself to US authorities, he put all his faith in the imaginaries of the United States of America.

And yet, in doing so, he subjected himself to the actual and empirical world that so defines the everyday politics of this country and its racial capitalist ethics—indefinite detention for millions in for-profit conditions, functionally devoid of rights, and at the heart of an immense political economy of racialized order. This system that is so vital to the protection of a tiny minority of the world's population but nearly all of the world's wealth—that he hoped against hope would embrace him—was ready to spit him right back out again.

The judge returned to the courtroom, ready to state his decision.

JUDGE: Mr. Souza, sir. I am not going to grant your relief today. I'm going to deny your application for asylum, for withholding of removal and for relief under the provisions of the Convention against Torture. Now, sir, because you've not been in the United States for at least one year, I'm also going to deny voluntary departure. . . . Is Portuguese the language you speak and understand best?

MATIAS: Yes, sir.

JUDGE: Sir, do you choose Brazil as your country of departure or did you want to choose a different country?

MATIAS: Your Honor, are you going to deport me?

JUDGE: Yes, sir, I'm going to order that you be removed from the United States, but I want to know if you want to go to your home country of Brazil, or did you want to choose a different country?

MATIAS: No, sir, why am I being, where am I going? Why am I going to be deported if my case is possible to get asylum?

JUDGE: Well, sir, I've denied your application for asylum. So, I guess what I want to know is if you want to go to a country, you can choose a different country than Brazil, if you would like to, and if you do that, I will list Brazil as an alternative, in the event that the country you choose does not agree to accept you. So, sir, do you want me to list, do you want me to list only Brazil, or did you want to choose a different country?

MATIAS: I want to appeal your decision.

JUDGE: I understand, sir, but my question is, do you want to go back to Brazil, or did you want to go to a different country?

MATIAS: No, sir, I want just to appeal, sir.

JUDGE: Yes, sir, but before we can get there, I need to know whether you choose only, you want me to list only Brazil, or if you want me to list a different country?

MATIAS: Sir, I want to be, I want to be true to you, I'd rather die than going back to my country.

This was no unfamiliar territory for the judge. Between 2015 and 2020, this was his decision in more than nine out of every ten of his cases. According to records, he moved to deport in 92.4 percent of his cases (477 out of 516)—far above the national average of 66.7 percent for immigration judges.[1]

ICE claims that 17,000 Brazilians were apprehended in one single United States border sector, El Paso, Texas, in the fiscal year ending in November 2019—one of whom would have been Matias. In December 2019, 16,952 Brazilians were in a caseload backlog, all awaiting deportation hearings. That same year, 2,485 Brazilians would be ordered deported from the United States. In keeping with this, and for the first time in nearly two decades, the Brazilian government, under the leadership of Bolsonaro, began accepting chartered deportation flights from the United States. Previously banned in 2006 by President Lula da Silva, deportation flights once again began to land, starting in October 2019—all at the same Brazilian airport, Confins, outside of Belo Horizonte. Journalists write that Brazilians arriving at the airport are left to beg for money for bus tickets to travel on to locations that are often several thousands of kilometers away, across this vast country.

ICE's spectacular numbers of Brazilians crossing at El Paso, circulated in press releases with similarly spectacular reportage, now motivate a new and proactive, and yet highly selective, kind of search for the disappeared. This search is vested in new technological solutionism, and a kind of capitalist power increasingly rooted in identity verification, and training machines to rationalize political problems with bio-informatics and personal identifiers.

That same year, 2019, the Microsoft Corporation waded directly into the politics of disappearance in Brazil. Far from Redmond, Washington, they reached out to the Mães da Praça da Sé, the São Paulo organization that was set up in the 1990s by a mother with hopes of finding her son. Ever since, she has sought to provide solutions and knowledge to assist mothers and fathers of the disappeared in what has become an ever-expanding community of suffering. As part of their work over the previous twenty years, Mães da Praça da Sé had developed an expansive database of the contemporary disappeared, including personal data and photographs. All of those images were vital for spreading the word and raising public awareness about the missing so that they might be seen and recognized, allowing for parents to be notified, tips to be gathered, and people to be found.

For Microsoft, this problem of mundane disappearance in Brazil was no longer something that could be restricted to Brazil—it was no longer to be approached myopically as a problem of Latin America for Latin Americans alone to deal with. Their interest in this database implied something of greater magnitude: that people being reported missing may be out there; they may have deliberately left. Their interest was not in who these people were or why they had vanished, much less whether they had died or been buried in a mass grave. Instead, they needed to know where they *actually* went, if they went, but only in the event of something in particular. Microsoft wanted the data set—in case these missing people, or others like them, might materialize in a place like El Paso, Texas. Just like Matias did.

As part of a program that it calls "AI for Humanitarian Action," Microsoft asked for the pictures from the more than ten thousand cases of missing men and women kept by the organization since 1996. For their part, Mães da Praça da Sé would have been remiss not to provide them, given the desperate need for solutions and dramatic inattention that usually exists for the missing, and the ability of a company of this stature to find at least one person. Microsoft touted a solution: that the images and life histories could be used to fortify the search, including through technological innovation.

From a different angle, though, Microsoft's goal seemed something quite different: that these images and data could be aggregated, digitized, and incorporated into Microsoft's Azure cloud infrastructure for use in practical applications and advanced computing. With its focus on the missing in São Paulo, Microsoft would take data from this distinct population and add their characteristics to a database of images and data that the company has collected on what it calls "modern migrants"—people outside the Global North, including refugees, displaced people, and the missing. With little in common otherwise, the categorization of a population on these lines rests on a common denominator that is eminently clear; these are people that might desire to enter the United States, Europe, Australia, or Canada—among other places. The aggregation of data on these

predominantly non-White populations who may be on the move, and perhaps in flight, is part of a new search to foreclose opportunity—fully at
odds with these populations' search for a better life.

This goal is far from obscured in how Microsoft described how it would
use the data for the benefit of the Mães da Praça da Sé in São Paulo. As
Microsoft put it in a press release at the time, the partnership with Mães
da Praça da Sé envisions "the creation of an application that uses facial
recognition . . . to strengthen the search for the missing and to ally with
the work of searching by public entities in partnerships with police, hospitals, emergency rooms, shelters and other institutions." Fully bypassing
any consideration of the role these institutions play in reproducing the
politics of disappearance, it continues:

> The platform uses cognitive tools, artificial intelligence and storage on
> Microsoft's Azure cloud software. With it, it will be possible to identify a
> person suspected to be in a state of abandonment with facial recognition.
> A user will just have to take a picture of the person and compare their physi-
> ognomy with the organization's database. The app will search and display if
> the characteristics are compatible with someone who is missing. It will also
> be possible to search for people by physical characteristics (skin, hair and
> eye color).[2]

"[This partnership] is a powerful example," wrote Brad Smith, Microsoft
CEO, "of how we can apply technology to help solve the greatest challenges
in our society." Missing people, people on the run, and the mundane mass
graves emergent, are indeed one of the great challenges of our time. But, at
best, this technological effort is a light-touch solution. Instead, technology
is making use of these absent and missing people in the vestiges of their
images and personal data that remain. Here, the concern is that these
people must be identified—not because they are missing, but because of
where they might turn up.

The images and data of missing people might seem discrete. But they are
past, present, and future. Their past is a history shrouded in doubt, suspicion, and concern about who they really were before they vanished. Their
present is a condition of both hopefulness—for family—and threat—that
they might emerge on the other side of a border. Their future is being determined through the vast database of their images and personal identifiers
that Microsoft, and others, use to teach "intelligent" machines about the

"physiognomy" of people who are likely to disappear, to be disappeared, or to flee to somewhere they should not. Unlike the data collected by Microsoft, the app is not available to users outside of Brazil. Moreover, users in Brazil roundly write that the app is "useless" in their reviews. They say the design is absurd, since it implies that people can go around taking pictures of others on the street and running them through the app. But even if police wanted to use it to take a picture of someone they have arrested, they wouldn't get past the interface, which constantly freezes.

One of the most notable clients who use Microsoft's Azure cloud database is ICE. With several contracts in place, totaling in the tens of millions of US dollars, Microsoft has written openly and prominently about providing its data and cloud services to ICE to enable it to "modernize" its work, stating: "ICE's decision to accelerate IT modernization using Azure Government will help them innovate faster while reducing the burden of legacy IT. The agency is currently implementing transformative technologies for homeland security and public safety, and we're proud to support this work with our mission-critical cloud."[3]

This selective attention to lives—not to their well-being or conditions of life and death, but to what they might do or where they might go—underscores a project of global bordering. People like Matias who would flee the streets of a Brazilian city matter only insofar as they might seek to come to the United States. Living, dying, or disappearing under any other condition doesn't matter. They are known only via this eventuality, with this knowledge used to further reassert the importance of a Global North population and capitalist regime that must be protected at all costs.

I met Matias when his appeal was picked up by a pro bono legal group, the Catholic Legal Immigration Network (CLINIC), at the Board of Appeals. Through his attorney, and colleagues at the University of Texas, Austin, and University of Indiana, Bloomington, I agreed to serve as an expert witness on his appeal, tracing existing research on Brazilian policing to show the pattern of persecution he had suffered on the basis of his race.

In our many conversations then and since, Matias described a much more complex picture of his circumstances. Speaking by himself and through an interpreter, he had no idea there would be a specific terminology or way of speaking that would determine the value of his life. The judge—who is also on the board of the Western Hemispheric Institute for

Security Cooperation, previously known as the School of the Americas—had also only thinly inquired into details about the context of Matias's persecution by police.[4]

Under the United Nations Convention against Torture, a discrete case emerged—one that in almost any other case of violence at the hands of police would have fallen away. That Matias lived on the street, had to beg for food, and had suffered police violence would not be sufficient grounds to grant him asylum. Instead, his potential for asylum rested on the fact that he had been subject to a pattern and practice of persecution against Afro-Brazilians such that he could demonstrate a well-founded fear of future persecution specifically on account of his race and ethnicity. Matias's description of the violence he suffered was important only insofar as it could demonstrate repeated persecution by the police *because* he was Black. The violence he suffered happened because the police ascribed Blackness upon him.

Absent legal representation and lacking in knowledge of processes, legal discourse, and documentation, Matias had previously never been able to articulate that he had been targeted by police as he fled three separate cities, police who did not know him and whose violence against him was not of a personal or individually targeted nature. No police officer knew him by name, and he had never seen any of them ever before. Instead, the violence he experienced demonstrated specific police intervention based on his being a poor Black person present in public spaces and appealing to people for help. When police harmed him, they targeted him specifically, while leaving others—poor but not Black—alone. That Matias fled one city, went to another, then again to another before leaving Brazil—with different police accosting him, threatening death, and doing harm at each stop—constituted a specific pattern legible for the standards of the Convention against Torture.

In January 2021, seventeen months after Matias was taken into ICE detention—almost all in the midst of COVID-19—I waited for a call to testify. I would be patched into the courtroom inside that private prison in Southern Georgia to answer questions and be cross-examined about the report I had written about Matias's case. But in place of a call, and the words of an officious judge, a text message came from Matias's attorney: "Graham, we will not be needing you today. Thank the Lord, the Court granted asylum."

Matias now lives in Massachusetts with an aunt. Four months after leaving detention, and just before this book went to production, he had not received a cent in refugee support from the United States government, has not been able to enter school, and is struggling to make do as a Black man in America.

The story of missing people and disappearance must be about people like Matias. And yet it cannot only be so. Matias's case should be celebrated for his life and what it enables a critical onlooker to see: a horrifying regime of exception and expulsion with vast capillaries of wealth generation. The conditions that compelled Matias to disappear from Brazil and embark on a continental search for a life to live cannot be disaggregated from the place he ended up. Brazil's maintenance of unequal human life is, in many ways, little different from the United States and its own ongoing history of post-slavery racial inequality, mundane disappearance, and unequal life. Most obvious, Brazil's and the United States' prison systems are kin—similar but different, their genetic code rooted in racial order, accumulation, and the reproduction of unequal life. Via these logics, their systems and governance tirelessly reassert the idea and practice of the "criminal" that becomes central to municipal and state taxation and budgeting, whether through the emission of bonds for prison construction, through everyday fines at the street level as property tax values wane, or through the legalized theft of civil asset forfeiture. While expressly local in iteration and suffering, production and management, the political conditions of disappearance—that people can disappear into prisons and need not be pursued when they do—are guided by a set of normative assumptions about racial difference and especially about what lives, wherever in the world, can end prematurely or disappear.

Gatekeepers at places like Stewart Detention Center oversee an increasingly global condition of disappearance and searching. As of May 2021, 38,202 Brazilians were stuck in a deportation backlog. In both sheer numbers and proportion per capita, this pales in comparison to countries like Guatemala (290,476, total population 17.9 million), Honduras (255,063, total population 10 million), and El Salvador (188,152, total population 6.5 million). While these dynamics are different in some obvious ways—people disappearing from their home countries to get to the United States *and* being disappeared from their families and social relations in

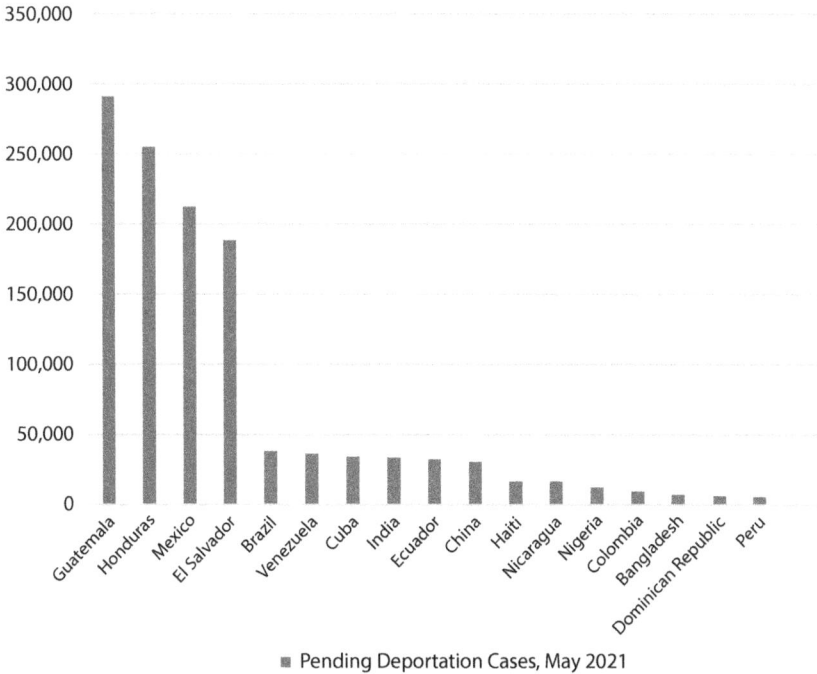

Figure 6. Pending deportation cases, May 2021 (graph by author with data from trac.syr.edu).

the United States—the political project of disappearance remains much the same.

Getting out is desperately important. People flee. They flee police. They flee the PCC and groups like it. They flee within Brazil, within the politics of disappearance and the machinery of the state itself. They disappear to the streets, and to the urban *cracolândias* ("cracklands"). They disappear into criminal asylums, cemeteries, and medical study. They enter cemeteries and leave three years later—partially, really—in unmarked bags. People disappear, reappear, and disappear again as they move through state bureaucracy. People disappear, too, because they've never really existed at all—no documents, no personhood, no ability to ever cast a vote. None of this disappearance is "into thin air."

At the same time, in another world and time, perhaps someone like Matias would have taken shelter in a different place, beneath a criminal organization like the PCC that serves to so deliberately attenuate the suffering, death, and disappearance that the thousands of Matiases are forced to bear. In spite of the world of violence that surrounded him, and the need to survive, Matias eschewed such an option, existing instead in a space between criminal organizations that reassert the value of life on new terms and Brazilian society writ large, which so forcefully sought for him to disappear. Between the selective care of the state and the police that tied him up and threw him in a dank pit—very much a *vala*—and the tedious care of an organization like the PCC and its mundane mass graves, he ran for something better.

The air that fills the void of someone's disappearance is thick with global political order. And perhaps it always has been, whether viewed through chattel, missing insurgents, or the ongoing devaluation of life in comparative exercises. While expressly local in iteration and suffering, production and management, disappearance is guided—facilitated—by a set of global conditions and normative assumptions about what life, wherever in the world, must be held aloft. None of this is specific to São Paulo. It is global in diverse ways, existing in variations throughout Latin America and beyond, circumscribed in a sharpening concern with global migration, movement, and keeping some people—labor, especially—in place. But the boundaries of that "place" are not defined by each nation-state. Instead, specific and particular borders matter and take precedence, requiring fortification and reassertion more than others. These borders, between states of great wealth and regions and countries comparably without, increasingly define the global order and the place of populations within it. This happens especially in mechanisms of moralistic sorting that defy an interest in global inequality, insidious capitalism, or a racist political economy, like those falling acutely on Matias at CoreCivic's Stewart Detention Center in Lumpkin, Georgia (pop. 2,630)—the largest of all such immigration detention centers in the United States. To keep the story of twenty to twenty-five thousand disappeared in São Paulo within the bounds of this city, state, and country is misguided, if not delusional.

The seductive question that courses through this book—"Where do they go?"—is in many ways a red herring that obscures the substance of the problem: that people are enabled to disappear. Beneath the indifference to human life—which should ultimately remain the focus—I have tried to trace some of the common patterns, the logics, the moral infrastructures of disappearance that surround how people are neither dead nor alive, and neither present nor entirely absent. People are disappeared by and killed by police, and perhaps buried. People are disappeared by the PCC, and groups like it. Some are buried after having died on the street, buried under wooden stakes numbered with a black marker. Others, like Matias, muster an awe-inspiring motivation to get out and search for something better. Only rarely are they embraced for doing so. Where this motivation comes from, uncodified but decisive, and against the countervailing weight of inhumanity, is not clear.

A politics of disappearance is never complete foreclosure; it reveals a world of searching, seeking, and demanding; it is a fragmented and transient project of hope and care. This project deigns to not forget Kaio, Felipe, Matias, and Madalena—and all the bones, which must be held aloft, and kept alive. It is a causeway to a politics of life that exists beyond the mundane and material disappearance that so defines the world today.

Reading Life through
Disappearance

A NOTE ON METHOD

In May 2016, the *New York Times* published an article about a little-known island in the sound off Queens in New York City. Hart Island, the author Nina Bernstein wrote, was a place "where overgrown nineteenth-century ruins give way to mass graves gouged out by bulldozers and the only pallbearers are jail inmates paid 50 cents an hour." The multimedia article begins with drone footage of an extremely flat island with patches of leafless trees, as though lifeless in its shadow-season brown. The camera circles above as two vehicles leave the ferry dock. One is a white Ford pickup truck, and the other is a white school bus, which winds its way along a single-lane road toward an encampment in the background. Along the way are ruins; buildings of various stories, all quadrangular in footprint, but which all speak of a kind of state institutionalism materialized in bricks of white and dark red.

Paragraphs in, the drone footage then captures a backhoe lifting pine boxes from the back of a white trailer truck, lifting them with the assistance of three men, dressed in orange garments, into a trench where they are guided by three others. This pine box is being placed on top of two others in a trench that looks like a strip mine. The white school bus and the pickup truck are in the frame too. All the vehicles have the typeface of the state, "New York Department of Corrections." Swallowing the foreground is flattened plant-less earth, barren except for white markers spaced about thirty feet apart, but not consistently, that must mark trenches beneath.

The article is distinctive, and it gazes on a space, in image and text, that the reader feels they should not see. There are activities going on here, a political economy, an elsewhere space, where things come together in a quiet but material production: human containment, bodies, bureaucracy, and ruin with a kind of banal orderliness. This place is off limits, such that I, personally, am left with a feeling: Should I be seeing it? The title of the article, "Unearthing the Secrets of New York's Mass Graves," pushes this sense further.

But the article does something else distinctive; it frames this space, a burial site for the unclaimed, as something other than a cemetery. Rather, it deploys a heavy term: this is a "mass grave." Here, although "everyone has their own little pine box," as Foucault once quipped, there is no earth between them. Pine rests on pine on all sides. But the neatness and rationalized linearity of this stacking, far from jumbled or haphazard, pushes a kind of ethical boundary about how "mass graves" are widely understood. As though there is too much order here for this to be a mass grave. The alternative: Does the state make mass graves all the time? And what is the difference between the space itself—an island like Hart Island, morphologically, socially, and politically extracted from the city—and the existence of mass graves within it? The existence of the former seems deterministic of the latter.

Hart Island is also routinely described as a "potter's field," a necessary ground for burying people who are left behind. It is a space of "social death" for those who have disappeared from society in a way that isn't even known. Though spoken of differently and under contextual guise, every city has a potter's field to dispose of populations that are not claimed, are expulsed, and made absent from social and political recognition. While a space of death, the potter's field is nonetheless dynamic with social and political assumptions. Its materialization and variation, across societies, manifest a real-world, tactile, sensorial space from which to read society, politics and historical—material—social change.

I became troubled by the mundane but dramatically under-described confluence of no less than four major threads, all of which imply structural conditions in varying degrees: (1) death and body disposal; (2) cities and human density; (3) emplacement—who? why? how?; and (4) materiality. From each, a text; a means to read society and capital, ethnographically, politically, and critically. In New York and elsewhere, a Hart Island becomes a means to locate and point a finger at capitalism's universalization of individuality and its making of something that can be called "social nothingness" or "social death" without irony, concern, or distress. As though such a thing, such a place, were not as unnatural as plastics clogging the ocean and global temperatures rising.

Less than a month later, on June 11, 2016, I found myself in the potter's fields of São Paulo. On a planned trip for a seminar examining questions around my first book, *The Killing Consensus*, I took two extra trips. One to Vila Formosa, on the east side of the city, and another to Dom Bosco, in the far North, beyond the city limits. These two spaces, I came to see, were both substantially different and substantially the same. Both worked as spaces of disposal, having entire sections that had no tombstones. Instead, these spaces had wooden stakes, hand-numbered with a marker. There were plain wood boxes. Moreover, few, if any, questions were being asked about who these nameless people were, why they were there, or why it was necessary to have such a place at all. Critical, too, was the racialization of the spaces. In two global cities, each with stock markets and exceptional concentrations of wealth, all were dramatically about poor non-White populations.

But the differences were of crucial importance, too. São Paulo's potter's fields are also cemeteries for the urban poor, whose commemoration, presence, and materials of memory made the spaces less bleak, even amid aching sadness and sorrow. They are less off-limits. Very little seemed still, even in the unevenness of the disturbed earth, much of it not yet compacted. These cemeteries were at a distance from society—deliberately so, as I learned later—but they weren't run under a regime of criminalization, with burial being done by prison labor. Most startling, I learned, was that there was—had been—a dictatorship mass grave inside Dom Bosco cemetery, and that the place was likely created *for this very purpose*. In this case, a place where bodies had been deliberately jumbled, coffin-less, with hundreds of others by Brazil's military dictatorship.

It was here that disappearance—a convergence of burial conditions, social death, anti-human politics, and furious capitalist inequality—came into view both materially and conceptually. Soon after, I came to know the horrific scope of disappearance in this city via an ominous figure: *twenty to twenty-five thousand every year*. Soon after that, Neide, Débora, and others allowed me into their lives.

In some ways, the starting point of this book is absence, dearth, and an epistemological struggle to make sense of that which we know may, or may not, exist in the form ascribed. How does one describe or relate something, someone, that is not "there" in material existence, but that one knows is present somewhere, whether in life or death? Much of my effort has been in keeping with what Yael Navaro (2020) recently described as a "negative methodology," the mitigated effort to know a black hole by tracing the outlines of the space that it occupies. Black holes are replete with forces and power beyond the human imagination, but their absorption of matter and magnitude of density makes rigorous observation of them difficult with dominant methodologies. Prove a black hole from its outside, its "event horizon," yes. Observe its force on the rest of the universe and contiguous objects, sure. Disappearance, like a black hole, is a question of what happens after or around the event, and of not yet knowing or centering the event in itself. Or, as Navaro puts it in speaking about sense-making in the aftermath of violence, "Against the assumption of the presence of evidence, I begin from an observation of its absence: its erasure, denial, misappropriation, inaccessibility, unavailability, or irretrievability in sites in the long-term aftermath of mass atrocity" (162).

But the metaphor doesn't stretch much further, thankfully, because black holes, unlike disappearance, are not created in the defense of capitalism, by people. Disappearance, unlike black holes, can be undone and made knowable without dramatic advances in methods. And so, while Navaro and others are very rightly concerned with knowing in the aftermath, this book appreciates a negative methodology, pointing to the politics of an ongoing aftermath rooted in the banal and globalizing conditions of disappearance as everyday life—in other words, to the idea of disappearance as being made by capital and society, and to the possibility of its unmaking with a different kind of sociality and political ethics.

In terms of evidence, I've attended to four epistemes in this book, all guided by ethnographic research that I carried out over a four-year period, from 2016 to 2019. First, I focused on relationships with a small handful of parents of the recently disappeared, seeking an appreciation of the multitude of factors surrounding their trauma, the event of disappearance, and all that happens amid absence. In so doing I attended to their condition and location in the city, visiting them when invited in, for long interviews and life-history recitations. My time with them was often too truncated to accompany them on active searches—which happen in acute moments when some snippet of news crops up—but these discussions flowed into elaborate WhatsApp voice messages that continue today.

Second, in a number of research trips, I focused on specific spaces, institutions, and life worlds within them, spending extended time in cemeteries, the coroner's office (IML), prisons, and police stations. To access these places I sometimes went alone, walking in through the gates of a cemetery, and finding ways to start conversations. I also went back to the homicide division to revisit old connections. In other cases, I came to rely more on interlocutors and partners in humanistic ventures, scholar-practitioners like Viviane, or globally important scholars, like Samira Bueno, for access to spaces. And it is with these people, and in authored partnership, that I continue to write and think. In all of these places, my inquiry hinged on informally structured conversations and observations of practices and material spaces, all of which motivates how the narrative I present here raises and works through everyday ethical and institutional paradoxes at different scales and from different positions. Attending to these spaces of disappearance, where families and relatives come—and later avoid—spending time with disappearance meant grasping its valences in working conditions, discursive construction, documentation, and materiality.

Third, I attend in specific detail to a set of crucial documents about the internal organization of the PCC. These documents, which I obtained in 2012, came originally from a wiretapping effort in the state of São Paulo. These documents became public in a series of indictments in 2013, and I describe the contents of this trove of data in detail in a 2019 article (Lessing and Denyer Willis, 2019). I have drawn on these documents to think through the relationship between punishment and moral order in *The Killing Consensus*, and to understand how the PCC manages to sustain itself across space and prison walls in that 2019 article. Here, though, I attend to the muted set of patterns about disappearance and sociality that I did not recognize until very recently. Disappearance plays a twofold role in these documents, one systemic—the relationship between the organization, prison, and "the state"—and the other institutional, within the organization itself. The documents illustrate a lifeworld that the state has created and continues to shape by disappearing hundreds of thousands into a penitentiary system or by lethal violence on the street.

In important ways, though, much of my understanding of the politics of disappearance is informed by nearly three decades of personal and scholarly engagement with Brazil. It is because of my attention to these disparate sources that my authorial voice is sometimes more present than I would like it to be, as I have sought to make links between things that are obviously adjacent and moved by the forces of each other, but with the processes that move them obscured and made under-knowable. It has been my effort too, though, to not make such links too explicit, clear, and asserted, since reducing the problem of disappearance to a linear relationship between things, between people, or between people and things, is not the point.

In particular, this book follows immediately on from several years spent accompanying detectives of the civil police, which I describe in *The Killing Consensus*. In that research, I observed the other side of what I saw here, how the logics of bureaucratic disinterest are performed and shaped by those charged with investigating, where yet another case walking into the room becomes yet another thing that cannot get done, and where the metric becomes not solving (or even resolving) a case but, instead, paperwork filed.

But it is not that simple either. The burden of "yet another case" does not mean that everything becomes a matter of the overwhelming weight of "one more homicide," or "another disappearance" to add to the last twenty-four thousand. Even amid twenty thousand cases of missing people, these detectives will find the needle in a haystack when they need to, burning down the haystack if need be. A homicide that matters, a disappearance of someone who shouldn't have, will compel action. For the rest, the haystack remains too huge, too impossible to search through. Such a reality is not resolved only by more resources. It is this logic, where the disappeared are already disappeared, and the found are already found, that I hope I have described toward a greater understanding of the maintenance of unequal life in Brazil and beyond.

Notes

INTRODUCTION

1. Counting the dead and disappeared is always both a project of illumination and obscuration. See Winifred Tate's 2007 book *Counting the Dead: The Culture and Politics of Human Rights Activism in Colombia* for a crucial discussion about naming and claiming violence, victims, and what might be left behind.

2. There is a vast and insightful body of work in this line, which traces the efforts, contestations, and claims about searches in the aftermath and the battle for memory. Such work includes: Verdery (1999); Adams and Byrd (2014); Drexler, Wagner, and Sanford (2010); Ferrándiz (2013); Ferrándiz and Robben (2015); Filippucci, et al. (2012); Grandin (2011); Rosenblatt (2015); Sanford (2003); Stover and Weinstein (2004); Wagner (2015).

CHAPTER 1. DISAPPEARANCE AND THE SEARCH

1. Atrocity, war, and the acute ethical-political rupture that surrounds many kinds of disappearance can create space for a greater attention to scientific methods and the use of DNA to discover and identify bodies. This is especially true where the ethical condition shifts in favor of those representing the disappeared, as Rosenblatt (2015) traces in Argentina, or where the impetus is on

reclaiming bodies for the reproduction of national identity, as Wagner (2015) describes of the United States' efforts to identify bodies in Vietnam.

2. Jonah Rubin (2018) describes how Francisco Franco, the Spanish fascist, continues to govern from the grave, in an ornate tomb in the "Valley of the Dead." Contestation over his body and its commemoration, which has been the site of efforts to disinter, is an ongoing battleground for the political discourse of the living in a continuing war between socialism and fascism.

3. Just as some life is socially dead, "ungrievable," as Judith Butler understands it, so are some bones. Just as "to assert the grievability of human life under conditions in which those lives have already been abandoned is to make a political claim against abandonment" (Butler 2021: 177), the same can be said of bones that animate no ethical or political response, save a very local response that is centered upon those who suffer with acute political indifference. For Butler, then, a claim against the ungrievability of bones or the disappeared—though not the "bodily existence" they imagine—might be formative of a "radical politics . . . as a form of persistence."

4. For example, Rafael Chambouleyron (2005) describes an early colonial condition in the Amazon region where the pursuit for resources was always tied up in the use of Indigenous and, later, Black populations to seek out wild goods like cocoa and clove bark. This extractive economy, which pushed inland in many directions, required such bodies to extract both for export and to finance the evangelizing and "captivating" work of missions.

5. See, for example, Dutra (2018).

6. Padre Vieira, cited in the extensive work of Luiz Felipe de Alencastro (2018: 144) detailing the South–South slave trade and its particular Atlantic characteristics in the formation of what is now known as Brazil.

7. There are many crucial considerations of these logics. Among them: dos Santos Gomes (2002); Dantas (2004); Freitas (1994); Schwartz (1996).

8. Crucially, Miki notes that those who sheltered slaves, like this or otherwise, were often the subject of severe repression. But far from always, and indeed "slave hiders were hardly eradicated, much like the *quilombolas* themselves."

9. As Immanuel Wallerstein writes, this is the basic contradiction of capitalism as a social system. "It results from the simultaneous desirability of freedom for the buyer and its undesirability for the seller—freedom of labor, freedom of the flow of the factors of production, freedom of the market. The combination of freedom and unfreedom that results is the defining characteristic of a capitalist world-economy. This ambivalence about freedom pervades its politics, its culture, its social relations."

10. In an interview in the *Boston Review*, Roy (2019) expands further, relating this logic to the resurgence of ethnonationalism. Here, the prospect of "an endless flow of unwanted immigrants with the wrong skin color or the wrong religion is now being used to rally fascists and ethno-nationalists across the world." This ethnonationalism is about the perpetuation of the nation-state, its requisite

of economic growth through the securitization of both state and global practices of resource and labor extraction, including the need for extreme fluidly alongside certainty of containment.

11. Melissa Wright (2017) describes the governance of the missing in Mexico in this way, where the first stage of recognition is to prove that the missing ever existed in the first place. As she puts it, "All of the modern trappings of biopolitical governance—birth certificates, educational and medical records, digitized government identification records, marriage licenses, property titles—fail to prove the disappeared's existence. And, without proof of existence, there is no proof of a crime when that non-existing subject fails to surface. Without crime, there is no injustice. And, thus, nothing to demand. As such, while we plummet from this logical precipice, the lack of empirical data (a lack generated by the government that directly or indirectly authorizes the disappearance) contributes to an epistemological ignorance (there is nothing to know and no way to know this nothingness), which, the governing elites then claim to be an ontological condition: the disappeared simply are not" (254).

12. The logic of disavowal, disappearance, and "cemeteriness" is at work in widespread ways, and not just in borderlands, or the Global South. Hannah Dreier writes of the way that the Suffolk County police on Long Island denominated a particular space as "the killing fields," after associating it with "Central American gangs." Dreier tracks the way that, after eleven young Latino men went missing between 2016 and 2017, the police framed these disappearances as a kind of "misdemeanor murder," shrugging it off on the supposition that all involved were either "runaways" and/or part of the MS-13. As a result, many ended up in this mundane burial space, widely spoken of and concerned about by families, but dismissed as irrelevant for investigation by virtue of the kinds of lives and bodies interred there. See: H. Dreier, "The Disappeared," *Pro Publica*, September 20, 2018, https://features.propublica.org/ms13-miguel/the-disappeared/, also, an associated *This American Life* episode "The Runaways": https://www.thisamericanlife.org/657/the-runaways.

CHAPTER 3. UNEARTHING LIFE

1. Eduardo Cunha, a representative from Rio de Janeiro State, was charged with diverting money to, among other places, an HSBC bank account in Switzerland. He was also the primary figure orchestrating the "soft coup" of then sitting president Dilma Rousseff.

2. A full interview is revelatory and shows the lifelong project of Erundina, which has not had the international profile of other Brazilian leftists. See https://revistamarieclaire.globo.com/Mulheres-do-Mundo/noticia/2020/09/candidata-vice-prefeita-de-sp-erundina-tem-pressa-velhice-nao-impede-o-sonho.html.

3. When Erundina was first elected in 1988 she ran with the same party, the Worker's Party (PT), as Luiz Ignacio "Lula" da Silva. Lula was elected president in 2002 with widespread union support and went on to govern with unprecedented popularity, in spite of a series of corruption scandals. But Lula's political path, and the PT's path, moved toward the center. None of the PT's elected mayors since Erundina have taken an interest in the urban poor, and their cemeteries.

4. In 2004 the federal government created the Força Nacional de Segurança Pública, a standing body deployed by local invitation. The FNSP, which aggregated police from state bodies, were deployed on invitation by local state governors or governments, especially in response to acute crises, cyclical unrest. The FNSP has also since been deployed, in 2019, in Mozambique, as a quasi-peacekeeping force.

5. Cemeteries are under municipal jurisdiction, by and large, with the cost of burial contributing directly to city budgets. However, the majority of city budgets are provided via decentralized funds from the federal government through portions of taxes, including business and personal income taxes.

6. Human and animal, as O'Neill describes. Some seek money for burial costs and corpse preparation, while others fly, lope, hover, and "eat themselves." O'Neill's depiction of vultures and disinterment in Guatemala City is evocative and troubling—if entirely necessary. The ghostly specter of systemic violence is heavy and well revealed in the human and animal symbiosis that lingers and predates the bodies, living and dead, of the urban poor. See O'Neill (2012a: 511).

CHAPTER 4. DISAPPEARANCE AND THE CEMETERY

1. For examples of the breadth of this substantial transdisciplinary work, see Arditti (1999); Brysk (1994); Comaty (2019); Coupland and Cordner (2003); Crossland (2000); Kovras (2013); Peake and Lynch (2016); Robins (2011); Smith (2017); Tidball-Binz (2012); Tully (1995).

2. While particularly deleterious to remains of the poor in Brazil, routine exhumation is a common practice in cemetery governance around the world, and with fascinating differences that work across demands for spaces, religious belief, unequal recognition of life, class, and political economies. For especially distinctive work on such questions, see Toulson (2012) and O'Rourke (2007).

3. The burning of bodies looms in questions of disappearance in Latin America. Isaias Rojas-Perez (2017) documents a struggle by Quechua mothers to memorialize and search around La Hoyada, a former military site with industrial furnaces used to hide and eliminate the missing from eventual exhumation and discovery.

4. The work of José Cláudio Souza Alves is a touchstone for understanding the suburbs of Rio, relating how violent groups exist in a highly consequential political economy of extraction and order imposition.

5. The Rio de Janeiro State Truth Commission was in many ways more extensive and incisive than the National Truth Commission. The Rio de Janeiro commission attended to contextual considerations, including race and the subjectivities of those being policed amid urban poverty. This commission included some of the most revelatory testimony, including that of Coronel Malhães. See Comissão da Verdade do Rio (2015).

6. The *Brasil: Nunca mais* report stands out among many civil society efforts to reclaim knowledge about Cold War disappearance. Cataloging all known disappeared and murdered political actors, including their places of burial and conditions of burial—name, pseudonym, unnamed, and so on—the report has been vital to the making of a notion of justice in post-dictatorship Brazil. See Arns (1985) and Godoy (2014).

7. Image available at: https://blogs.uai.com.br/opiniaosemmedo/wp-content/uploads/sites/67/2017/04/lula-e-dilma-presos-e1492295517165.jpg

8. Indeed, the work of Brodwyn Fischer across various contributions (2004; 2008; 2014) argues that the very materialization of favelas into the city, especially in Rio de Janeiro, is derived from the lack of synthesis between the Brazilian Left and its fractious relationship with the urban poor and its own movements and situated demands. While appearing to be the rational community for overwhelming demands for systemic political change, the urban poor's actual needs remained largely severed from institutionalized leftist politics, dominated by other class interests. The demands made by the urban poor for rights and infrastructure, largely in spite of leftist parties, worked through their own committees and coalitions, tethered to material and everyday questions and struggles for basic subsistence.

9. Jenny Edkins's *Missing: Persons and Politics* (2011) is among the only works that engages with disappearance as a valuable political category. Edkins focuses on "the Western Individual" after the Second World War to ask how disappearance matters, for both the "missed" and the "unmissed." The politics that surrounds both, and that unites them, reveals, as she puts it, "the status of the rest of us" (14). Disappearance, for Edkins, is a means of revealing power, which she does not stretch to the point of asking how disappearance, itself, reproduces politics.

10. Image available at: https://www.redebrasilatual.com.br/cidadania/2019/04/bolsonaro-encerra-grupos-que-identificavam-ossadas-de-vitimas-da-ditadura/.

11. There is a long history of sensitive records being destroyed in Brazil, and often by fire. At the Dawn of Emancipation in 1890, Brazilian authorities burned all records of slavery, obliterating an immense archive that could continue to implicate those engaged in all of its violence. But such efforts were not always done nefariously. Rather, in this case, the burning was intended to foster the logic of emancipation, and to not look back. Commissions were set up to gather all known records, and to "proceed to immediately burn and destroy them, in the municipal warehouse of the capital city, in whatever way is deemed most

convenient to the commission"—as the decree put it (Barbosa, quoted in Aidoo 2018: 12). Aidoo (2018: 12) writes of this now ominous creation of silence in the name of progress, "The records were so extensive that it took several years to destroy them." For the case at hand, see http://www.arquivoestado.sp.gov.br /revista_do_arquivo/05/artigo_11.php.

12. In the 2020 elections, Erundina ran for "vice mayor" of São Paulo alongside Guilherme Boulos for mayor, after years of being a federal representative.

CHAPTER 5. THE USEFULNESS OF CAPRICIOUS KNOWLEDGE

1. Centered on gold mining, Mariana was the first capital of Minas Gerais and a place of historical, religious, and political significance. As the town grew, it became central to efforts to revolt, such as the Inconfidência Mineira, a 1789 secessionist effort inspired by the American Revolution. The leader, a man nicknamed "Tiradentes," was publicly hanged and had his body torn to pieces, which were then displayed in Mariana and elsewhere. In 2015 the tailings pond of a mine jointly owned by a Brazilian company, Vale, and a British company, BHP Billiton, burst, releasing toxic sludge through two towns and killing at least nineteen.

2. A copy of the document is available at http://www.arqanalagoa.ufscar.br /pdf/recortes/R07227.pdf.

3. That his burial was separate made his identification easier, owing to obvious known features like his lack of front teeth. See Silva (2017).

4. Though it was widely celebrated, the commission had much of its reach circumscribed by military influences, channelled through the Amnesty Law signed at the end of the dictatorship.

5. For more details, see http://www.mpf.mp.br/sp/sala-de-imprensa/docs /denuncia-harry-shibata/view.

6. The rights of the dead, and the expansion of citizenship toward the dead and disappeared are long-standing debates, that while "philosophically unworkable" (Rosenblatt 2010: 921) are vital to the ongoing struggle for everyday justice. Also see Bonner (2021).

7. For reflections on the need for cadavers in medical study in São Paulo, see https://piaui.folha.uol.com.br/materia/aula-de-anatomia/.

8. Juquery has a difficult history, being the subject of many calls for investigation and inquiry. See https://www1.folha.uol.com.br/fsp/cotidian/ff25099813.htm.

9. This has included appeals to the public, and awareness-raising campaigns for body donation. https://jornal.usp.br/atualidades/faculdade-de-medicina -aceita-doacao-de-corpos-para-pesquisas/.

10. See Governo do Estado de Sao Paulo, Secretaria de Estatda de Saude, "Doação de órgãos e tecidos tem o melhor ano da história em SP," http://www

.saude.sp.gov.br/ses/noticias/2007/janeiro/doacao-de-orgaos-e-tecidos-tem-o
-melhor-ano-da-historia-em-sp.

11. More background and discussion of this case is available at http://g1.globo
.com/São-paulo/noticia/2016/06/familia-doa-orgaos-de-jovem-morto-apos
-perseguicao-policial-em-sp.html.

12. Record of the motion to create a law: https://www.camara.leg.br/proposicoes
Web/prop_mostrarintegra?codteor=1710238&filename=PL+727/2019.

13. Record of the motion to create a law: https://www.camara.leg.br/proposicoes
Web/prop_mostrarintegra?codteor=1710240&filename=PL+729/2019.

14. In a deeply historical logic, police violence has long been justified by the
ends. Until just recently, victims of police violence were legally categorized not as
victims, but as protagonists whose supposedly active role in resisting arrest justi-
fies the immediate and logical response—death. In varying ways, such a set of justifications are both legally codified and discursively constructed, leaving the dead
or the violated without an ability to contest their legal condition as guilty. This logic
of guilt in victimization, where the real victim of violence is constructed as the protagonist of the event, is described similarly by Aidoo (2018). Here sexual violence
under slavery was constructed as caused by slaves themselves who did not decline
to participate in the violent interaction. The act of being sexually violated, without
contesting the act, implicated the victim as the active agent causing the violence.

15. Ten different organs plus many different kinds of tissue can be extracted
and transplanted. Currently, these include kidneys, liver, lungs, heart, pancreas,
and intestines. As of 2014, in some countries, hands and faces have become
transplantable organs.

16. In his book *The Anti-Black City*, Jaime Alves (2018) describes parts of this
crucial movement. For the city of Salvador, see Christen Smith's *Afro-Paradise*
(2016a).

17. See discussion at: https://www.cartamaior.com.br/?/Editoria/Direitos
-Humanos/Cadaver-negro-estudante-de-medicina-branco/5/35926.

CHAPTER 6. THE DISAPPEARABLE SUBJECT

1. After he was eventually imprisoned and escaped, then imprisoned and
released in 2012, Cabo Bruno was assassinated outside his home within days of
release. The killers were never found.

2. This "deprivation scheme" is currently the subject of a class action lawsuit
being advanced by the Southern Poverty Law Center. Now at the appeal stage,
the lawsuit argues that the for-profit detention company CoreCivic "threatens
detained immigrants who refuse to work with serious harm, including deprivation of privacy and safety." Ongoing case files are accessible at: https://www
.clearinghouse.net/detail.php?id=16613.

3. Kevin Lewis O'Neill (2012b) describes the religious valences of this project, where work and dedication to employment is the means of both moral and economic rebirth.

4. This kind of regime is legible at scales, and in historical scripts, such that efforts to change regimes of containment should not seek a return to previous state moments but a move toward abolition. See, for example, Tansel et al. (2021).

5. For an accessible and effective discussion, see: Gordon's (1999) interview with Davis.

6. Among others, this includes work from across the region, including Salvatore and Aguirre (2010); Garces (2010); Lemgruber and Paiva (2010); Drybread (2016); Alves (2016); Godoi (2016); Fontes and O'Neill (2019); Weegels (2016); Darke, Garces, Duno-Gottberg and Antillano (2020).

7. I discuss this logic at length in *The Killing Consensus*. For an example, on pages 29–30, "According to bureaucratic practice, a police killing is immediately categorized as 'resisting arrest followed by death,' more colloquially known as '*resistências*.' Under this rubric there is a presumption of guilt for the person shot, and a presumption of innocence for the officer who shot them. Homicide detectives are tasked with investigating these killings and arbitrating whether these presumptions are 'appropriate.' When not appropriate, homicide detectives must overturn these categories—a *resistência* becomes a homicide and the offending police are arrested."

8. For more vital work on understanding the "*bandido*" as a social and political category, see Misse (2010).

CHAPTER 7. FROM DISAPPEARANCE, PRESENCE

1. This ongoing effort to invest, and to stimulate the economy, has consistently focused on security—and especially on prisons and one-off infrastructure. See https://São-paulo.estadao.com.br/noticias/geral,governo-alckmin-vai-retomar -projeto-de-construir-46-presidios-no-interior-imp-,662108.

2. Image available at: https://veja.abril.com.br/wp-content/uploads/2016/12 /massacre-carandiru-20161001-004.jpg?quality=70&strip=all.

3. Image available at: https://acervo.folha.com.br/leitor.do?numero=20828& anchor=6043222&origem=busca&originURL=.

4. The ongoing construction of memory, and its reinvention, is of constitutive importance for codifying identity in what can be highly disassociated social groups. See Biondi and Marques (2010).

5. As I document (2009), the PCC's spread in the early 1990s was further catalyzed by a public policy of "dispersion," which sought to separate the various early-days leaders of the organization from each other. The result was to the contrary; it helped to spread the organization throughout the prison populace in new prisons.

6. In *Sharing This Walk: An Ethnography of the PCC in Brazil*, Karina Biondi (2016) describes this process and how it matters in great depth, associating it with the very logic of PCC ordering.

7. See, for example: de Jesus Rodrigues (2019); Nunes, M. (2017); Araújo (2018).

8. He was forced to resign for a statement that has since become banal, under the current president. Quote available at https://blogs.oglobo.globo.com /panorama-politico/post/sobre-chacina-secretario-de-temer-diz-que-tinha-era -que-matar-mais.html.

9. Quote available at https://blogs.oglobo.globo.com/panorama-politico/post /sobre-chacina-secretario-de-temer-diz-que-tinha-era-que-matar-mais.html.

10. Statistics compiled at https://www.justica.gov.br/news/mj-divulgara-novo -relatorio-do-infopen-nesta-terca-feira/relatorio-depen-verSão-web.pdf.

11. For a brief summary, see https://oglobo.globo.com/brasil/plano-de-dilma -para-presidios-cria-28-das-vagas-prometidas-20784569.

12. This *salve* was originally published in Manso and Dias (2018). Emphasis in the original. The original text is as follows:

Salve Da Conscientização
Comunicado de conscientização do resumo do disciplinar.
Na data do 05/08/2014 saudamos a todos com um forte abraço

O resumo disciplinar vem através deste comunicado, deixar todos cientes daimportância da participação de cada um com os trabalhos da organização. Temos objectivos constantes com as verbas arrecadadas através destes trabalhos, onde este dinheiro é revertido em benefícios para os menos favorecidos e aqueles que se encontram nas trancas federais e estaduais. Hoje a organização trabalha em forma de fortalecer irmãos e companheiros que somam constantemente, onde fazemos uma seleção visando fortalecer financeiramente, como gravatas, passagens para visita, cesta básica, agasalhos, assistência médica, casas de apoio, medicamentos e velórios daqueles que venham a perder a vida.tudo isso só ocorre se os irmãos e companheiros agirem de forma pontual e responsável com os pagamentos das rf, cebola, 100%, bob. Em fim todos os trabalhos dos progressos da organização dentro e for a do sistema.

Muitas vezes nos deparamos com irmãos cobrando: onde está o apoio? Mas nós perguntamos será que esses irmãos e os nossos companheiros estão levando para a geral do estado sua dificuldade. A geral do estado tem elaborado relatórios e arremessado para o resumo fazendo pedido ou apresentado projetos?

Somos uma corrente onde os irmãos fortalecem a organização participando dos trabalhos com dedicação e responsabilidade e a organização fortalece os necessitados através da precisão de cada um. Hoje nos deparamos com vários estados carentes e é de extema importância que os integrantes da organização dentro do estado analisem a necessidade dos companheiros e dos irmãos para que possamos fortalecer, frisando sempre que este fortalecimento é fruto dos trabalhos da organização.

Esse comunicado deve ser passado em mãos para que todos leiam e reflitam na *importância da evolução disciplinar e financeira* da organização.

No mais um forte abraço a todos

OBS: qualquer dúvida podem buscar a sintonia para esclarecimentos.
ASSINADO RESUMO DA DISCIPLINAR

CHAPTER 8. MUTED MARTYRDOM

1. I discuss this case at length in a previous work (2015) *The Killing Consensus: Police, Organized Crime and the Regulation of Life and Death in Urban Brazil*, chapters 2 and 6.

2. Sven Beckert (2015) documents this triangle in *Empire of Cotton: A New History of Global Capitalism*. See also Williams (1973).

3. Britt's work details the historic and contested relationship between race, space, and urban planning, especially as early twentieth-century urban renewal sought to write over the spaces of Black identity and incipient freedom in post-emancipation São Paulo. As a supposedly progressive project, urban planners demolished key Black churches and sites of the early Black movement in the city, under guises of modernity and as a way to foster new immigrant populations, such as the Japanese, who are most associated with the Liberadade neighborhood today.

4. Experiences with death and its banality in Brazil have many variations, and historical moments, including those described by Nancy Scheper-Hughes (1993). Responses to such a condition, particularly as it advances through acute modes of containment in the current historical moment, stand in some contrast to the ways that death has been made mundane, both by the Brazilian state, whether in "public health" or "public security," and by those who suffer it.

5. For a news release describing this incident, see https://www.hnt.com.br/imprime.php?cid=105927&sid=206.

6. As Amira Mittermaier (2015) explores, when Tunisian fruit seller Mohammed Bouazizi set himself alight in Algeria in 2010 after having his cart of goods destroyed by police, his suicide was an act of frustration and an amorphous ethical outcry that sparked protests and political revolutions across the Middle East and North Africa. See also Allen (2009).

CHAPTER 9. MAKE LIVE, MAKE DISAPPEAR

1. The PCC is a highly bureaucratized organization with expansive spatial coverage that transcends prison walls. Their use of highly regimented documentation, which includes providing templates of how to keep proper records, has created a system where, in the absence of obvious trust in a criminal world, membership, personal histories and trustworthiness can be established—and consulted by telephone. For more, see: Lessing and Denyer Willis (2019).

2. This selection of the cases omits very similar or duplicate entries. They include all relevant cases that relate different rationales for disappearance, whether directly related to nonpayment or flight from the organization for other reasons, such as suspicion of having broken the rules.

3. "O mesmo foi covardemente assassinado por dois indivíduos desconheci-dos num palio."

4. Lazzarato's work on debt and capital in the post-Fordist economy argues that this means a hyper-subjectification of the individual. Where it is made to seem that "you can do anything" and "you are your own boss," such an emphasis on the radical self and autonomous personal advancement means an accumulation of debt. For Lazzarato, such a configuration mediates relations between individuals, taking on (in this case) a fragmented disciplinary function that forces individuals into a cog-like existence—whether that existence is a 9–5 job or as a fee-paying member of a group like the PCC.

5. The PCC's written codification of its identity, as its emergence from an acute terrain of violence, is not anomalous. Indeed, it echoes many of the different "criminal constitutions" that dot the world in contemporary times, and historically. These constitutions, which vary in their sophistication, durability and oral or written nature, have a remarkable historical staying power, reaching from pirates in the seventeenth-century Atlantic—at least 25–30 percent of whom were Black, on average—to gangs in California, Polish prisoners, and Sicilian *mafiosi*.

6. I discuss this case, which is pseudonymized, in "Before the Body Count: Homicide Statistics and Everyday Security in Latin America" Denyer Willis (2017).

7. https://gauchazh.clicrbs.com.br/seguranca/noticia/2019/08/cemiterio-clandestino-em-porto-alegre-tem-cem-corpos-diz-mp-cjzn6y1jio55wo1paavurnkfj.html.

8. https://noticias.r7.com/cidades/policia-encontra-cemiterio-clandestino-usado-por-grupo-de-exterminio-em-goias-31052013.

9. http://g1.globo.com/rs/rio-grande-do-sul/noticia/2013/05/policia-investiga-suposto-cemiterio-clandestino-atras-de-presidio-no-rs.html.

10. https://epoca.globo.com/tempo/noticia/2016/07/numero-de-corpos-desovados-em-São-paulo-sobe-191.html.

CHAPTER 10. "I JUST WANT TO LIVE"

1. Data from the TRAC Immigration database at Syracuse University, www.trac.syr.edu.

2. Official news release, Microsoft, https://news.microsoft.com/pt-br/maes-da-se-microsoft-parceria-aplicativo-inteligencia-artificial-localizar-desaparecidos/.

3. For a basic description of how Microsoft uses Azure for militarized government agencies like ICE, see Microsoft's development blog: https://devblogs.microsoft.com/azuregov/federal-agencies-continue-to-advance-capabilities-with-azure-government/.

4. The School of the Americas, renamed the Western Hemispheric Institute for Security Cooperation in 2006, is a US government facility established in

1946 to train members of Latin American militaries. Currently located in Fort Benning, Georgia, its own internal documents, such as training manuals, have shown that their training includes specific attention to counter-subversive tactics, including torture and disappearance. In her ethnography of the School of the Americas, Lesley Gill (2006) richly describes how the institution sits behind a region-wide regime of violence, manifested through secretive campaigns and military legitimization. In her opening prologue, and throughout, disappearance figures centrally, including in descriptions of SOA-trained military figures tied to people like Amparo Tordecilla in Colombia, who "disappeared, kidnapped by a group of men who approached her in a taxi. Her cadaver and those of others were later discovered in a clandestine cemetery on the outskirts of the city" (xvi). Fort Benning is thirty-nine miles from Stewart Detention Center in Lumpkin, Georgia.

References

Abreu, J. C. de. (1998). *Capítulos de história colonial (1500–1800) e os caminhos antigos e o povoamento do Brasil.* Brasília: Editora Universidade de Brasília). Retrieved from https://www2.senado.leg.br/bdsf/bitstream/handle/id/1022/201089.pdf?sequence=4.

Adams, B., and Byrd, J. (2014). *Commingled Human Remains: Methods in Recovery, Analysis, and Identification.* Amsterdam: Academic Press.

Aidoo, L. (2018). *Slavery Unseen: Sex, Power, and Violence in Brazilian History.* Durham, NC: Duke University Press.

Alencastro, L. F. (2018). *The Trade in the Living: The Formation of Brazil in the South Atlantic.* Albany, NY: SUNY Press

Allen, L. A. (2009). "Martyr Bodies in the Media: Human Rights, Aesthetics, and the Politics of Immediation in the Palestinian Intifada." *American Ethnologist,* 36(1): 161–80.

Alves, J. A. (2014). "Neither Humans nor Rights: Some Notes on the Double Negation of Black Life in Brazil." *Journal of Black Studies,* 45(2): 143–62.

———. (2016). "Blood in Reasoning: State Violence, Contested Territories and Black Criminal Agency in Urban Brazil." *Journal of Latin American Studies,* 48(1): 61–87.

———. (2018) *The Anti-Black City: Police Terror and Black Urban Life in Brazil.* Minneapolis: University of Minnesota Press.

——. (2019). "Refusing to Be Governed: Urban Policing, Gang Violence, and the Politics of Evilness in an Afro-Colombian Shantytown." *PoLAR: Political and Legal Anthropology Review*, 42(1): 21–36.

Alves, J. C. S. (2003). *Dos barões ao extermínio: Uma história da violência na Baixada Fluminense.* Rio de Janeiro: Associação de Professores e Pesquisadores de História, CAPPH-CLIO.

——. (2007). "Assassinos no poder: Ação de grupos de extermínio dá lucro à contravenção e favorece a ascensão de políticos ligados ao crime na Baixada Fluminense." *Revista de Historia da Biblioteca Nacional*, 25: 36–9.

Araújo, F. (2012). "Das consequências da 'arte' macabra de fazer desaparecer corpos: Violência, sofrimento e política entre familiares de vítima de desaparecimento forçado." ["On the consequences of the macabre 'art' of making bodies disappear: Violence, suffering and politics among families of victims of forced disappearance"]. Tese de doutorado [doctoral dissertation], Programa de Pós-Graduação em Antropologia e Sociologia, UFRJ.

——. (2018). De perto e de dentro: Globalização, violência e o poder das facções criminosas no Brasil. Doctoral dissertation, Instituto Superior de Ciências Sociais e Políticas.

Arditti, R. (1999). *Searching for Life: The Grandmothers of the Plaza de Mayo and the Disappeared Children of Argentina.* Berkeley: University of California Press.

Arns, P. E. (1985). *Brasil: Nunca mais.* São Paulo: Vozes.

Bales, K., and Mayblin, L. (2018). "Unfree Labor in Immigration Detention: Exploitation and Coercion of a Captive Immigrant Workforce." *Economy and Society*, 47(2): 191–213.

Bank, L. J. (1990). "The Making of the Qwaqwa 'Mafia'? Patronage and Protection in the Migrant Taxi Business." *African Studies*, 49(1): 71–93.

Beckert, S. (2015). *Empire of Cotton: A New History of Global Capitalism.* London: Penguin.

Bernstein, N. (2015). "Unearthing the Secrets of New York's Mass Graves." *New York Times.* At: http://www.nytimes.com/interactive/2016/05/15/nyregion/new-york-mass-graves-hart-island.html (last accessed July 30, 2017).

Berry, D. R. (2017). *The Price for Their Pound of Flesh: The Value of the Enslaved, from Womb to Grave, in the Building of a Nation.* Boston: Beacon Press.

Biondi, K. (2016). *Sharing This Walk: An Ethnography of Prison Life and the PCC in Brazil.* Chapel Hill: University of North Carolina Press.

Biondi, K., and Marques, A. (2010). "Memória e historicidade em dois 'comandos' prisionais." *Lua Nova: Revista de Cultura e Política*, 79: 39–70.

Blakely, R., and Harrington, J., eds. (1997). *Bones in the Basement: Post-Mortem Racism in Nineteenth-Century Medical Education.* Washington, DC: Smithsonian Institution Press.

Bloch, M., and Parry, J., eds. (1982). *Death and the Regeneration of Life.* Cambridge: Cambridge University Press.

Bobadilla, K. (n.d.). *A ditadura militar em São Paulo: O caso da ossadas dos desaparecidos de Perus.* At: https://www.fespsp.org.br/seminarios/anais3 /KassiaBobadilla.pdf (last accessed January 13, 2022).

Bonefeld, W. (2010). "Free Economy and the Strong State: Some Notes on the State." *Capital and Class*, 34(1): 15–24.

Bonner, M. (2021). "Reclaiming Citizenship from Police Violence." *Citizenship Studies*, 25(3): 317–32.

Britt, A. (forthcoming). "Spatial Projects of Forgetting: Razing the Remedies Church and Museum to the Enslaved in São Paulo's 'Black Zone,' 1930s–'40s." *Journal of Latin American Studies.*

Brown, V. (2008). *The Reaper's Garden: Death and Power in the World of Atlantic Slavery.* Cambridge, MA: Harvard University Press.

Brysk, A. (1994). "The Politics of Measurement: The Contested Count of the Disappeared in Argentina." *Human Rights Quarterly*, 16: 676.

Bueno, S., and Denyer Willis, G. (2019). "The Exceptional Prison." *Public Culture*, 31(3): 645–63.

Butler, J. (2021). "Bodies That Still Matter." In Halsema, A., Kwastek, K. and Oever, R, eds. (2021). *Bodies That Still Matter* (pp. 177–94). Amsterdam: Amsterdam University Press.

Carneiro, E., and Gennari, P. (2016). "O Ministério Público em busca de pessoas desaparecidas: Desaparecimentos forçados por omissão do Estado." *Revista Liberdades*, 22: 39–55.

Carter, J. H. (2014). "Gothic Sovereignty: Gangs and Criminal Community in a Honduran Prison." *South Atlantic Quarterly*, 113(3): 475–502.

Castells, M. (1989). *The Informational City: Information Technology, Economic Restructuring and the Urban-Regional Process.* Oxford: Basil Blackwell.

Chamayou, G. (2012). *Manhunts: A Philosophical History.* Princeton, NJ: Princeton University Press.

Chambouleyron, R. (2005). "Opulência e miséria na Amazônia seiscentista." *Raízes da Amazônia*, 1(1): 105–24.

Chazkel, A. (2020). "Toward a History of Rights in the City at Night: Making and Breaking the Nightly Curfew in Nineteenth-Century Rio de Janeiro." *Comparative Studies in Society and History*, 62(1): 106–34.

Comaty, L. (2019). *Post-conflict Transition in Lebanon: The Disappeared of the Civil War.* London: Routledge.

Comissão de Verdade do Rio. (2015). *Relatório.* Retrieved from: http://www .memoriasreveladas.gov.br/administrator/components/com_simplefile manager/uploads/Rio/CEV-Rio-Relatorio-Final.pdf.

Costa, M. I. S. (2017). "Política de saúde mental política de segurança: Manicô-mio judíciario, entre o hospital e a prisão." *Revista do Arquivo do Estado*, 2(5): 144–60.

Coupland, R., and Cordner, S. (2003). "People Missing as a Result of Armed Conflict: Standards and Guidelines Are Needed for All, Including Health Professionals." *BMJ*, 326: 943.

Crossland, Z. (2000). "Buried Lives: Forensic Archaeology and the Disappeared in Argentina." *Archaeological Dialogues*, 7(2): 146–59.

Dantas, M. L. R. (2004). "'For the Benefit of the Common Good': Regiments of Caçadores do Mato in Minas Gerais, Brazil." *Journal of Colonialism and Colonial History*, 5(2).

Darke, S., Garces, C., Duno-Gottberg, L., and Antillano, A. (2020). *Carceral Communities in Latin America: Troubling Prison Worlds in the 21st Century*. Cham, Switzerland: Palgrave-Springer Nature.

Davis, D. (2016). "'The Bone Collectors' Comments for Sorrow as Artifact: Black Radical Mothering in Times of Terror." *Transforming Anthropology*, 24(1): 8–16.

de Jesus Rodrigues, F. (2019). "Mercados ilícitos, ambivalências e agressividade: Condições estatais e mercantis de um circuito de bailes de reggae em 'periferias' de Maceió, AL1." *Contemporânea*, 9(1): 199–227.

De León, J. (2015). *The Land of Open Graves: Living and Dying on the Migrant Trail*. Oakland: University of California Press.

Denyer Willis, G (2021). "Mundane Disappearance: The Politics of Letting Disappear in Brazil." *Economy and Society*, 50(2): 297–321.

——. (2019). "Life and Death Insurance." *SSRC Items*. Retrieved from: https://items.ssrc.org/insights/death-insurance-the-pcc-and-the-protection-of-life-in-the-twilight/.

——. (2018). "The Potter's Field." *Comparative Studies in Society and History*, 60(3): 539–68.

——. (2017). "Before the Body Count: Homicide Statistics and Everyday Security in Latin America." *Journal of Latin American Studies*, 49(1): 29–54.

——. (2015). *The Killing Consensus: Police, Organized Crime and the Regulation of Life and Death in Urban Brazil*. Oakland: University of California Press.

——. (2009). "Deadly Symbiosis? The PCC, the State and the Institutionalization of Violence in São Paulo." In Rodgers, D., and Jones, G. A. (2009). *Youth Violence in Latin America*. New York: Palgrave, 167–81.

Dias, C. N., and Darke, S. (2016). "From Dispersed to Monopolized Violence: Expansion and Consolidation of the Primeiro Comando da Capital's Hegemony in São Paulo's Prisons." *Crime, Law and Social Change*, 65(3): 213–25.

DiGirolamo, V. (2002). "Newsboy Funerals: Tales of Sorrow and Solidarity in Urban America." *Journal of Social History*, 36(1): 5–30.

dos Santos Gomes, F. (2002). "A 'Safe Haven': Runaway Slaves, Mocambos, and Borders in Colonial Amazonia, Brazil." *Hispanic American Historical Review*, 82(3): 469–98.

Drexler, E. F., Wagner, S., and Sanford, V. (2010). *Transitional Justice: Global Mechanisms and Local Realities after Genocide and Mass Violence*. New Brunswick, NJ: Rutgers University Press.

Drybread, K. (2016). "Documents of Indiscipline and Indifference: The Violence of Bureaucracy in a Brazilian Juvenile Prison." *American Ethnologist*, 43(3): 411–23.

Dutra, S. (2018). "Heroes of the Sertão: The Bandeirantes as a Symbolic Category for the Study of Brazilian West Colonization." *Territórios e Fronteiras*, 11(1): 60–76.

Economist. (2018). "The Life Insurance Industry Needs New Vigour." May 18. Retrieved from: https://www.economist.com/finance-and-economics/2018 /05/17/the-life-insurance-industry-is-in-need-of-new-vigour.

Edkins, J. (2011). *Missing: Persons and Politics*. Ithaca, NY: Cornell University Press.

Ermakoff, I. (2014). "Exceptional Cases: Epistemic Contributions and Normative Expectations." *European Journal of Sociology/Archives Européennes de Sociologie*, 55(2): 223–43.

Ernst, F. (2019). *The Life and Death of a Mexican Hitman*. Crisis Group International. Retrieved from: https://www.crisisgroup.org/latin-america-caribbean /mexico/life-and-death-mexican-hitman?fbclid=IwAR0_gYssLbOV-J_4Rjah TDZROvOsl31YNFlTj19bPouXPMPqUGKqJh109Ts.

Feltran, G. (2018). *Irmãos: Uma história do PCC*. São Paulo: Editora Companhia das Letras.

Ferrándiz, F., and Robben, A. (2015). *Necropolitics: Mass Graves and Exhumations in the Age of Human Rights*. Philadelphia: University of Pennsylvania Press.

———. (2019). "Unburials, Generals, and Phantom Militarism: Engaging with the Spanish Civil War Legacy." *Current Anthropology*, 60(S19): S62–S76.

———. (2013). "Exhuming the Defeated: Civil War Mass Graves in 21st-Century Spain. *American Ethnologist*, 40(1): 38–54.

Filippucci, P., Fontein, J., Harries, J., and Krmpotich, C. (2012). "Encountering the Past: Unearthing Remnants of Humans in Archaeology and Anthropology." *Archaeology and Anthropology: Past, Present and Future*, 48: 197.

Fischer, B. (2004). "Quase pretos de táo pobres? Race and Social Discrimination in Rio de Janeiro's Twentieth-Century Criminal Courts." *Latin American Research Review*, 39(1): 31–59.

———. (2008). *A Poverty of Rights: Citizenship and Inequality in Twentieth-Century Rio de Janeiro*. Stanford, CA: Stanford University Press.

——. (2014). "The Red Menace Reconsidered: A Forgotten History of Communist Mobilization in Rio de Janeiro's Favelas, 1945–1964." *Hispanic American Historical Review*, 94(1): 1–33.

Fontes, A., and O'Neill, K. (2019). "La visita: Prisons and Survival in Guatemala." *Journal of Latin American Studies*, 51(1): 85–107.

Foucault, M. "Of Other Spaces: Utopias and Heterotopias. *Architecture/ Mouvement/ Continuité*. Accessed December 10, 2017, at: http://web.mit.edu /allanmc/www/foucault1.pdf.

Freitas, J. (1994). "Slavery and Social Life: Attempts to Reduce Free People to Slavery in the Sertão Mineiro, Brazil, 1850–1871." *Journal of Latin American Studies*, 26(3): 597–619

Garces, C. (2010). "The Cross Politics of Ecuador's Penal State." *Cultural Anthropology*, 25(3): 459–96.

Geschiere, P., and Nyamnjoh, F. B. (2000). "Capitalism and Autochthony: The Seesaw of Mobility and Belonging." *Public Culture*, 12(2): 423–52.

Gill, L. (2006). *The School of the Americas: Military Training and Political Violence in the Americas*. Durham, NC: Duke University Press.

Gilmore, R. W. (2007). *Golden Gulag: Prisons, Surplus, Crisis, and Opposition in Globalizing California*. Berkeley: University of California Press.

Godoi, R. (2016). "Intimacy and Power: Body Searches and Intimate Visits in the Prison System of São Paulo, Brazil." *Champ Pénal/Penal Field*, 13.

Godoy, M. (2014). *Casa da vovó: Uma biografia do DOI-Codi (1969–1991), o centro de dsequestro, tortura e morte da ditadura militar*. São Paulo: Alameda.

Golash-Boza, T. (2016). "Racialized and Gendered Mass Deportation and the Crisis of Capitalism." *Journal of World-Systems Research*, 22(1): 38–44.

Goldstein, D. M. (2016). *Owners of the Sidewalk: Security and Survival in the Informal City*. Durham, NC: Duke University Press, 2016.

Gordon, A. F. (1999). "Globalism and the Prison Industrial Complex: An Interview with Angela Davis." *Race & Class*, 40(2–3), 145–57.

Grandin, G. (2011). *The Last Colonial Massacre: Latin America in the Cold War*. Chicago: University of Chicago Press.

Grinberg, L. T., de Lucena Ferretti, R. E., Farfel, J. M., Leite, R., Pasqualucci, C. A., Rosemberg, S., . . . and Brazilian Aging Brain Study Group. (2007). "Brain Bank of the Brazilian Aging Brain Study Group: A Milestone Reached and More Than 1,600 Collected Brains." *Cell and Tissue Banking*, 8(2): 151–62.

Hattori, M. L., de Abreu, R., Tauhyl, S. A. P. M., and Alberto, L. A. (2014). "O caminho burocrático da morte e a máquina de fazer desaparecer: Propostas de análise da documentação do Instituto Médico Legal-SP para antropologia forense." *Revista do Arquivo*, 2(6): 1–21.

Hurren, E. (2004). "A Pauper Dead-House: The Expansion of the Cambridge Anatomical Teaching School under the Late-Victorian Poor Law, 1870–1914." *Medical History*, 48(1): 69–94.

Jamieson, R. (1995). "Material Culture and Social Death: African-American Burial Practices." *Historical Archaeology*, 29(4): 39–58.

Karasch, M. C. (1987). *Slave Life in Rio de Janeiro, 1808–1850*. Princeton, NJ: Princeton University Press.

Kovras, I. (2013). "Explaining Prolonged Silences in Transitional Justice: The Disappeared in Cyprus and Spain." *Comparative Political Studies*, 46(6): 730–56.

Kovras, I., and Robins, S. (2016). "Death as the Border: Managing Missing Migrants and Unidentified Bodies at the EU's Mediterranean Frontier." *Political Geography*, 55: 40–49.

Laqueur, T. (1983). "Bodies, Death, and Pauper Funerals." *Representations*, 1: 109–31.

———. (2016). *The Work of the Dead: A Cultural History of Mortal Remains*. Princeton, NJ: Princeton University Press.

Lemgruber, J., and Paiva, A. (2010). *A dona das chaves: Uma mulher no comando das prisões do Rio de Janeiro*. Rio de Janeiro: Editora Record.

Lessing, B., and Denyer Willis, G. (2019). "Legitimacy in Criminal Governance: Regulating a Drug Empire from Behind Bars." *American Political Science Review*, 113(2): 584–606.

Lomnitz, C. (2019). "The Ethos and Telos of Michoacán's Knights Templar." *Representations*, 147(1): 96–123.

Manso, B. P., and Dias, C. N. (2018). *A guerra: A ascensão do PCC e o mundo do crime no Brasil*. São Paulo: Editora Todavia SA.

Marighella, C. (1969). *Mini-Manual of the Urban Guerilla*. Retrieved from: https://www.marxists.org/archive/marighella-carlos/1969/06/minimanual -urban-guerrilla/index.htm.

Mbembe, J-A. (2017). *Critique of Black Reason*. Durham, NC: Duke University Press.

Mbembe, J-A., and Meintjes, L. (trans.). (2003). "Necropolitics." *Public Culture*, 15(1): 11–40.

Medeiros, F. (2016). *Matar o morto: Uma etnografia do Instituto Médico Legal do Rio de Janeiro*. Rio de Janeiro: EDUFF.

Miki, Y. (2012). "Fleeing into Slavery: The Insurgent Geographies of Brazilian Quilombolas (Maroons), 1880–1881." *The Americas*, 68(4): 495–528.

Misse, M. (2010). "Crime, sujeito e sujeição criminal: Aspectos de uma contribuição analítica sobre a categoria 'bandido'." *Lua Nova*, 79: 15–38.

Mittermaier, A. (2015). "Death and Martyrdom in the Arab Uprisings: An Introduction." *Journal of Anthropology*, 80(5): 583–604.

Nascimento, A. (2002). *O quilombismo: Documentos de uma militância pan-africanista*. Brasília: Fundação Cultural Palmares.

Navaro, Y. (2020). "The Aftermath of Mass Violence: A Negative Methodology." *Annual Review of Anthropology*, 49: 161–73.

Nunes, M. (2017). "Dinâmicas transfronteiriças e o avanço da violência na fronteira sul-mato-grossense." Repositorio do Conhecimento do IPEA. http://repositorio.ipea.gov.br/handle/11058/7916.

Nuzzi, V. (2015). "Última etapa para as ossadas de Perus: Perto, talvez, da identificação." *Rede Brasil Atual.* At: http://www.redebrasilatual.com.br /cidadania/2015/02/ossadas-de-perus-9472.html (last accessed July 29, 2017).

O'Neill, K. L. (2012a). "There Is No More Room: Cemeteries, Personhood, and Bare Death." *Ethnography,* 13(4): 510–30.

———. (2012b). "The Soul of Security: Christianity, Corporatism, and Control in Postwar Guatemala." *Social Text,* 30(2): 21–42.

O'Rourke, D. (2007). "Mourning Becomes Eclectic: Death of Communal Practice in a Greek Cemetery." *American Ethnologist,* 34(2): 387–402.

Peake, S., and Lynch, O. (2016). "Victims of Irish Republican Paramilitary Violence: The Case of 'The Disappeared.'" *Terrorism and Political Violence,* 28(3): 452–72.

Pereira, T. A. Z. (2018). "The Rise of the Brazilian Cotton Trade in Britain during the Industrial Revolution." *Journal of Latin American Studies,* 50(4): 919–49.

Pires, T. R. D. O. (2018). "Estruturas intocadas: Racismo e ditadura no Rio de Janeiro." *Revista Direito e Práxis,* 9(2): 1054–79.

Povinelli, E. A. (2008). "The Child in the Broom Closet: States of Killing and Letting Die." *South Atlantic Quarterly,* 107(3): 509–30.

Prefeitura. n/d. *Falecidos IML/SVOC.* At: http://www.prefeitura.sp.gov.br /cidade/secretarias/obras/servico_funerario/falecidos/index.php?p=229658.

Reineke, R. (2016). "Los desaparecidos de La frontera (The disappeared on The border)." In: Rubio-Goldsmith, R., Fernández, C., Finch, J., and Masterson-Algar, A., eds. *Migrant Deaths in the Arizona Desert: La vida no vale nada,* 132–49. Tucson: University of Arizona Press.

Reis, J. J. (2003). *Death Is a Festival: Funeral Rites and Rebellion in Nineteenth-Century Brazil.* Chapel Hill: University of North Carolina Press.

Rezende, E. (n.d.). "O enigma dos cemitérios da cidade de São Paulo." At: http:// www.cemiteriosp.com.br/pdf/Enigma_cem_%20cidade_SP.pdf (last accessed July 29, 2017).

Roberts, R. (1990). *The Classic Slum: Salford Life in the First Quarter of the Century.* London: Penguin UK.

Robins, S. (2011). "Towards Victim-Centered Transitional Justice: Understanding the Needs of Families of the Disappeared in Postconflict Nepal." *International Journal of Transitional Justice,* 5(1): 75–98.

Rojas-Perez, I. (2017). *Mourning Remains: State Atrocity, Exhumations, and Governing the Disappeared in Peru's Postwar Andes.* Palo Alto, CA: Stanford University Press.

Rosas, G. (2019). "Necro-Subjection: On Borders, Asylum, and Making Dead to Let Live." *Theory and Event*, 22(2): 303–24.

Rosenblatt, A. (2015). *Digging for the Disappeared: Forensic Science after Atrocity*. Palo Alto, CA: Stanford University Press.

———. (2010). "International Forensic Investigations and the Human Rights of the Dead." *Human Rights Quarterly* 32(4): 921–50.

Roy, A. (2019). How to Think about Empire. *Boston Review*. Retrieved from: http://bostonreview.net/literature-culture-global-justice/arundhati-roy-avni -sejpal-challenging-"post-"-postcolonialism.

Rubin, J. S. (2018). "How Francisco Franco Governs from Beyond the Grave: An Infrastructural Approach to Memory Politics in Contemporary Spain." *American Ethnologist*, 45(2), 214–27.

Salla, F. (2007). "De Montoro a Lembo: As políticas penitenciárias em São Paulo." *Revista Brasileira de Segurança Pública*, 1(1): 72–90.

Salvatore, R. D., and Aguirre, C., eds. (2010). *The Birth of the Penitentiary in Latin America: Essays on Criminology, Prison Reform, and Social Control, 1830–1940*. Austin: University of Texas Press.

Samet, R. (2019). "The Subject of Wrongs: Crime, Populism, and Venezuela's Punitive Turn." *Cultural Anthropology*, 34(2): 272–98.

Sánchez-Jankowski, M. (1991). *Islands in the Street: Gangs and American Urban Society*. Berkeley: University of California Press.

Sanford, V. (2003). *Buried Secrets: Truth and Human Rights in Guatemala*. New York: Palgrave Macmillan.

Sappol, M. (2002). *A Traffic of Dead Bodies: Anatomy and Embodied Social Identity in Nineteenth-Century America*. Princeton, NJ: Princeton University Press.

Scheper-Hughes, N. (1993). *Death without Weeping: The Violence of Everyday Life in Brazil*. Berkeley: University of California Press.

———. (2001). "Commodity Fetishism in Organs Trafficking." *Body and Society*, 7(2–3): 31–62.

Schmitt, C. (2010). *Political Theology*. Chicago: University of Chicago Press.

Schwartz, S. B. (1996). *Slaves, Peasants, and Rebels: Reconsidering Brazilian Slavery*. Chicago: University of Illinois Press.

Schwartz-Marin, E., and Cruz-Santiago, A. (2016). "Pure Corpses, Dangerous Citizens: Transgressing the Boundaries between Experts and Mourners in the Search for the Disappeared in Mexico." *Social Research: An International Quarterly*, 83(2): 483–510.

Sikkink, K., and Marchesi, B. (2015). "Nothing but the Truth." *Foreign Affairs*. Retrieved from: https://www.foreignaffairs.com/articles/south-america/2015 -02-26/nothing-truth.

Silva, G. S. da (2017). "Para além da repressão e da resistência: Uma releitura dos lugares de memória da ditadura civil-militar no Brasil." *Epígrafe*, 4(4): 125–48.

Smith, C. A. (2016a). *Afro-Paradise: Blackness, Violence and Performance in Brazil.* Urbana: University of Illinois Press.

———. (2016b). "Facing the Dragon: Black Mothering, Sequelae, and Gendered Necropolitics in the Americas." *Transforming Anthropology,* 24(1): 31–48.

Smith, L. A. (2017). "The Missing, the Martyred and the Disappeared: Global Networks, Technical Intensification and the End of Human Rights Genetics." *Social Studies of Science,* 47(3): 398–416.

Smith, N. (1996). "Spaces of Vulnerability: The Space of Flows and the Politics of Scale." *Critique of anthropology,* 16(1): 63–77.

Stevenson, L. (2012). "The Psychic Life of Biopolitics: Survival, Cooperation, and Inuit Community." *American Ethnologist,* 39(3): 592–613.

Stover, E., and Weinstein, H. M., eds. (2004). *My Neighbor, My Enemy: Justice and Community in the Aftermath of Mass Atrocity.* Cambridge: Cambridge University Press.

Strange, J. (2003). "Only a Pauper Whom Nobody Owns: Reassessing the Pauper Grave c. 1880–1914." *Past and Present,* 178: 148–75.

Tansel, C., Danewid, I., Axster, S., Wilcox, L., Goldstein, A., and Mahmoudi, M. (2021). "Colonial Lives of the Carceral Archipelago: Rethinking the Neo-liberal Security State." *International Political Sociology* 15(3): 415–39.

Tate, W. (2007). *Counting the Dead: The Culture and Politics of Human Rights Activism in Colombia.* Berkeley: University of California Press.

Tidball-Binz, M. (2012). "Global Forensic Science and the Search for the Dead and Missing from Armed Conflict: The Perspective of the International Committee of the Red Cross." In: Ubelaker, D. H., ed. *Forensic Science: Current Issues, Future Directions,* 337–65. Chichester, UK: Wiley.

Toulson, R. E. (2012). "The Anthropology of a Necessary Mistake: The Unsettled Dead and the Imagined State in Contemporary Singapore." In Chua, L., Cook, J., Long, N. and Wilson, L., eds. (2012). *Southeast Asian Perspectives on Power.* London: Routledge, 107–20.

Trouillot, M. R. (1995). *Silencing the Past: Power and the Production of History.* Boston: Beacon Press.

Tully, S. R. (1995). "A Painful Purgatory: Grief and the Nicaraguan Mothers of the Disappeared." *Social Science and Medicine,* 40(12): 1597–610.

Van Onselen, C. (2000). "Jewish Marginality in the Atlantic World: Organised Crime in the Era of the Great Migrations, 1880–1914." *South African Historical Journal,* 43(1): 96–137.

Veja. (2014). "Troca de tiros na Marginal Pinheiros termina com um morto." *Veja São Paulo,* May 21. http://vejasp.abril.com.br/materia/perseguicao -policial-interdita-marginal-pinheiros (last accessed July 29, 2017).

Verdery, K. (1999). *The Political Lives of Dead Bodies: Reburial and Postsocialist Change.* New York: Columbia University Press.

Wacquant, L. (2002). "Slavery to Mass Incarceration." *New Left Review,* 13: 41.

Wagner, S. E. (2015). "A Curious Trade: The Recovery and Repatriation of US Missing in Action from the Vietnam War." *Comparative Studies in Society and History*, 57(1): 161.

Wagner, S., and Rosenblatt, A. (2017). "Known Unknowns: Forensic Science, the Nation-State, and the Iconic Dead." In: Stojanowski, C., and Duncan, W., eds. *Studies in Forensic Biohistory: Anthropological Perspectives*, 237–66. Cambridge: Cambridge University Press.

Wallerstein, I. (2010). A World-System Perspective on the Social Sciences. *The British Journal of Sociology*, 61(1): 167–76.

Weegels, J. (2016). "The Prisoner's Body: Violence, Desire and Masculinities in a Nicaraguan Prison Theatre Group." In: Freks, G. *Gender and Conflict: Embodiments, Discourses and Symbolic Practices*, 151–73. London: Routledge.

Williams, D. M. (1973). "Abolition and the Re-deployment of the Slave Fleet, 1807–11." *Journal of Transport History*, ss-2(2): 103–15.

Wright, M. (2017). "Epistemological Ignorances and Fighting for the Disappeared: Lessons from Mexico." *Antipode*, 49(1): 249–69.

Zagaria, V. (2019). "The Clandestine Cemetery: Burying the Victims of Europe's Border in a Tunisian Coastal Town." *Human Remains and Violence: An Interdisciplinary Journal*, 5(1): 18–37.

Zarrugh, A. (2020). "The Development of US Regimes of Disappearance: The War on Terror, Mass Incarceration, and Immigrant Deportation." *Critical Sociology*, 46(2): 257–71.

Zilberg, E. (2011). *Space of Detention: The Making of a Transnational Gang Crisis between Los Angeles and San Salvador*. Durham, NC: Duke University Press.

Index

Note: figures and maps are indicated by page numbers followed by *fig.* and *map.*

construction of, 190n4; dead and, 136; martyrdom and, 139; of missing, 2; search for missing and, 10
Mexico: commemoration of bosses, 136; family searches for missing in, 26, 37, 158; governance of the missing in, 26, 185n11; mass graves in, 26, 37, 152, 158–59. *See also* United States–Mexico borderlands
Microsoft Azure cloud software, 168–70, 193n3
Microsoft Corporation: AI for Humanitarian Action, 168; database of modern migrants, 168–69; facial recognition software and, 11, 168–70; Mães da Praça da Sé database and, 167–68; militarized government use of software, 193n3
migrants: Brazilians at U.S. border, 7, 167, 172; detention centers for, 97; disappearance and, 172–73; environmental deterrence and, 25, 165; ethnonationalism and, 184n10; as exploitable bodies for labor, 23; Microsoft aggregation of data on, 168–69; necro-subjection and, 98
Miki, Yuko, 16, 18, 184n8
Mini-Manual of the Urban Guerilla (Marighella), 62
Missing (Edkins), 187n9
Mittermaier, Amira, 192n6
mothers of the disappeared: mobilization of, 10; multiple continuous violences and, 32–33; police abductions and, 119–20; protesting cemetery privatization, 29–30, 42–43; search for mass graves, 26, 37; search for missing and, 4, 9, 11, 26, 30–34, 41–42, 54
mundane mass graves: ethics of disappearance and, 10–11, 159; family searches for missing in, 5, 26, 41, 152; forgettable people in, 37, 46, 125; in hospitals and universities, 38; marginalization from political life, 21, 25; mundane disappearance and, 7, 9–10, 13–14, 28; ordering of disappearance in, 26; outside public sphere, 154–55; PCC and, 162, 174; politics of disappearance and, 162, 169; in São Paulo, 38, 46, 156, 156*map*, 157–59

Nascimento, Abdias, 65–66, 129
National Truth Commission, 26–27, 68–69, 71, 81–83, 187n5
Navaro, Yael, 179–80
necro-subjection, 98, 161

Neide (mother of Felipe), 3, *fig.*; dehumanization by state, 72; IML and, 78–81, 83; intimidation of, 27, 80; protesting cemetery privatization, 30, 42; search for Felipe, 1–5, 28, 152
Nyamnjoh, Francis, 23

O'Neill, Kevin Lewis, 186n6, 190n3
organ donation: criminality and compulsory, 91–92; government advocacy for, 88–91; police killings and, 90–93; public prosecutor approval of, 92; types of, 189n15
organized crime: Comando Vermelho and, 116, 137–38, 140–41; commemoration of dead, 137–38; control of prisons, 7, 138; disappearance and, 26–27; legitimacy and, 27; mass graves and, 38. *See also* Primeiro Comando da Capital (PCC)
ossadas (found bones), 153
ossuários (bone houses), 29
Otávio (gravedigger), 11, 46–54, 89, 122
Our Lady of Remedies, 131

Parry, Jonathan, 9
Pires, Thula, 65
Plano Nacional de Apoio ao Sistema Prisional (National Prison Support Plan), 118
police: abduction of political dissidents, 81; *blitzes* by, 66, 89; blood feud between PCC and, 123; disappearance and, 62, 108, 119, 175; discovery of mass graves, 38, 157–58; flight from, 161–62, 164–65; military hierarchy and, 101, 104; pacification policy and, 38, 153–54; prisons for, 94–96, 98, 100–106, 109; public knowledge of, 102–3; state investment in, 50; targeting of Black populations, 65–67, 78, 84, 107, 162, 164–65, 170–71; violence and, 102–8
police killings: of *bandidos*, 66, 85, 95, 102, 107; of Black populations, 21, 84, 96, 101–2, 107, 124; characteristics of, 65; death medals and, 103–4; death squads and, 13, 64; deservedness and, 85, 102–3, 107; disappearance of bodies, 62, 85–86; in favelas, 20, 66; femicide and, 106; IML and, 75–76; lack of accountability for, 107–8; mass graves and, 11, 62; mothers of young men and, 32; off-duty, 95, 98, 100, 103–5; order maintenance and, 103, 105; organ donation and, 90–93; PCC member massacre, 122–24; permissible, 108; of political dissidents, 72, 81; prison massacres,

Founded in 1893,
UNIVERSITY OF CALIFORNIA PRESS
publishes bold, progressive books and journals
on topics in the arts, humanities, social sciences,
and natural sciences—with a focus on social
justice issues—that inspire thought and action
among readers worldwide.

The UC PRESS FOUNDATION
raises funds to uphold the press's vital role
as an independent, nonprofit publisher, and
receives philanthropic support from a wide
range of individuals and institutions—and from
committed readers like you. To learn more, visit
ucpress.edu/supportus.

www.ingramcontent.com/pod-product-compliance
Lightning Source LLC
Chambersburg PA
CBHW030818270326
41928CB00007B/784

* 9 7 8 0 5 2 0 3 8 8 5 2 9 *